LAUNCH your LIFE

5 SECRETS TO KNOWING WHAT YOU WANT IN YOUR TEENS, COLLEGE YEARS, AND EARLY CAREER

MORGAN RICH, MA, PCC - The Play Huge™ Coach

Stone Pile Press
Portland, Oregon

LAUNCH YOUR LIFE:
5 Secrets to Knowing What You Want in Your Teens,
College Years, and Early Career

Published by:
STONE PILE PRESS
Portland, OR
www.stonepilepress.com

Rich, Morgan, 1970 –
Launch your life: 5 secrets to knowing what
you want in your teens, college years, and early career.

ISBN 978-0-9815544-3-3

1. Education/General

COVER ILLUSTRATION BY: Benjamin Dewey
COMICS BY: Benjamin Dewey
GRAPHIC STORY DIALOGUE BY: Nathan Staples, *www.meleecomics.com*
FRONT COVER DESIGN BY: Kathi Dunn, *www.dunn-design.com*
BACK COVER COPY BY: Susan Kendrick, Write to Your Market, Inc.
COPYEDITING BY: Kathy K. Grow, DoWriteEditing
CONCEPT EDITING BY: Michael Bremer, Kathy K. Grow, Steve Mintz
INTERIOR DESIGN BY: Erin Stark, © TLC Graphics, *www.TLCGraphics.com*

TO DAD—

Thank you for the gift.
It is still not worth it.
But I hope you would be proud. I wish I could know.
I miss you. I love you.

morgan

WHAT OTHERS are SAYING about MORGAN RICH and *LAUNCH YOUR LIFE*

"Who of us has not at times found ourselves astray along the path of life? Morgan Rich has written a remarkable guide for those of us who want to regain our footing, refocus our energies, and achieve all we're capable of. His voice speaks to us in words at once plain and profound. He writes with passion and persuasion. He is convinced it can be any committed reader's story. I am, too."

MARK BARMANN
Retired executive; Mentor; Friend

"Purposeful, joyful, meaningful, and powerful, *Launch Your Life* teaches, coaches, and cheerleads, pushing softly but persistently. Morgan Rich's intelligent and heartfelt approach is a guide to creating a life that is very, very full."

STEVE MINTZ
Educator; Camp Director; Coach; Father

"I have known Morgan and the impact he has when he enters a room for four years, and his 'playing huge' impact also comes through every page of this book. Morgan walks his talk, knows what it means to feel forced into configuration that is not his, and how to be authentically present, alive, and influential. Working with or reading Morgan's writing will entice you to live your own life authentically, playfully, and full out."

BJ LEVY, PCC, JD, MA
Partner, inviteCHANGE

"*Launch Your Life* is a motivational manifesto. Morgan Rich's unique style and 'user-friendly' format allow the reader to pursue his or her own path toward self-discovery and self-realization, all the while guided by the inspiring 'passionate compassion' that makes this more than your typical self-help book. In our ongoing search to finding deep meaning and purpose in our lives, Rich encourages us to *act*—to move forward with courage and dignity, with confidence and respect—in short, to 'Play Huge!'"

JOE RUGGIERO, PHD
Head of the Upper School
Francis W. Parker School

Table of Contents

Preface

I remember taking his hands. I held them gently but firmly. I spoke to him quietly, hoping beyond hope that he could hear me: "Take my energy. I am healthy. I have lots of energy; you are just hanging on. Use my energy to get healthy. Please, please, take what you need."

My dad died the next day.

My life has not been the same since. Something shifted dramatically.

As I think of it now, I believe that he did not take any of my energy, but rather gave me what remained of his, including his commitment to make a difference in people's lives. He was done fighting. Now it was my turn.

Something awoke in me that day. A *me*, way down deep. A *me* I was familiar with, but did not know well. A *me* who wanted to be known.

That day launched me into my life and toward my goals.

In the more than twenty years since, I have been observing, and learning and exploring and working with, people just like you—young people and not-so-young people who want to connect to your own *me*, way down deep inside.

My goal with *Launch Your Life*—as with my coaching, my speaking, and all my creations—is to help you launch your own life.

Here are some of the more common stories I hear from my coaching clients. Do any of them sound like you?

- I want to exercise, but just can't get myself to the gym. My brain knows that I want to go, but it just doesn't happen.

- I don't have any idea what I want to do with my life. I feel like I should know, but, when I really think about it, I just draw a blank.
- I know there is something else to life, but I feel totally alone in figuring it out.
- I want to make a difference, but don't know how.
- What do I major in? Do I go to college? Should I go to graduate school? What is my career going to be?
- For a long time, I have dreamed about starting my own business, but the idea of quitting my job and going for it is hard to imagine.
- I feel like I'm supposed to do well in school, but it is really hard for me. I don't like it. It's not interesting.
- My teenager is about to graduate, and we have no real or meaningful relationship. What have I been doing? How did this day get here so fast?
- I want to find someone to share my life with. Where are all the good people? Are my standards too high? Is something wrong with me? How can this be as difficult as it is?
- I have a secret. Oh, do I have a secret. But there is no way on earth that I can tell anyone, even though it is eating me alive from the inside out. I cannot imagine how people are going to react.

Because you picked up this book, odds are you have a Gnawing Feeling that something is out of whack. You are not settled. You come ready. You want to *Launch Your Life*.

And you come at an essential time.

This book is for you. I've done my best to make sure that all the ideas, thoughts, and stories are presented in ways that make sense, are easy to understand, and get you in action.

Because we're all different and learn in different ways, I've taken the various ways your brain may learn into consideration.

PREFACE

I present information in multiple ways, including through my personal stories, stories about other people (including my clients), metaphors, illustrations, graphic stories, concept examples, plus web resources and additional resources available on-line.

It's important for you to understand what I'm trying to say. And it's important for me to communicate in a way that makes this book useful to you. To that end, I've put together an advisory group of young people who have kept me honest and effective in my attempts to communicate with young people and their parents.

One more thing. While reading this book, you will very likely find yourself at some point saying, "Didn't I already read that?" or, perhaps, "Okay, okay, I get it." The reason for repetition is because that is how you learn. The reason for repetition is because that is how you learn. And another reason for the repetition is because many of the ideas in *Launch Your Life* are interrelated and, thus, apply to many sections of the book.

A project like this one takes an amazing amount of investment—of time, energy, money, focus, favors, passion, and vision—and there are many people to thank for this book happening because of their willingness to invest in it, too. For a more complete list, please visit *www.themeaningrevolution.com/launchyourlife/thankyou*. But a few must be mentioned here.

First, I offer a thank-you to the Counting Crows, Cold Play, Rusted Root, Deep Forest, and the ensemble of *The Lion King* for your hours and hours of companionship. You kept me focused, attentive, and—at times—awake, as revision after revision happened. You may never know or understand the impact you had on this project. I hope to have the same invisible impact on others that you have had on me.

Britany—not just as an employee of Play Huge Coaching, but as a friend, a caretaker of Ezra and Sylvie, and a thoughtful contributor, your presence has made this project happen. I am massively grateful for your thoughtful feedback, your honesty, and your taking the reins of keeping our coaching business moving in the direction we are committed to.

Ezra—during all the hours I sit at my computer and think and write and think some more, I look out at the garage door, knowing that behind it lurks the rebounder you love for us to play with together. Your joy of learning and your perseverance in figuring out the things you are curious about have informed many of the ideas in *Launch Your Life*. I hope all the people who read this book have the same joyful laughter, serious focus, committed toughness, and playful spirit you share with the world. I adore you. You inspire me. I love being the tickle monster. I love you deeply and completely. Let's have a catch.

Sylvie—you are five years and a couple of weeks old and a giant ball of energy and love. You have been flexible and understanding as I have spent time usually reserved for you to make this book happen. You are magically creative and imaginative, tenacious with your desires, and always playful. I watch you and remember the gift *Launch Your Life* is intended to convey. You have kept me going on many days with the snuggles, the imaginary games of baby, the wrestling, and the laughter that we share. I hope you feel at least a smidgen of the absolute overwhelming love I feel for you..."Tummy Time!"

Mom—there have been many, many trips across town to deliver kids home after long afternoons with Grammy. There have been many trips to the zoo, trolley rides, cartoons, milk shakes, and, most of all, love that you have contributed to this project. These efforts have saved me the time to capture those last thoughts of the day, and essential moments of insights.

Launch Your Life would not have been possible without your effort. You know the commitment this kind of undertaking takes, and you have supported me the whole way. Even when I have been fried and uncertain enough to not be forthcoming with details, you have stuck with me and offered your encouragement. I may not express it as often as I could, but I love you dearly, and am grateful to have you as part of our daily life here in Portland.

Marcy—my name is on the cover of this book, but your presence is in every sentence, on every single page, and in me. There is simply no earthly way *Launch Your Life* would have happened without your love, kindness, and tenacity. You believed in me when I did not. You pushed me when I needed it. You held me when I needed that. I cannot even begin to catalog the time and energy commitment you have made to provide me time to articulate my vision. How do I possible convey my gratitude?

I think the greatest gift we can give to anyone is the demand that they not compromise who they are. You do that for me. I feel held by you as the pure and absolute possibility of who I am. Your love and our togetherness makes every day of my life the best one I have ever lived. Thank you. I love you.

Launch Your Life is the culmination of twenty years of experiential research directed toward understanding what is important in life, how to get what matters, and how to Sustain a sense of Meaning and Fulfillment. It is about connecting to who you are, connecting to others, and being in conscientious and inspired action.

Again, odds are you picked up this book searching for something more in your life or a powerful direction to head. *Launch Your Life* can launch you into your life and toward your goals. You are capable of making happen everything you want in your life; all you have to do is act. Let's go!

Playing Huge.
morgan

Introduction

OUR JOURNEY BEGINS—LET'S GO!

I wish I had a month to talk to you about courage.
And another month to talk to you about passion.

Kobus Neethling

There is nothing enlightened in shrinking
so other people will not feel insecure around you.

Marianne Williamson

THREE KEY COMPONENTS

You need three things to make this book work for you:

- the desire to unleash the Real You—that is, being engaged in your life and ready to do what it takes to make it amazing
- the courage and passion to get in action—to Play Huge
- an idea of what path to take through *Launch Your Life*, based on an understanding that the structure of this book is made for you

I've done my best to make sure that all the ideas, thoughts, and stories are presented in ways that make sense and are easy to understand. Further, I have attempted to present the material in many ways to support the learning styles of as many of you as I can.

When you finish the Introduction and before you dive into the rest of *Launch Your Life*, I suggest you take some time to create a path through the book that works for you.

Launch Your Life will work best for you when you have a plan to unleash your desire, act with courage, and express your passion.

AWAKENING THE DESIRE...A BEGINNING

Each of us has the ability to be happy and fulfilled, but, sometimes, you need to dig deep and take action to make it happen.

Advertising, the illusion of prestige, and outdated school curricula obscure the human essence of meaningful relationships. Constant emails, text messages, and phone calls interrupt our face-to-face communication and community gatherings; high-stakes testing causes students to limit their learning possibilities, while also creating miserable learning situations and tangible self-doubt for many; parents are stuck in a rut of believing that getting good grades and going to college are the only ways to a successful life; as a culture, we are in a trance that material possessions provide something important. We are out of touch with the profound simplicity that makes life fulfilling—making a difference, leaving the planet better than we found it, and treating people with dignity and respect.

But—yikes!—there is more. Today we face daunting educational, economic, ecological and moral challenges. In our preparing you, our young people, for your lives in this increasingly uncertain and challenging future, we are out of touch with what gives meaning. At a time when you have the unprecedented capability to communicate and to be "connected," your ability and desire to authentically connect to other people—let alone other living things—is in crisis. And, despite a mountain of need, we are not prepared to do anything significant about it.

Insecurity and individualism prevail where community and intimacy are most needed.

What we—as educators, parents, children, friends, and learners—have lost, and what you, as young people, have lost in this process is profoundly disheartening. We have lost our care for one another, our emotional (and physical) health, the ability to listen, the love and friendships we all desperately crave, and the passion and courage to make a difference.

We have the ability and power to do something about it.

Launch Your Life is intended to be a wake-up call. When you get to know me, you will realize I am a playful and goofy guy, but I am also passionately serious——I aspire to be Mr. Play Huge. I hope my playfulness has the power of all good play: to reveal to you what is possible for your lives, and to so do with the combined flavors of fun and challenge that allow you to see and feel inspired that you too can live with joyfulness, love, and human connections, and remind you that you want to make a difference. I want to model for you that you can have all this, and that doing so will change the world for the better.

From the nice, fun, playful me, the wake-up call is a cute nudge to say, "Hey, you could be doing more with your life." But, from the passionately serious me, the (unfiltered) WAKE-UP call is, "Stop making excuses, get off your lazy/insecure/apathetic/uncertain ass, and figure it out. We need your brilliance, creativity, and passion, and you cannot afford to be complacent one more moment. Get. In. Action. Now."

Launch Your Life is my effort to scream out: LET'S GO! What is happening is not okay.

We have the creativity, ingenuity, power, and care for one another to make a huge difference.

I don't know if a book is the right way to make it happen. I have never undertaken anything like this before. I don't consider myself a writer. I consider myself a passionate person who refuses to sit on the sidelines and allow what is happening in our world to keep on happening. The words and concepts that follow will,

I hope, provide a guide for you to connect to your passion, Stand in your courage, and scream out with me: LET'S GO!

We have got to stop talking and complaining about it. There is no excuse to be complacent or complicit. It is time to get in action.

In this book, I aspire to inspire and remind you

- that life itself is bigger than material possessions, grades, test scores, college admittance, being right, a good résumé, the right clothes or latest gadget, or earning a certain amount of money. No hearse has an attachment for a U-Haul trailer. And your casket does not come with a self-storage unit.
- that you know this. You want to make a difference, and your life will be complete only when you work to live every day in zestful expression.
- that a moment of laughter, a walk in the country, a creative exchange of ideas, simple touching, eye contact, or shared tears can create aliveness in a way that material possessions never, ever, ever will. Your relationships with people are where life happens.
- that the only moment you are promised is right now! You are mortal, and death is always in the background. If you take yourself in passionate—but not graceless—significance, you can have more fun than you currently have now and be at least as effective.
- that all of us are humans. You are part of a we. And, yet, we are each unique.
- that you must unlock your listening. You must work to listen to and savor the uniqueness of other people. Real Listening challenges you to be present and engaged and to enter into the worlds of others, to where the gifts of meaningful friendship, love, peace, understanding, and shared laughter reside.

- that all of you, young people *and* parents, stand a better chance of making it through life's inspiring and challenging moments if you are intimate and respecting partners, friends, sons, daughters, moms, dads, husbands, wives, and community members. We are not meant to make it through life alone. It's About People. Humanity is essential. Your community of loved ones and supporters is critical for your success, your joy, your meaning, and your laughter.
- that humor, celebration, gratitude, courage, passion, compassion, humility, powerful assertiveness, love, and creativity are all crucial elements to a life of Meaning and Fulfillment.

So, readers—both young people and parents, and all you others—ready yourselves for a joyful shock as you go through these pages. Let yourself dream about how your life could be, how your children could live, or the joy your parents and friends could feel in their lives—and then be inspired into action. Explore the path offered on these pages and courageously live your dreams.

The Meaning rEvolution

Launch Your Life is part of a bigger vision and movement. It is my Stand to make a difference, and I call it the Meaning rEvolution. The simplest way to explain the Meaning rEvolution is to imagine a place where people's lives are filled up with meaning, and everyone lives passionately committed to making a difference.

In the next chapter, you will be introduced to the Real You. In the Meaning rEvolution, everyone is connected to his or her Real You, and willing and able to courageously act. You believe in yourself at a core level. You are inundated with positive messages that remind you how powerful you are, and allow you to make the biggest difference you are capable of.

The positive messages and the necessary support to make this happen in a Sustainable way can only come from one place: other people. The most significant thing that happens in the

Meaning rEvolution is that you are always meaningfully connected to and thoughtful about other people; you treat all living things (and our planet) with the respect and dignity they deserve. By creating relationships with people based on who you really are and who they really are, you spend your days in the freedom of feeling that the Real You is fully and zestfully expressed, Playing Huge, and loved.

In the same way people exercise in the morning or drink coffee to get themselves going, if you are in the Meaning rEvolution, then every day you connect with what you Stand for and reconnect with what you want to accomplish, and everyone else is doing the same thing. Then everybody shares their commitments for the day, they talk about challenges, and they give hugs and high fives to get ready to make today magical.

The Meaning rEvolution starts here. The way to learn how to make this happen is to read and implement the ideas in *Launch Your Life*.

BEGINNING TO CHART YOUR PATH—STRUCTURE AND ORGANIZATION

What follows are descriptions of the structure, organization, and simple idea of what to expect in *Launch Your Life*. This is intended to support the creation of your path/journey through the book. Having a bird's-eye view of a maze makes it easier to navigate the maze. Once you are inside, it is very difficult to identify where exactly you are, and nearly impossible if you have never seen it from above. But, if you have an idea of where you are going when you are inside trying to get out, you will have a better understanding of where you are. The intention of these structures is to provide the bird's-eye view of *Launch Your Life*.

I've structured the chapters to be consistent and to present information so it will appeal to many types of learning brains in order to make sure all the ideas presented in *Launch Your Life* are simple and clear. Each chapter follows this format:

- **Title Page:** the Main idea of the chapter and quotes
- **Mind Map:** the key concepts of that chapter arranged in a mind map
- **The Simple Idea:** an introduction to the main ideas of the chapter as well as the main concepts to take away
- **The Idea Explained:** an in-depth exploration of the concept
- **The Path to Get There:** the action steps you need to put the concepts to use in your life
- **Possible Barriers:** common challenges you may face on your path
- **Huge Outcomes:** a taste of what you can expect if you apply each chapter
- **Wrap-Up:** the chapter's information conveyed in yet another way, by using a metaphor. The metaphor will put you on the Play Huge Stage and, eventually, the Empathize Stage, where you get to play around with the ideas from the chapter.

There are several other layers of organization at play in *Launch Your Life* to enhance your understanding and make the material accessible, including the 5 Secrets, the three parts of the book, and five chapters. Throughout the book, you'll also find a *Graphic Story and Characters*—stories, examples, and situations to help illustrate important concepts and experiences. And the graphic story is a great story of people on the journey of launching their lives.

The 5 Secrets

Launch Your Life is structured around the 5 Secrets to knowing what you want. All the ideas and structure in the book are intended to coach you to implement the 5 Secrets into your everyday life. These five concepts that you will find useful in Launching Your Life are all simple, logical, and easy to put to use, but so few people seem to be aware of them that I think of them as secrets.

These secrets will be presented, in depth, one at a time, at the end of each of the first five chapters, but here's a very quick overview to introduce them.

SECRET #1—BELIEVE IN THE UPWARD SPIRAL

The journey to Meaning and Fulfillment isn't one of great leaps and bounds. It's one of small positive steps, each of which raises you closer to the life you want. With each step, you gain more momentum, more distinctions, and greater abilities. Believe in the Upward Spiral. Take a step forward today, another tomorrow, and then another. You may start slowly, but, no matter how small your steps, your commitment and perseverance in stepping forward will create results you want.

SECRET #2—BE THE OPERATER OF YOUR LIFE

OPERATER is an acronym for a set of steps you can follow when facing any plan, action, or decision.

When you are the OPERATER of your life, you take charge of who you are and where you're going. It is like getting that bird's-eye view of your life.

OPERATER is:

Organize and **P**lan	**E**xperience: be **R**ealistic, be **A**ccountable, call **T**ime-out	**E**valuate	**R**epeat

SECRET #3—PLAY ABOVE THE LINE

You are absolutely, 100% capable of making your life happen the way you want. You are in charge.

When you Play Above the Line, you take responsibility for your life. You stop playing the role of victim. You avoid the games of blaming others, giving up, and always having excuses. You control your responses to events that happen.

When you Play Above the Line, you engage in your life with the dignity and respect your life deserves. Playing Above the Line is living your life with integrity, grace, accountability, pride, humility, and passion!

(1992 Adapted from "The Line" Quantum Learning Network —Super-Camp—*www.quantumlearningnetwork.com* — Used with permission)

SECRET #4–IT'S ABOUT PEOPLE

Your relationships with the people you love, your friends, your colleagues, the natural world, even people you disagree with and people you don't understand yet, are where you will find Meaning and Fulfillment. *Launch Your Life* is all about connection to the people in your life.

We are not meant to go through life alone. The way to unlock our potential, creativity, and courage is to create an inspired community of people.

SECRET #5–ALWAYS HONOR SUSTAINABILITY

Launch Your Life is intended to impact your life now and into the future, and to make the kind of deep change in your life that you truly crave.

The only kind of change that matters is change you can Sustain through every day of your life. Honor the moments you feel truly alive and inspired, by making them happen every moment of every day!

Following the latest trend...doing what you think will make you cool... thinking a moment of inspiration is *the* answer... and any choice you make based on your immediate interest... will not deliver the long-term solution the Real You wants.

Basing decisions on what is Sustainable in the big picture will enhance your life. It will allow you to live your life in a way that honors the Real You.

Be consistent. Be insistent. Live Sustainably.

The Parts and the Chapters

PREFACE

The preface welcomes you to *Launch Your Life* and helps you understand how my book can be helpful to your creating the life you dream about.

INTRODUCTION: YOUR JOURNEY BEGINS

The introduction explains the structure and possible paths into and through *Launch Your Life*. Then it begins to awaken your desire to Play Huge with a word from me, and ushers in a foundational aspect of the book—Know Yourself—by challenging you to find your own way through the structure and organization of *Launch Your Life*.

PART I: GET IN THE GAME

YOUR LAUNCH PAD

The intended outcomes of this chapter are:

- to connect with the Real You, and
- to get in touch with your Gnawing Feeling and become aware that you want more from your life.

PLAY HUGE!

The intended outcome of this chapter is to get in action and honor the Real You by being courageous and passionate.

PART II: PERSONAL TRAINING

KNOW YOURSELF

The intended outcome of this chapter is to know your talents, your learning style, what you are passionate about, and know what you are willing to take a Stand for.

TRUST YOURSELF

The intended outcome of this chapter is to trust your Know Yourself enough to express it in the world.

PART III: INTO THE WORLD

EMPATHIZE

The intended outcome of this chapter is to enter into the world of other people by stopping being so focused on yourself. You will begin to understand other people and by activating your Real Listening learn how to treat people (and other living things and our planet) with dignity and respect.

CONCLUSION: OUR JOURNEY CONTINUES—LET'S GO!

The conclusion will review the highlights and essential components of *Launch Your Life*, and celebrate you and your new adventures.

Graphic Story and the Characters

The story of Jamie, Elly, Leslie, and the gang follows along the same trajectory *Launch Your Life* does. The characters work to learn the 5 Secrets and, then, put them into action in their lives by using Your Launch Pad, Play Huge, Know Yourself, Trust Yourself, Empathize, and all the other ideas in *Launch Your Life*.

You will find times when I reference the graphic story in the text with an icon.

These are places where I think an event in the story provides a good example of the idea in the text. I invite you to create your own connections, both from your own life and from the graphic story.

The characters introduced below are the main characters in the *Launch Your Life* story. They are meant for you to be able to identify with and/or learn from. Components of their adventures will show up throughout the book. They are intended to provide stories, examples, and visual representations in a nontext-based way. Because we all learn differently, the characters and their stories may be immensely helpful for you and your understanding of *Launch Your Life*. Or, it may be that you don't identify with them; if so, ignore them and use the text to drive your learning. The point is—whatever works best for you, go with it!

ELLY

Elly is Carrie and Mark's daughter, and she does everything they ask and expect her to do. She is a high school junior already thinking she will apply to colleges. She is a good athlete and well liked by her friends. She does well in school because she works hard at it, but she does not feel particularly excited about anything.

JAMIE

Jamie is Elly's older brother and a high school senior. He is popular and opinionated. He has strong musical abilities, but lacks self-confidence and an understanding that he has talents other than what are focused on in school. He knows there is more to life than just doing well in school and going to college, but is not sure how to make it happen. He has a good number of friends, but their habits support his apathy and lameness. He clearly feels his parents think he has failed them. He doesn't feel like they understand him.

CARRIE AND MARK

Carrie and Mark are the parents of seventeen-year-old Elly and eighteen-year-old Jamie. They want what is best for their kids and want to help. They don't put intentional pressure on their kids, but do have a clear image of what they believe to be the path to success (i.e., the traditional route of college and career). They both have jobs, but neither is particularly passionate about what they do, and so are struggling with their identities (although they may not think so).

NORA

Nora is a college sophomore in the process of choosing a major. She does well in school, but doesn't have a sense of what she wants to do with her life. She keeps going around and around on what to study, and everyone in her family has an opinion about what she should do—and she tries to listen to all of them. However, she especially looks up to her cousin Derek. She is a respectful kid who doesn't want to create unrest or disappointment in her family.

COREY

A junior in high school, Corey is an athlete who loves sports but still feels lost. He doesn't do particularly well in school—and doesn't like it—but feels like he is supposed to get ready to apply to college. Because he doesn't do well in school, he ends up in the middle of misinterpretations of his behaviors. He is labeled as the classic stupid jock, but has a lot of pride and is wicked competitive. When someone challenges him, he does not easily step back. This, of course, can get him in more and more trouble.

DEREK

Derek is a young professional. He does work that makes him a good amount of money, but he doesn't love the work. He has never seriously thought about changing his work, but does talk about it sometimes. He has always done what was expected of him, and done it quite well. But, when he looks around at his life and his friends, he wonders what exactly everyone is doing. No one else seems to be worrying about the stuff he is worrying about. Whenever he expresses any of these feelings, people say he should go back to school—get an MBA or go to law school, or maybe try to get into a PhD program.

LESLIE

Leslie has had some tough things happen in her life, including the death of her mom when she was an early teen. She never liked school and didn't do particularly well. These struggles fueled her creation of alternative ways to learn. She has big dreams and ideas, and, although she struggles with believing she can make them happen, she does not lack the courage to try.

Key Concept References

ANCHOR ICON

When a concept is being explained for either the first time or the most significant time in *Launch Your Life* you will find an Anchor icon. This icon will serve as a reference point for the concept.

BOOK ICON

When a concept is brought up and there is a link to another place in the book that I think you might find helpful or interesting, you will find a book icon with a page number. It might reference you back to the place where the concept is anchored, a story, or another place of interest.

Additional Resources

I am constantly creating alternative ways to convey the ideas in *Launch Your Life*. Along with my life coaching, speaking, and forums, *Launch Your Life* is part of what I call the Meaning rEvolution. I believe the ideas in *Launch Your Life* can have a tremendous impact on people's lives, and I Stand for making that difference in the world.

I encourage you to check out the web site to see the latest ideas and efforts. There you'll find more stories, examples, songs, and images about the ideas in *Launch Your Life*. You'll see and hear videos of me speaking, slide shows, and podcasts, all conveying the same ideas contained here in the book. (Like Leslie, I am not afraid to try things.)

Further, I suspect that, as you read and explore *Launch Your Life*, you will come up with your own ideas, examples, stories, songs, and so much more. Please go to www.themeaningrevolution.com/launchyourlife to share your creations, as well as to connect with other people who are launching their lives, like you. After all, It's About People.

Some Possible Paths

Here is just a sampling of some of the ways you can make your way through *Launch Your Life*:

- You could start by checking out the mind maps and simple concepts in each chapter. Then you could read the graphic story and search for explanations in the text of what is happening with the characters.
- You could read the Huge Outcomes and all 5 Secrets, then decide which section(s) will address the challenge(s) you are dealing with in your real life.
- You could realize that you already Know Yourself, and, therefore, go directly to Trust Yourself and figure out how to Stand powerfully for who you are.
- You could begin by looking at all the mind maps and simple concepts, then read all the way straight through the book.
- You could choose to read from front to back, but, before starting each part and each chapter, make sure you have a big-picture idea of what you are about to read. You might do this by looking at the structure, the concepts, the stories and examples, the part of the graphic story that (loosely) goes with each section, and checking out the Huge Outcome mind map and review.

What is your way? The Real You is ready and waiting.

IT FEELS DIFFERENT BUT IT'S GOOD TO BE HOME AGAIN. I'VE GOT TO CHECK OUT THE COMMUNITY CENTER.
Half way isn't en...ugh...
...lay huge or d... try.
I must share w...
I have learned...
AS MUCH FUN AS IT IS TO STAND HERE AND SECOND GUESS MYSELF I'VE GOT WORK TO DO. ALL RIGHT! LET'S DO THIS!

WHAT WILL IT TAKE?

NEAT!
BIOLOGY
DENTISTRY
JAZZ
PSYCHOLOGY
PAINTING
COURSE CATALOG
COOL.
KISS
FIGHT!
YOU CAN'T DO THAT HERE GUYS...
CHECK IT OUT.

WHAT WILL IT TAKE?

— PART ONE —

GET in the GAME

YOUR LAUNCH PAD

"Having a future to look forward
to is INCREDIBLY powerful.
When you give yourself a positive
outlook it is amazing what you can do."

Kobus Neethling

"I refuse to be drawn into accidentally
energizing and rewarding negativity.
I refuse to not purposefully
energize and nurture successes."

Howard Glasser

"It's not that I do not get on it;
it's that I get off it much, much faster than you."

Landmark Forum Leader

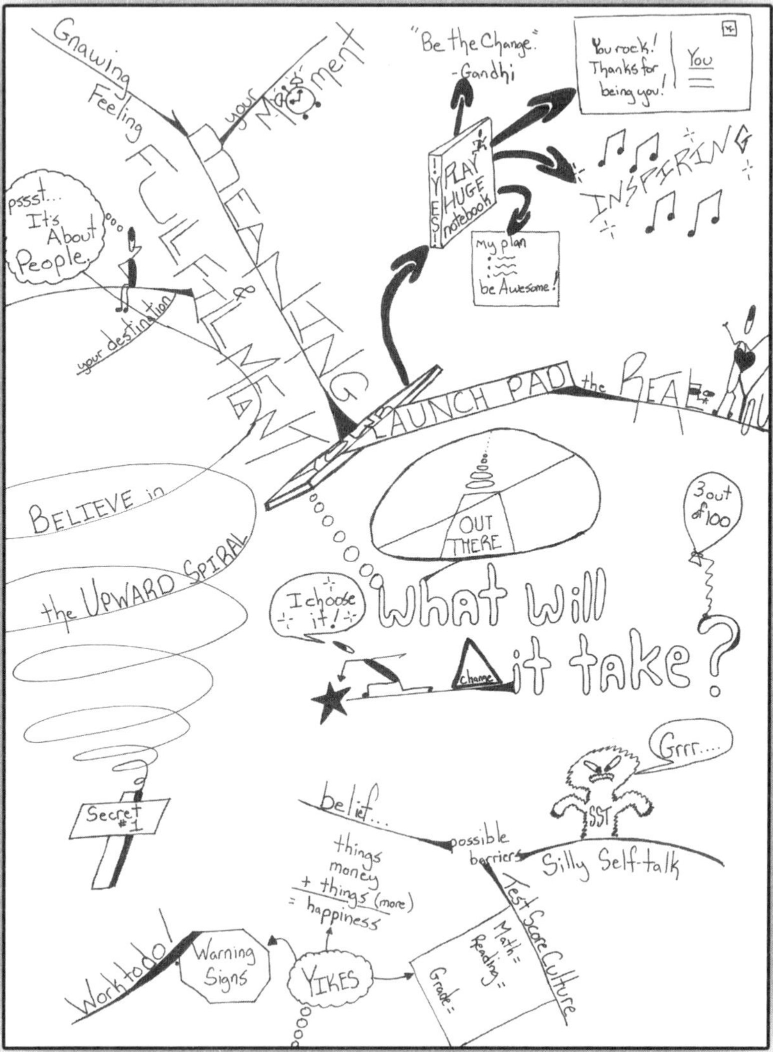
Gnawing Feeling
your Moment
MEANING
& FULFILLMENT
"Be the Change."
-Gandhi
You rock! Thanks for being you!
You
PLAY HUGE notebook
YES!
INSPIRING
my plan
be Awesome!
pssst... It's About People.
your destination
LAUNCH PAD
the REAL
BELIEVE in
the UPWARD SPIRAL
OUT THERE
3 out of 100
I choose it!
What will it take?
change
Grrr....
SST
Secret #1
belief...
possible barriers
Silly Self-talk
things
money
+ things (more)
= happiness
Test Score Culture
Math =
Reading =
Grade =
Work to do!
Warning Signs
YIKES

YOUR SIMPLE LAUNCH PAD

Your Launch Pad will move you beyond that Gnawing Feeling.

Don't wait for some life event to blast you awake. Your journey begins in the moment you decide to do something about it. And you *can* do something about it. The Real You knows you want more from your life, so, right here and right now, is the opportunity for the Real You to make a choice.

For every day to have a purpose, you want to feel your power. You will feel your power when you make your life what you want it to be and what you believe it can be. It feels great when you develop your character and your potential, and make a difference in people's lives.

Getting there is not easy. There are barriers and cultural messages that throw you off the track. But, the Meaning and Fulfillment you seek comes in the challenge. Meaning and Fulfillment are about living in the complexity, the uncomfortable moments, and the challenges of life.

Now is your time to choose. What will it take for now to be the moment the Real You stands in your passion and says, "It's time to launch my life!"?

YOUR LAUNCH PAD EXPLAINED

The Real You

Who are you really? How do you want to live your life? If you were free from the influences of school, parents, peers, and society, what would you do with your life? How would you be living?

Launch Your Life is based on the following three premises:

67

- Everyone wants to make a difference and leave the planet a better place than he found it.
- Everyone wants passionately to fulfill her potential.
- Everyone wants to be liked.

In *Launch Your Life*, I call the authentic expression of what *you* most want for your life, the Real You.

What is your authentic expression?

You certainly have had moments of absolute clarity and excitement about who you are, how you want your life to be, and, perhaps, a vision of how to get it.

The message may have come in the shower. The message may have come during exercising. What you most want may have emerged while talking with friends. The message may be in the feeling you have after a movie or performance, in the tears, inspiration, or reflections in the moment before you leave the theatre.

Life As A House

I remember watching the movie *Life as a House*. I cried throughout the movie and then more when the movie was over. It is the story of a man who is diagnosed with cancer. He has difficult relationships with his ex-wife, his son, others, and even himself. He had spent his lifetime busy with work, and not paying enough attention to things he cared about—spending time with his family, enjoying his work, and building his dream house.

In the moments after the movie, I remember vowing to myself that I would do everything I could to be a conscientious husband, a present and engaged dad, and a courageous person. The funny thing is that I know these things about myself, but they are really easy for me to forget. When I watched the movie, they all became crystal clear for me again.

When I connect to my Real You, I realize the power of movies for me. There are things in my life I really want, but, when I start going through the motions of each day, I find it very easy to forget the things I care most about. There are certain movies—as well as stories, books, personal experiences, and more—that help connect me with who I am way down at a core level. This core connection is the Real You.

LOVING LINGUISTICS

My friend Isabel worked for a company that created guides for doing well on tests. She shared that the job was okay, but what made the hard work worthwhile was the time after work. That is when she would have these magical conversations with her co-workers/friends. They all loved words and language, so they would have long intense conversations about anything linguistic. She remembers talking for hours and hours about the history, the use, and the power of words.

What my friend Isabel realized through these conversations and her reflections was what her Real You wanted. Now, looking back, she realizes those conversations were the expression of the things she loved most in the world—words and language. Based on her realization of what matters for her, she now has a business with which she helps people put words to the things they are most passionate about. And she loves it.

While I remember having the kind of conversations Isabel has in this example, mine were not about words and language. They were about sports and the meaning of life. But this is exactly the point. We all have different things we are passionate about and different ways of making our lives mean something. Your Launch Pad is about discovering what the Real You feels like saying and feels like doing.

As you search for the moments when your messages come through, remember that, whenever the moments happened, they were moments of clarity and excitement. They aroused the possibility of what you can create, and what you want to create, with your life.

These messages made your inner knowing get excited because they were not filtered through what is possible, or practical, or what is easiest, or what you should do, or what others want you to do. They are an honest and inspired connection to you from way down deep inside—the Real You.

Throughout *Launch Your Life*, I will refer to the Real You, and to the tremendous power that honoring it has on believing in yourself.

Elements of a Fully Launched Life

A life ready to be launched and lived to its fullest is based on an understanding of these elements that are described in the following pages:

1. Your Moment
2. Your Gnawing Feeling
3. Your Destination

Your life will be ready to be launched when you have answers to this question:

What will it take for me to make my dream my reality?

YOUR MOMENT

375

And then one day it happened…

I was blasted into being awake. I got shoved into a journey of being connected to and expressing that *me* way down there—my Real You.

My blast came the day my dad died. Through the tears, anger, confusion, and absolute disbelief, something awoke in me. That *me*, way down deep, stirred. I had no idea what to do or which way to go or how to deal with the feelings, but I had a whole new perspective on life. And, while I did not understand it then, that new perspective was a gift. But it was a very costly gift.

What Will It Take to Make Your Joy Happen?

The question I ask myself constantly is, "What will it take?" What is it going to take for you, for my clients, for my kids, for my friends—for everyone—to wake up, get in action, and stop being complacent? I want to give you the same gift I got when my dad died, but at a far less significant cost.

You will have it a bit easier, and a bit harder than some others. What do I mean? You certainly have heard or seen stories of significant events like these. Or maybe you have experienced them.

- Someone in the family gets hit by a drunk driver and is killed. The family then becomes active in anti-drunk-driving campaigns.
- A child is diagnosed with childhood diabetes. That defines the family, and they become consumed with curing their child and finding a cure for childhood diabetes in other children.
- Your mom is diagnosed with breast cancer, and you become an active member of breast cancer awareness campaigns.

There are two dynamics at play in these cases. There is an emotional and significant event that creates action—the blast. And there is an immediate issue to rally for and get involved in—the Stand.

The way you have it easier than these people is that you don't have to deal with a highly emotional or tragic event. You, hopefully, have a choice whether to engage in your life or not.

The way you have it harder is that you have to figure out what it *is* going to take for you to engage because there is no blast.

You also have it harder because there is no clear issue for you to get involved in. You get to choose. Your Stand does not get determined by the implication of the blast.

When there is not a blast (and, actually, even when there is), what creates Meaning and Fulfillment is connecting with that *you* deep down, the Real You, and beginning to live in the full, zestful expression of that you.

Whether you have had a significant event, as I did, or you have not, the place where *Launch Your Life* begins is with your desire to engage. It is perfectly fine to have a clear idea what you Stand for. And it is perfectly fine to have no idea what you want to do, or what your cause is, or how to deal with your situation.

Remember: there is no experience required. But you absolutely must be ready to engage in the process.

What will it take for you to engage in the process?

YOUR GNAWING FEELING

One thing it is going to take is becoming aware of the Gnawing Feeling in your gut, that feeling that there is more to life than you have been led to believe. In your most honest moments, you know there is more to it, and to Launch Your Life will require awakening that Gnawing Feeling.

My Coaching Clients

When my clients come to coaching, they often describe a feeling that there is something more to their life. They seem to be doing okay, but there is something there that just doesn't feel right. They're not interested in school; they don't have a lot of energy; they don't love their job; they wish they were more courageous, or engaged, or passionate, or something.

Your Peers

When you listen to people in your class, they may describe an absolute lack of interest in school. They may not like certain subjects. Or maybe they love school, but find it boring and not challenging enough. Or they may believe that what they are learning in school is stuff they are never going to use in their lives, and they have seen other graduates who are out in the world struggling, even though they completed their schooling.

They have that feeling that there is something more to life than what they are currently experiencing, but there seems to be some agreement ("out there") that what they are doing is the way to make their lives successful, so they don't pay much attention to that feeling that there must be something more, or another way.

Your Families and Friends

When you see your friends and family members moping around, complaining, and with low energy, you may wonder how much fulfillment they are feeling in their lives. They may be able to put on a happy face, or make the best of the situation, or even make their apathy seem cool, but you know they are not happy or feeling fulfilled.

Your Co-Workers

Sometimes, when things are going well and your company and you are making money, you find you don't feel right about the way the company and/or individuals in the company are conducting themselves. Perhaps they are exploiting people, or being negative around the office, or being deceitful, but the money and acknowledgment are rolling in. And everyone is going along with it.

Even when your common sense tells you there is a different way to be doing something, you keep justifying the actions because of the apparent benefit(s).

Your Classmates

It happens not only in the work world, but in school, too. Consider SAT/ACT test scores and grades. Sometimes, when things are going well and your test scores are good and you have good grades, you still don't feel good about the way you spend your time.

Perhaps you have not treated people well, or you just aren't happy and something is missing, but the acknowledgment is rolling in. There is certainly a perceived benefit in having good scores and grades, so, even when your common sense tells you there is a different way to be doing something, you keep justifying the actions because of the apparent benefit(s).

The gist of all these situations is some version of, "I have a sense that there is something more to my life, and there is a different way to be. But I don't know what it is. I don't even know how to start to figure it out. And, even in the fleeting moments when I have some idea what I want, I don't believe I can get it."

And then this tension ends up in the questions, "Am I crazy?" or "Is there something wrong with me?"

My answer is no.

What I found in my years of research is that you are simply not in touch with what will bring Meaning and Fulfillment to your life. You skate along the surface of life, doing what you are told in the way you are told to do it. You do what you perceive you are supposed to do, hoping and trusting that meaning will somehow magically show up. But it never does.

I also found that you *know* there is more to life. You know you can change your perspective. And your knowing shows up in your most honest moments as an instinct, a vision of something different, a curiosity about people who have that "it," a song that awakens some inspiration or a new idea, a fellow student with a positive attitude, the tears after a movie, the admiration of a passionate friend, the inner knowing that there is a more honest and honorable way to conduct business or represent yourself, or an insight while exercising or showering, I have found that when you are challenged and pushed to think about what you want from your life, you are generally able to sense there is more to it than a glib "provide for my family" or "make lots of money" or "this is the way it is meant to be" or "whatever." Your knowing is a sense that your life can be full of Meaning and Fulfillment.

In *Launch Your Life*, I call this feeling the Gnawing Feeling.

What will it take for you to engage in the process?

One thing it is going to take is connecting to your Gnawing Feeling, because moving beyond Your Launch Pad will demand the desire and the courage, first, to acknowledge your Gnawing Feeling and, second, to do something about it—which is the next chapter, Play Huge. *Launch Your Life* begins with your commitment to engage.

My commitment began the day my dad died.

Remember, there is no experience required. You don't need to know what you are going to do, but you do need to know that you are going to do *something*.

When will your commitment begin?

YOUR DESTINATION

Meaning and Fulfillment

My belief is that a life with Meaning and Fulfillment is the life you all truly desire. Be honest with yourself and imagine being on your deathbed. I think you will want to look back and feel your life was worthwhile, and that you lived with a purpose. I think you will want to be able to look back and feel you tried your hardest to fulfill your character and your potential.

I coach my clients with this foundational understanding, and I wrote *Launch Your Life* with the intention of providing ideas, secrets, and motivation for you, my readers, to take steps toward filling up your life with Meaning and Fulfillment. I am hoping that, as you read, reread, and refer back to *Launch Your Life*, the outcome you create for yourself is increased Meaning and Fulfillment.

ENJOYING MY FAMILY

I think about this all the time with my wife and my kids. I can't imagine if one of them were to die. (Phew, that is even hard to write.) I would be absolutely devastated. It's hard to imagine what my life would be like without my family.

Then I think, you know what I have? What I have is today, and I'm not guaranteed tomorrow. And I'm not guaranteed ten years from now. I'm highly optimistic and hopeful for our future togetherness, but—today—I can love Sylvie's hugs and imagination. And I can enjoy Ezra's joyfulness and massive curiosity. I can be grateful for Marcy's thoughtfulness, our shared vision, and her absolute support. And I can embrace these and enjoy these and be fulfilled with these right now. I get to choose it.

Then, if something happened, I am hopeful I could look back and say, "You know what? I couldn't have gotten any more love and any more life out of each day than I did."

That's fulfillment.

I think you want to be able to look back at your life and feel you made a difference in the lives of people you shared life with and, especially, the people you cared about. This is what I mean when I say, It's About People.

In the culture of the United States, people feel a lot of pressure to be a certain way and have a certain kind of life. You spend a lot of time and energy trying to achieve what you think you are supposed to do, what school you are supposed to go to, and what kind of job you are supposed to have. You have an image of how you are supposed to look, what you are supposed to wear, how much money will make you happy, and so much more.

You work hard to live this life, and you do the things you have been told you are supposed to do to make yourself happy, but, somehow, it doesn't deliver all that was promised. So, you try harder and you buy more. You pull up your bootstraps. But, again, the results are not what you were expecting. Maybe you begin to believe that this is what's in the cards for your life, and you begin to accept your plight. Or, maybe you keep on fighting and making an effort.

But, wherever you are on your journey—despite feeling like a failure, despite feeling like you have let people down (including yourself), despite feeling (or, perhaps, accepting) that you are on the road to nowhere—in your most honest moments, you have that Gnawing Feeling.

And when you make the commitment to listen to your Gnawing Feeling and to engage in the process of Launching Your Life, you will realize that the destination is Meaning and Fulfillment.

- It is about living in the moment. What you want is not "out there" somewhere.
- It is about seeing life as an opportunity, not as a failure. It is about taking charge of change.

- It is about honoring your common sense and your sense of what is right—working to become one of the 3 out of 100. 35
- It is about believing in yourself.

My Commitment

My commitment is to Stand for the highest iteration of what is possible for the Real You. I know you are capable of creating the change you want and making each day the best it can be. I know that everyone, no matter how deep down, wants to make it happen. *Launch Your Life* is a commitment to creating a place where you can enjoy your life and eliminate that Gnawing Feeling that tells you there is something not right in your life. My commitment is for you to connect with your passion, and then live every day honoring the Real You.

THE PATH TO YOUR LAUNCH PAD

Establishing Your Launch Pad is about your making the decision to go for it. In order to make *Launch Your Life* work for you, you have to have the desire to unleash the Real You. The quote at the beginning of the Introduction is all about this desire:

> I wish I had a month to talk to you about courage.
> And then another month to talk to you about passion.
>
> *Kobus Neethling*

Courage is the next step, when you take your desire and put it into action—Play Huge. But, without passion, there is not much use for courage.

To establish your path to Your Launch Pad, you will connect with the Real You, learn how to quiet your Silly Self-Talk, and 23 answer this question for yourself: "What will it take?" But, more than anything else, you will awaken your passion.

Connect with the Real You

You certainly have had those moments of absolute clarity and inspiration about who you are, what you want your life to be, and how you want to feel each day. Perhaps you even have a vision of how to get it. This is connecting to your inner knowing. You know that, if what you want is not filtered through what is possible or practical or what you should do or what others want you to do, it would be really amazing.

Again, in *Launch Your Life*, I call that you who is sending these messages the Real You.

But how come those moments of clarity and inspiration are so hard to come by? They are an authentic expression of you from way down deep inside—the Real You—yet they happen at such odd times. And, even when you try, they can be hard to remember.

One of the challenges in connecting with the Real You is that the voice from your inner knowing and authentic self is quiet. Another might be that you hear the messages, but they are hard to understand. Or, you have the moments, but they don't seem so significant. But you do know something is not right and you are not on-target.

In *Launch Your Life*, I call this sense that there is something more you could be doing, that Gnawing Feeling.

As you begin this journey, it is important to remember that the Real You may be scared and too intimidated to come out. This is okay and quite common. The gnawing is the Real You's effort to get your attention.

It is quite possible that at some point you have expressed the Real You and received less than stellar support. Perhaps your friends laughed at you. Maybe your family told you it was a silly dream. It could be that someone said you would never amount to anything, and now you cannot get that out of your head. It is time to quiet these voices and change the messages.

In the next section, you will learn about your Silly Self-Talk. I often characterize the emergence of the Real You as it struggles against your Silly Self-Talk and cultural messages with this image:

INVITATION

Know that the Real You is in there, and, as you work the *Launch Your Life* process, your quiet little voice will grow stronger and stronger. For now, extend an invitation to the Real You to share and to come play.

With your open invitation, you are saying to yourself that you will protect the Real You when your Silly Self-Talk gets strong and mean. Your open invitation *opens* the possibility to Stand for yourself when others offer that less-than-stellar support.

LISTEN FOR MESSAGES

Once the invitation is extended, the Real You will begin to send messages. The challenge, and opportunity, is to begin to listen for the messages.

By doing this, you will begin to be able to connect to the messages and capture the moments when the Real You speaks up. By paying attention to the existence of messages from the Real You, you will realize that the Real You might want some of these kinds of things (or others):

- to be in better shape and/or eat more healthfully
- to have a positive attitude every day
- to make a difference in your community
- to make your job feel amazing, and be the job you love
- to date someone you really like
- to make the softball or baseball team
- to find a mentor from whom to learn a skill, a trade, or a way of thinking
- to make choices and decisions and feel powerful about them

What is on your list?

132 *NOTICE WHERE YOU ARE NOT ENTHUSIASTIC*

Another way to connect with the Real You is to begin to notice the times when you are not enthusiastic about what you are doing. At these times, you have that feeling there is something else you would like to be doing.

As you pay attention to, and listen to, the gnawing, ask yourself what it is about the activity you are doing that does not resonate with you. You will naturally start with obvious things, then move to more challenging things, and, eventually, move to the deeper levels of what is going on.

IMAGINE THINKING ABOUT HISTORY

For example, let's say you don't like one of the classes you are taking in school. It would be easy to say, "This is the most boring class I have ever taken." If you did some more reflection, you might realize that the reason that you don't like it is, "I don't like history. The teacher talks too much." Eventually, you might realize that school is a very challenging place for you because your learning style is not compatible with the way schools typically teach. Maybe the way you best understand history is by traveling to a place and hearing about that place from the people who live there.

Or, let's say you are wandering down the path of graduating from high school, going to college, getting a job, and doing exactly what you are supposed to do. When people ask about your dreams you say, "I want to provide for my family." But, when you are honest with yourself, you don't like your work. Still, it is easy to say that the gnawing is "just a phase" or "part of the price I pay." But there is more to it than that.

BE HONEST WITH YOURSELF

You want to figure our what the gnawing is about, so, another step is being willing to be honest with yourself.

When you do more reflection, you begin to realize, "There are some interesting things about my work, and I like the pay, but it is not very meaningful." And, eventually, when you are really honest with yourself, you realize there is more you can be doing about it. But, when you passively accept the way things are and try to ignore the challenges, you compromise the Real You.

And, in that real honesty with yourself, you know that not liking how your job is going, being away from your family, and not being happy are *not* accomplishing your goal of providing for your family. You realize that the greatest gift you can give your family is making your life (and work) meaningful, and becoming an engaged part of their lives.

GET TO DEEPER LEVELS

Eventually, as your journey on the Upward Spiral (Secret #1) continues, you will be able to connect easily and consistently with the Real You. You will know what you value and what you Stand for. And you will know when your choices are compromising the Real You.

You will not be lost in the place of "I don't know what I want to do with my life" or "What should I do this weekend?" or "How do I make this situation better for myself?" or "I don't care what kind of job I get." You will know the answers that honor the Real You. You will believe in the gifts you can share with the world.

When you get to that deeper level, you will likely have a beautiful vision of what you want your life to be and who you want to become. You will be clear on a way of being that *you* believe is powerful. You may not always make choices that honor the Real You, but you will not be unclear on what you want.

When you learn to be the OPERATER of your life (Secret #2), you will be able both to analyze and to see the big picture of the situation, and also not get drawn into the temptation to compromise the Real You through your choices. Or, when you do get drawn in, you will be able to reflect about what happened and figure out how to avoid it happening again.

What will your life be like when you can create moments of clarity and inspiration? What will happen when, instead of having them occur randomly when you're not expecting them, you can access those feelings on demand? How can you make it so that, instead of waiting and waiting for those moments of inspiration and clarity, they are at your fingertips?

How do you get from the place of just beginning to be aware that there is, somewhere deep down, the Real You, to a life of aligning all your choices and your stands with the Real You?

The Play Huge Notebook.

PLAY HUGE NOTEBOOK

My Play Huge Notebook includes music, articles, movies, quotes, and anything I can get my hands on that I know kicks me into that powerful space the movie Life as a House did. The requirement for anything that goes into my Play Huge Notebook is that it inspires me, gets me energized, and/or gets me focused. It gets me connected to my Real You.

The Notebook includes quotes I read that help remind me who I want to be, how I want to live each day, and keep me committed to my Stands.

There are letters and notes that people have written me over the years, that help me feel appreciated, loved, and powerful. Here are some examples:

- *Thank you, Morgan, for being there for me.*
- *I really appreciate your effort in helping me with my idea yesterday.*
- *I really appreciate your honesty.*
- *I appreciate your giving me a hug. I really needed it.*
- *I appreciate your work and I appreciate you.*

There are movies that I know always trigger my sense of justice and my desire to make a difference—movies about teachers, about people doing justice in the world, about people inspiring one another and holding each other to a really high level, and about people connecting to each other in meaningful ways. But, again, my criteria are that they inspire me and blast me into a resourceful space.

Certain music gets me juiced, excited, energized, focused, and makes me courageous.

I include certain articles (and some books) to read, that I know will get ideas flowing and my creativity engaged.

And there are activities I know will help get me grounded and feeling ready to Stand powerfully.

Finally, an essential part of the Play Huge Notebook is called the Powerful Portfolio. In my Powerful Portfolio, I keep track of things I am doing that keep me moving in the right direction.

I accumulate actions during which I navigate the Cusp (see page 80) and say Yes! to what I want; this helps me see my pattern of breaking through the barriers that are holding me back, and then being able to Sustain new and effective patterns.

I capture ideas for my Know Yourself so I can keep building and tracking my development. And, because I am creating a portfolio of moments in which I am powerful and in charge, I can grow my Trust Yourself.

By putting all these resources in one place—where I can always remember where they are and don't have to go on a wild goose chase to locate them—I make it easy to know that all I have to do when I am feeling funky or lost or uninspired is open up my Play Huge Notebook.

I know that, when I cannot find resources when I need them, the search can easily throw me farther down a downward spiral. I also know, when I am in a funk or having trouble getting in action, that I don't have the capacity to figure out how to get out of it. I cannot think what will help me get out of it, or what my Real You wants. But the Play Huge Notebook provides a list of resources from a time when I was in a powerful space and I *was* able to figure out what would help.

When you have your Play Huge Notebook, you can always—even when you are in a funk—go in and read some of your quotes, or you can go watch the movie, go on a hike, or do an activity. You know that, with your Play Huge Notebook, you can get yourself out of the funk and into a positive place. You can blast yourself into a more positive space where getting in action is much easier.

Creating Your Play Huge Notebook

How did I create my notebook? I started.

And I started with a three-ring binder, some dividers, and a plastic pouch for letters and notes. The dividers were labeled Quotes, Articles, Lists (movie, song, and book), Activities, and Powerful Portfolio.

My first entries included three quotes, one article, one book, four movies, seven songs, one activity, and two things on my Powerful Portfolio list. I also had a letter of recommendation written by one of my high school teachers.

I would share the specific items in my Play Huge Notebook, but the specifics don't matter. What gets you inspired and focused will be unique to you. To find these things, explore situations in which you were having fun and feeling inspired.

By collecting these resources, you set yourself up for a life of Meaning and Fulfillment.

I suggest you start your Play Huge Notebook right now.

Quiet Your Silly Self-Talk

Like everyone, you have a voice in your head.

Unfortunately, the voice in your head does not tend to be helpful. Instead, the voice in your head tends to take normal, everyday situations and make them into false stories and imaginings. For example, think about talking to someone you have a crush on. Before you have that conversation, you will play out the possible scenarios in your head. You might come up with some imaginings that go like this:

- We start to talk. I say something stupid. He laughs at me and walks away.
- I call her on the phone and she has no idea who I am. Then I have to try to explain how she knows me, and I will sound like a dummy.
- He will not be interested in me and will not talk to me, or, if he does, he will be mean.
- She will think I am uncool.

There are a lot more possibilities of what might happen, and every false story you make up decreases the likelihood you will actually have that conversation.

Sometimes you try playing out entire conversations in your head: "Okay, if I say this, then he will say that, then I will not know what to say, and…um…well…phew…that will be awkward. Okay, so I will not say that. Instead, I will ask about his classes. Good. But what if he does not like his classes? Then what will I do?" And so on and so on and so on and…

Here's another example of Silly Self-Talk in action:

IMAGINE WRITING A PAPER

Imagine you are writing a paper and are not feeling very good about it. You already don't trust yourself and your ability to write a good paper, and then you hear a couple of your friends talking and laughing.

Even though you didn't hear what they were talking about, you are certain that they understood the paper topic and are already done with their papers, and their papers are really good.

While you are writing the paper, your Silly Self-Talk is making up all kinds of false stories: "My paper is not very good, and it is definitely not as good as my friends' papers. The teacher is going to think I am completely stupid when he reads this. He is going to think that I didn't do any of the reading. He is going to think that I don't care about his class. I also bet that everyone else's paper is going to be really good. Whenever someone else talks in class, they say things that make sense, so I am certain that they understand what is going on. Ugh."

Then, after you turn your paper in (if you even do turn it in after the false stories your Silly Self-Talk already has going), you might begin worrying about what grade you are going to get. The story you make up will be something like this: "I am sure that I will get a D. Phew, that will be so bad. I bet I will get the worst grade in the class. When my friends find out, they are going to think I'm a dummy. My parents will be angry, and I probably won't be able to go out this weekend."

> Because of this, you are in a bad mood every day until the paper gets returned.
>
> Then, when the paper comes back, the story you might make up could be something like this: "I cannot believe I got that grade. I am now certainly going to do badly in this class. The teacher doesn't like me and thinks I'm dumb. All my classmates are doing better in the class and are smarter than me. I probably will not get into college either."

In *Launch Your Life*, I call these false stories and imaginings your Silly Self-Talk.

Whether the particular false stories in these examples are true for you is not significant. The important thing to take from this is that we all have Silly Self-Talk and we all make up false stories. Noticing what you say to yourself, and understanding when it is helpful and when it is harmful, is one of the skills that will help when you stand powerfully for yourself. Why? Because when you do this, you will generate many different kinds of reactions from other people, and that means a lot of opportunity for you to make up false stories in your head about what those people are thinking and saying.

Stories are very powerful to us as humans. They resound with our psyches, and bestow lessons and understanding. But not all stories are good, useful, or true, and false stories can be as influencing as true ones. The stories your Silly Self-Talk tells are based on fear and avoidance, not on truth.

Your Silly Self-Talk usually prevents you from taking risks and from connecting with people through communication. And, the worst part is, the reasons you don't have the conversations are not even real! They are imaginings from your Silly Self-Talk. I call it not dealing with reality. And when you don't deal with reality, you waste a lot of time and energy.

But, worse than wasting time and energy is that, when you start to figure out how to manage all the possibilities your Silly Self-Talk has created, you get farther and farther from the Real You. Before you even have the conversation with the person you have a crush on, you have already made them someone who doesn't like you, who makes fun of you, thinks you are uncool, thinks you are not cute enough, thinks you are lonely, thinks your friends are lame, thinks you...thinks you...thinks you...

But, really, you have no idea what how the person will react. *All these possibilities exist only in your head.*

Sadly, after dealing with all this, you forget the simple premise that the Real You has a crush on someone and you want to talk with them.

It takes courage to get in touch with the Real You and what you believe is right about you and right about the world. In every part of *Launch Your Life*, you will get to deal with your Silly Self-Talk.

And, to help you quiet it, here are four steps to control your Silly Self-Talk:

FOUR STEPS TO CONTROL YOUR SILLY SELF-TALK

Step 1—Identify your Silly Self-Talk

You first have to identify the voice in your head. Ready? Answer this question:

Do you have a voice in your head?

You answered either "Yes," "No," or "I don't know," and you very likely did so with—the voice in your head.

We all have it, and it is perfectly normal.

Once you realize what your Silly Self-Talk sounds like, it's important to get familiar with the kinds of false stories and imaginings you have. Here are some examples of things your Silly Self-Talk might say:

- I am not good enough to do that.
- I can't do this.
- I'm not as talented as they are.
- I'll look stupid if I say anything, and everyone will laugh at me.
- That will be embarrassing.
- Obviously, everyone else understands, but not me.
- Who do I think I am?
- I don't know how to do that.

You make a conscious effort to identify your Silly Self-Talk by beginning to notice when your thinking is clouded by these kinds of messages, and then by acknowledging it. Say, "Hi, Silly Self-Talk." It seems crazy! But, by doing this, you will begin to recognize the voice more quickly. Then, as you get better at that, you can quiet it.

You can also begin to notice when other people are sending negative messages to you. Often negative messages come across as people making assumptions about how you feel, how you will react, or your abilities. Or, they come at you as teasing, sarcasm, or joking. And, before you dismiss that as kids just being kids (or parents being parents), know that your Silly Self-Talk loves any and all affirmations, even the sarcastic and joking ones. It uses these to learn where you are vulnerable, and to create new messages to stop you.

When you are familiar with your Silly Self-Talk, another step is beginning to identify situations in which your Silly Self-Talk thrives. You will have your own unique circumstances in which your Silly Self-Talk is the loudest and the harshest. It might be in a math classroom ("I am terrible at math and will never be any good at it"); it might be when you have a crush on someone; it might be when talking about colleges; it might be with your parents. It doesn't matter what it is—just know when to look out for it.

Step 2—Jam Your Silly Self-Talk

Once you are able to identify your Silly Self-Talk, the second step is to jam it—to stop it. Your Silly Self-Talk can easily create a running commentary on everything you do, but there are many different ways to jam the false stories, the imaginings, and the scenarios. You will have to find the ways that are most effective for you.

Here are some suggestions about things you can do to jam the Silly Self-Talk:

- Flood yourself with affirmations.
- Do a reality check by describing exactly what really happened.
- Use positive words and body language, and shift your environment.
- Use your Play Huge Notebook and its resources (music, quotes, etc.).

Using the scenario above, in which you imagine you are writing a paper and not feeling very good about it, here's one way you might jam your Silly Self-Talk:

JAMMING YOUR SILLY SELF-TALK

When you began worrying—"I am sure I will get a D. Phew, that will be so bad. I bet it will be the worst in the class. When my friends find out, they will think I am stupid."—you could say, "Hey, wait a second. This is my Silly Self-Talk. Jam it. Jam it. Yes. Yes. Yes. Yes. I Play Huge. I say useful things all the time. I am awesome!"

Step 3—Figure Out What Really Exists

The better you get at identifying and jamming your Silly Self-Talk, the more you will be able to distinguish between false stories and reality. Instead of wasting time and energy wondering what a teacher thinks about your work or whether someone wants to go out with you, you ask them. Then you know what they really think.

But, beware. You can still get caught in your Silly Self-Talk even after you know what they think. At some point, you certainly have said this kind of thing to yourself: "I know she said she would go out with me, but she is only doing it because she is being nice. She doesn't really like me."

But, once again, if you find yourself thinking this, then it is an opportunity to talk to that person about it.

It is a constant cycle of making sure you are dealing with what really exists.

Step 4—Handle It

The farther you travel on the Upward Spiral, the quieter your Silly Self-Talk gets, and the better you get at dealing only with what really exists. You handle situations with honesty and accountability, because, with courage and confidence and a clear head, you quickly stop the false stories and scenarios. In this place, you will find a tremendous amount of extra time, more energy, increased health, and greater opportunities.

But, more importantly, you will begin to learn you can deal with the complexity, awkwardness, and discomfort of actual outcomes and what people really feel. You honor the Real You and what you feel by letting go of reactions that exist only in your Silly Self-Talk. Oh, and you begin to handle the success that you create, as well.

It might be the case that you wrote a bad paper. It might be that your teacher is disappointed. It might be that you will get a bad grade in the class. It might be that someone thinks you are uncool or not cute enough. If that is the case, then you deal with that reality. Trust Yourself enough to be able to handle the challenge, the complexity, and the opportunity created when you deal with what really exists.

One way to do this is to be honest. As a teacher, I know that almost every teacher would appreciate the following effort:

HANDLING IT HONESTLY...

Mr. Rich, I am disappointed with my effort on this paper. I apologize that I turned it in late. My commitment is to have it in early next time.

I knew weeks ago that this was going to be a busy time for me. Next time, I will anticipate my schedule, and, as soon as I can, I will ask you if we can work something out.

When you *Launch Your Life*, you deal with the things that really happened. You deal with the actual outcomes and what people really feel. You let go of reactions that exist only in your Silly Self-Talk. Stress and excess energy expenditure come from time spent dealing with false stories that don't exist. False stories become, at best, a waste of time and, at worst, a trigger that sends you onto a downward spiral. In order to connect with your Gnawing Feeling and get connected to the Real You, you will have to quiet your Silly Self-Talk.

Answer "What Will It Take?"

"OUT THERE"

When I was a kid, I began my search for Meaning and Fulfillment in the place I had always known with absolute certainty was the source of the Gnawing Feeling. I knew the life I wanted was "out there" somewhere. Many of my friends had it. My teachers had it. People in my family had it. Older kids definitely had it (especially the ones who could talk to girls). And, in my head, none of these people had that Gnawing Feeling. It was just me, and, because of that, there was obviously something wrong with me.

I began my journey thinking it would happen when I got to a certain place in life. The people not still in their first year of college seemed to have a certain confidence about them. But, when I became a college sophomore, my Gnawing Feeling persisted. Then I was sure that, when I chose a major, it would go away, because my path would be clear and others who had majors had a certain confidence about them. But, when I chose my major, it was really hard, and I felt more lost even than I had previously.

Okay, it will become clear when I become a senior. No.

Um, my path will become clear when I graduate from college. No.

Then it will happen when I get a job. No.

It must happen when I start making more money. No.

The life you want is not out there somewhere.

In all my years of thinking there was something wrong with me, of fluctuating between being oblivious and caring too much, and of being convinced that everyone else had their lives all together, and, someday...maybe, I would figure it out for myself, I thought that something would happen to get me to the place everybody else already was.

THE ENVIRONMENTALIST WITH THE PAPER CUP AND THE BOTTLED WATER

She had started a program called the "The Sustainability Minute" on a well-known radio station in a big city and was getting lots of acclaim. It was an honor to have her come speak to my environmental science class.

However, when she walked into our classroom, she had a double paper cup, with "cozy," from a local coffee merchant, and a disposable bottle of water. There could have been a reasonable explanation for these items, but the message to my students was still clear: she believed the solution to Sustainability was somewhere "out there," and talking about Sustainability on the radio would solve the problem.

My students brought up questions about her integrity. Did her values match her actions? How could she be doing a radio program on Sustainability issues, while using several products that were not Sustainable, when talking to a group of students about that very issue? They wondered if she were aware of the inconsistency, or if she did not care about the inconsistency.

When I asked later what she had talked about during her forty-five-minute discussion, none of my students could tell me. Before she began talking, they had stopped listening because, as they described it, they sensed a credibility issue.

Eventually, my class and I realized that we live thinking there is an "out there" somewhere. We think there is some magical occurrence when we get into college, get a job, graduate, move away from home, fall in love, get married, have kids, make a certain income, retire, etc., that will make our lives all we want them to be.

As a kid, I had always imagined people were doing something I was not doing; thus, by doing what they were doing, I would like my life. But I became confused because, when I did those things, nothing changed. I still felt lost, confused, uncertain, and that I must be missing something. What my class and I realized is that Meaning and Fulfillment are very personal.

When you Stand for something, and you do something to express that, it feels good. When you talk about Sustainability and your actions are congruent with your belief, it feels good. When you love drawing and you draw, it feels good. When you care about people and you spend time with them, it feels good.

Events are just events. What matters is participating in events in a way that honors the Real You.

In this way, life is not "out there" anywhere. It is right here. Sustainability is not just about doing a radio show; it is about living Sustainably. Life happens when you saturate every moment of your days with thoughtful action. Making your life what you want it to be will not happen someday or somewhere. It will only happen in your every action.

Life is a process, not an event.

Your life is happening right here and right now. How is it going for you?

What will it take for you to engage in the process?

It will take making all your choices matter, so, when you act, you honor the Real You.

It will take realizing that what you want is right here, and all it takes is active engagement by you.

TAKING CHARGE OF CHANGE

Beyond believing life is "out there" somewhere, my research has also made it clear that you believe change is something that happens to you. You get the job. You get into the school. You win the lottery. Or not.

You believe that the way your life turns into what you want it to be is because an event happens, or a series of events happens, or they don't happen. You have fallen into a trance of forgetting that change happens through action and perseverance. You overlook your ability to create change, and you are uncertain in your ability to enjoy the current moment.

Here's an alternative to letting life happen to you that serves as a preview of what is to come in the next chapter.

THE TOLLBOOTH WORKER

Working in a tollbooth can be very boring, repetitive, unfulfilling work, or—in a word—tiresome.

But it was not tiresome for a guy who worked in a tollbooth near the Golden Gate Bridge in San Francisco. Why? Because he took charge of change. No, not dimes and quarters, but of his attitude.

Instead of being bored, he thought, "I get to be outside all day, looking at the woods and one of the most beautiful bays in the world. I get to interact with thousands of people every day, and I can make them smile. I can listen to music I love, and dance in my office all day."

People were constantly amazed at the tollbooth guy. He was in such a good mood, and he made his own day and the days of others around him so positive. He chose to make his work meaningful. He believed he had the opportunity to touch many, many lives each day, and provide a smile for people.

Meaning and Fulfillment will NOT happen someday until it happens today. And tomorrow. And the next day. When you are in your power, you can do it. It is your choice.

Think of the number of people you know who don't like school, are mad at a friend, or are unhappy in their job. Perhaps you are one of those people. You have a choice. You can figure out how to make that not-so-great situation matter.

In fact, the only way it can happen for you is to make it happen. It will never happen *to* you. You will always create it.

What will it take for you to engage in the process?

It will take your being in your power and making powerful choices about creating your life in a way that honors the Real You.

BE ONE OF THE 3 OUT OF 100

When I am in large groups of people, there are usually a couple of people I am drawn to. Something about them differentiates them from others. I call them the "3 out of 100." What draws me to them is an intangible sense of confidence they exude. It isn't the boisterous, hip, trendy, or popular people. It is not the "out there" stuff or their accomplishments or résumés. It turns out that it is people with character. It is the people who are honest, have integrity, are respectful, thoughtful, playful, who have present and engaged relationships with people, and treat people with dignity and respect. Oh, and they are the people who laugh at my jokes.

The characteristics have become clear and consistent in my years of reflection. They have gained greater clarity when I have encountered people who are living their lives passionately and in congruence with who they are and what they value.

When I have gotten to know people like this, I find they do far more listening than talking. They don't spend time explaining/justifying their lives. They typically know what they Stand for and are clear in their values, while also being curious about learning, exploring, and asking hard questions about their lives. They don't particularly care what they are "supposed" to be doing or about the things that they "should" be paying attention to. They are in action, making things happen in their community and their lives, but they are not caught up in the mantra of our time—"I am too busy." They are very good at protecting their word. They enter into the challenging parts of relationships. They go into the messy situations that are complex, challenging, and uncertain. They are willing to take risks and learn from their mistakes. They Stand up for common sense, so, when something seems too good to be true and they know in their hearts that the premise is faulty, they don't allow themselves to get drawn into behavior or actions that compromise their integrity.

Simply put, every little moment and interaction is a committed step on their paths.

But, more than anything else, they are good people who care about other people. They treat every person with respect and with dignity. They are not willing to gain personal advantage on the backs of others. They have time for friends and family. They are engaged in the lives of their kids and partners. They are available for people.

They have character.

What will it take?

Live in integrity with the Real You. Make your actions match your values.

POSSIBLE BARRIERS

If it were easy to fill your life with Meaning and Fulfillment, there would be no purpose for a book like *Launch Your Life*. But it is not easy, and there are many barriers that currently exist in your life, and more you will experience as you move forward. This section will highlight many of those possible barriers, and will also explain several warning signs intended to raise a flag on behaviors that indicate help is needed.

Challenges You Face

OUR TEST SCORE CULTURE

In my research, I looked at the things that bring Meaning and Fulfillment, the "out there" and "right here" issue, the ability to take charge of change, the lack of confidence issue, and Meaning and Fulfillment being about people.

What became evident is that most of us do believe change is "out there" in the world somewhere beyond our grasp, that people who are successful have somehow managed to enter the "out there" world, and that the most important things are things.

THE SICK HUSBAND

A client shared this story about spending the day with her husband who wasn't feeling well. She told me, "I took the day off. I took care of him. I made him soup. I got him juice. I kept the house quiet so he could sleep. I spent the day helping him get healthy and be comfortable.

"Then, Tuesday morning, I got up and went to work. When I got there, I felt completely behind. I felt like I hadn't done anything. I felt that I wasn't productive."

And I will never forget my client then saying, "The world does not value the way I spent my day. What the world values is production. It values getting through your to-do list. It is more important for me to get things done than it is to take care of my sick husband."

She was feeling bad about spending her day with her sick husband. She was feeling bad about taking care of him, getting him juice, making him soup, and helping him rest.

SCHOOLS, TEST SCORES, GRADES

In our culture, you are inundated with messages that tell you to have the right external appearance, the right products, to do the right things to impress people. We have become the Test Score Culture. You learn to look at all the impressive places people have gone to school and worked. You learn to look at all the cool and hip stuff people have. You have learned to value how much money you make. You have learned to value only things that you can put on a résumé. You get very little acknowledgment for who you are.

Here's a list of things test scores will never convey:

- You want to make a difference in the world.
- People respect you.
- You are creative.
- You work hard.
- You are a good friend.
- You care about people.
- You have integrity.
- You are committed to being a conscientious and engaged family member and friend.
- You complete any task you take on, early and with a high level of excellence.
- You are a good listener and inspire people as a leader.
- You love to share your sense of humor.
- You love playing music.
- You love to listen to birds singing on a spring morning.
- You want to have lots of close friends, and feel sad that you have had challenges finding people to hang out with.
- You are struggling in school because you feel trapped in a classroom.
- You love being outdoors, and, at camp last summer, you learned how to identify the names and ages of trees.
- You talk to your parents every day, despite the fact that you don't have a great relationship, and you are working on understanding one another.

Here is a list of things test scores can convey:

- You are good at taking tests.
- You are not good at taking tests.

- You have an aptitude for math.
- You have an aptitude for the meaning of words.
- You can perform under pressure—on high-stakes tests.

Which list do you feel represents who you are?

The reason people don't like these tests is because the stakes are very high, but they don't represent who you are.

Further, unfortunately, when you apply to college these days, less and less often do you get a personal interview. *Who you are* is the materials you have presented, your SAT/ACT scores, your grades, and an essay you prepared.

The pattern of the Test Score Culture does not end with test scores and grades; the next stage is using a résumé to get a job. You could duplicate the lists from above with résumés. Résumés don't convey who you are; they convey things you have done.

The message behind this method of admitting students and evaluating candidates is, who you are is not important. What is significant are your test scores, grades, and things you have done.

On top of the challenges with test scores, applications, and résumés, is our culture of advertising. The object of advertising is to sell products. The way products get sold? Create insecurity in a customer, and then offer a solution to feeling bad about himself with the product.

So, even if you are able to navigate the test scores, applications, and résumés, you are inundated with messages that flash in neon lights and with massive repetition: "You are not okay. You would be so much happier, successful, hip, good-looking, etc., if you had our product." The culture piles on here, because, on top of the message that *what you do* is the only thing that is important, you get the message that *who you are* is not okay.

THE (PERCEIVED) VALUE OF MONEY AND THINGS

184

You think that, as you accumulate experiences you can add to your résumé, you will have a better life. You begin to think of yourself as the things you have and the accomplishments you have achieved. There is a principle called the Hedonic Treadmill, which says that, as you accumulate things, your identity becomes the things you have. And, when you "are" your material possessions, you have the false perception that the more things you have, the happier you are. You forget about the essential elements that make up the Real You—what you value, how you treat people, how engaged you are with the people who matter most to you, and what you Stand for.

THE PARKING SPOT

I know a person who raises millions of dollars for green technology innovations. When I was first introduced to her, I was massively impressed. My perception was that she was doing good things for the world. Then she got into a dispute with a friend of mine about a parking space that she owned and my friend was using. The way she handled the situation was enlightening to me.

She wanted to use the parking spot for her Mercedes one time a week. My friend used it every day. They were trying to negotiate a solution. When they were talking, she did not listen. She was a bully. She was absolutely consumed with her own interest, being right, her own situation, and what would make her life more convenient. She completely disregarded my friend.

Here is a person seemingly doing something beneficial for the environment and for people, but treating someone she knew with disrespect and self-righteousness. By external appearances, her life was on-target, but, by the internal measures of her character—how she treated people and who she was—she was off-target. She had become the material possessions she owned, and the things that filled her résumé.

The amount of money you make, or raise for something, is not who you are, just as a résumé is not who you are. The amount of money you make has zero—absolutely nothing—to do with the importance of your work (look at teachers as an example—low pay, important job), just as a résumé is about what you've done, not about how good a person you are.

Oftentimes these days, you don't even get a chance to interview for a job. All you get is the opportunity to submit your written materials. Only if you get past the initial screening process do you get to meet a real person.

PREJUDICE AND THE CHALLENGES OF NOT BEING ACCEPTED

In addition to our Test Score Culture, and the (perceived) value of money and things making you feel like you're not good enough, many of you are not accepted because of the color of your skin, your sexual orientation, or your gender.

This is perhaps the biggest challenge that nonwhite men have to deal with in our culture, the biggest and brightest message that "you are not okay." The message comes in many, many ways, from inequality in getting hired for jobs to making less money in jobs, from how the high-stakes tests are designed to the school buildings kids attend, from our language to messages in advertising and music, and so much more.

Prejudice can have a powerful impact on your abilities. Not being accepted for who you are has a powerful conscious and subconscious impact on your ability to connect with and express the Real You.

I have a friend who is gay. His is (sadly) the stereotypical story of the long and slow acceptance of himself, followed by the stage of knowing this about himself but not being able to tell anyone. It ate him up. Everything he did in his life was compromised because he could not be true to himself. His Real You was really hurting and really lonely. He could not bring himself to face the rejection and ridicule he imagined would happen if he came out to his friends and family.

I believe one reason inner-city schools face such challenges is that everything experienced in those environments tells you that you're not okay. Bathrooms that don't work, graffiti, metal detectors, teachers reading the newspaper throughout the whole class period, buildings that are not maintained, and high-stakes testing—all carry a profound message that you don't matter. Connecting with the Real You in those circumstances is immensely challenging, if not impossible.

When you experience prejudice, the message conveyed is that you are not okay. There is something wrong with you. Thinking there is something wrong with you that you can't do anything about creates a feeling of hopelessness. And, when you feel hopeless, it is hard to be passionate about anything. It compromises the core of the Real You, way down deep, and that makes life very challenging.

ASKING FOR HELP INDICATES POWERFUL SELF-CARE

My experience shows clearly that, when you reach out—showing up for coaching, asking for help, taking responsibility, asking the hard questions, or taking a Stand—that means you have figured out that you are caught in the Test Score Culture of external appearance and achievement. When you reach out, you muster the courage to figure out who you are and what you Stand for. This effort shows you are ready to be one of the 3 out of 100 who have character and are willing to Play Huge.

You might think there is something wrong with you, or you are weak, if you seek support. You might think you should be able to figure it all out on your own. Almost every one of my clients says something like this at some point early in our coaching relationship. They all have to fight through the idea that asking for help makes them seem weak, or unable, or stupid, or something.

But. But. But. But.

But, my experience makes me believe quite the opposite. When you seek support, you are being courageous, bold, powerful, and open-minded. When you seek support, you are the minority who has gotten to a place in which you refuse to continue to live with that gnawing in your gut. You are the one saying, "Enough of this craziness. I am going to do whatever it takes to do something about my Gnawing Feeling." By taking the courageous step to figure out who you are, and then to express it in the world, you are escaping the Test Score Culture and entering the world of Play Huge.

Warning Signs That You Have Work to Do

This section is about warning signs that prevent you from connecting to the Real You.

When I talk with young people about launching their lives, there are always those who immediately come back with the shallow response that "Everything is fine" or "I don't need any help." Along with the shallow response comes the attitude that, "That stuff you talk about is for people who are screwed up."

Others come immediately full of arrogance and body language indicating they believe they have it all together. I call it the "I'm too cool" attitude. I have seen it enough to know not to buy it. In my experience with young people, there is always curiosity about how to *Launch Your Life*, even though sometimes it is buried deep down inside, behind a whole lot of grandstanding.

Over the years, I have learned that beneath the shallow responses are real questions about how to make life awesome. I believe this desire is inside everyone; it's just a matter of finding the right set of keys to unlock the passion.

It takes different people different amounts of time and different motivations to get past the shallow responses and the grandstanding. And, sometimes, there is a lot of resistance to finding the keys that unlock the passion. What follows are behaviors I have seen (and I imagine you have, too) that, to me, are indications there is gnawing that is creating inner turmoil. These behaviors indicate some challenges in your understanding of the Real You. Somehow, you are compromising who you are.

Your shallow responses and acting too cool are efforts to deflect attention away from the vulnerability and confusion you feel. The more unwilling you are to acknowledge the presence of your vulnerability and confusion, the more likely you are to have the following warning signs.

If any of these warning signs are happening in your life (or the life of someone you know), it's an indication that some self-discovery and self-exploration are needed.

PLAY BELOW THE LINE

204

One of the secrets to knowing what you want in your life is a concept I call Play Above the Line. Remember: part of having a meaningful and fulfilling life is being in charge of change. When you Play Above the Line, you take responsibility and ownership for your actions.

When you play *below* the line, you assume the position of being a victim of circumstance. You make excuses for everything. The world happens to you and you have no control over it. When something happens in your life, you explain it by justifying it, laying blame on someone or something, denying there is an issue, and/or giving up.

Here are some examples of what you might say when you are playing below the line:

- The teacher screwed me.
- I was late because the bus was late.
- Everyone else was also talking.
- My dog ate my homework.
- We lost because the referee made a bad call.
- Who cares?! It's a stupid game anyway.

These are all excuses. And, if you find yourself saying stuff like this often, it's a warning sign that you have work to do.

SHALLOW THINKING

When I asked one of my former students what she wants to do with her life, she said, "Provide for my family." Another former student said, "I don't care. I just want to make a lot of money and, truthfully, party." Yet another former student said, "I want to get good grades; I want to get into a good college; I want to graduate at the top of my class. Then I want to get a good job and keep going from there." All these people are in their early twenties now.

Because I know these people, I know they are only skimming the surface of what is possible for them. And I know that shallow thinking is not the only warning sign they are exhibiting. When they talk about what they want for their lives, I know they are reciting the party line of what they feel they are supposed to say, and doing what they feel they are supposed to be doing. My experience says, at some point in the coming years, they will begin to do some deeper thinking about what they really want their lives to be like.

I also know my peers, around forty years old, who said the same things and are now grown-up examples of the outcomes of shallow thinking in their early twenties. They are what my former students are on the path to becoming. I have seen the shallowness lead to many job changes, lack of satisfaction with life, substance abuse (and other warning signs below), and challenges finding meaningful relationships.

Some are married now or in committed relationships, but have settled for these relationships in desperation. These are not relationships based on honesty, passion, shared vision, and commitment. And this is not happening just with my former students and current peers; it is happening all over our country. I believe this is one of the reasons so many marriages/committed relationships end in divorce/break-up, and many of those that don't are surviving, not thriving.

If you find you are skimming the surface, reciting the party line of what you are supposed to be doing, and living exactly the way you "should" be living, be aware. Doing only what you "should" can be a warning sign that some deeper thought and consideration could help you connect to the Real You and find your path.

SUBSTANCE- AND SELF-ABUSE

The next category of warning signs is any kind of substance- or self-abuse. If you smoke, have an eating disorder, are doing drugs or any kind of self-harm or self-mutilation, or if you have an overreliance on appearance or getting a lot of tattoos or piercings, know that these are warning signs. If you are engaged in any of these things, some self-discovery and self-exploration are needed. They are signs that you have a real opportunity to connect with the Real You in a really, really different way than you currently do.

These activities are based on a profound compromise of the Real You. These behaviors are happening because you are groping for something more, but you cannot figure out what. When you connect with the Real You and get the message that who you are is okay, the substance- or self-abuse will be much easier to stop.

GAMBLING

I know many young people, especially boys, who have gotten involved in gambling. In sports, gambling tends to be a way to make events that aren't interesting (for example, a Thursday night football game between two teams you don't care about) worth watching and spending time on. Other kinds of gambling seem to be an effort to escape reality.

I have heard the arguments that playing poker is a way to be social. I have even seen situations where friendly poker games bring together people who probably would not otherwise be hanging out, and they can be a fun activity for good friends. When it happens like that, it can have social value. But be careful. It is easy to use "it's a good way to be social" as a justification for your gambling and as a cover-up for your vulnerability.

If you are gambling, pay attention. It may be just a fun activity, but it can very easily become a warning sign that you have exploration to do, and you have strayed from a path that will get you what you want in your life.

OVERINDULGENCE–THINGS

If you are always dressed in the nicest clothes...if you have all the new stuff, all the time (whether clothes or gadgets, electronics or haircuts)...that can be a smoke screen for a vulnerability that's underneath. If you want people to be impressed by your appearance or the stuff you have, it can be because you don't feel good about who you are. This is quite common in U.S. culture, and it is a warning sign.

OVERINDULGENCE–FOOD

It is also possible to overindulge in food. Usually in this scenario, the kind of food that gets eaten is classic junk food or something indulgent. It is not healthy. This habit is also often accompanied by a lack of exercise, and that is not a recipe for long-term fulfillment. This kind of overindulgence, as well as all the others, can be a warning sign that some deeper work, some deeper self-exploration, and some search for honesty should be done.

OVERINDULGENCE–TV, VIDEO GAMES, WEB SURFING

If you spend a significant amount of time watching television, playing video games, or surfing the web, you should pay attention to those habits. They are often indications of loneliness, lack of clarity, or hopelessness. When you spend many consecutive hours doing these things, it creates a trance state in which you escape reality—which is often the reason you do it. And that is exactly the point. If you constantly feel the need to escape your reality, take that as an indication that deeper self-exploration and self-reflection could help get you moving in a more healthy direction.

MEANNESS

If you are mean and disrespectful to people, or people think you are mean and don't feel respected by you, there is likely an opportunity to reflect and to do some evaluation on your way of being.

THE OUTRAGEOUSNESS TRAP

I had a camper one year who always wanted to take all activities to the extreme. If we were rock climbing, he wanted to climb the hardest climb or wanted to climb without safety ropes. If we were backpacking, he would suggest we take unsafe routes, hike at night, or ignore our need to replenish water reserves. If we were rafting, he would want to run (or swim) the most dangerous path.

The reason for his outrageousness was that, whenever he talked about it, the staff and the campers reacted strongly, and would end up spending a lot of time and energy focused on him and his requests.

I also worked with a young person with a lot of piercings. Through the years I knew her, the piercings became more and more outrageous (provocative). The pattern worked like this:

Piercings, Piercings, and More Piercings

Teachers, parents, and peers reacted to her piercings, and she would get attention for what she looked liked and what she had done.

Later, after everyone had gotten used to her appearance, another, more edgy piercing would appear. The conversation around her would always be "Doesn't that hurt?" or "What if you want to take it out?"

More months would go by, everyone would get used to that, and the attention would dissipate. Then she began the conversation about what she was going to do next. And it was important that the next idea was more edgy than the previous one.

The pattern was piercing, reaction, dissipation of reaction, discussion of what's next, reaction, more discussion, more reaction, new piercing, reaction, dissipation of reaction, and so on.

I was always conscious of my reactions. I felt like the more appalled I was at the new idea or the more I talked through the idea with her, the more I was adding to what she perceived as a challenge. But, the more I did not engage, the more outrageous the next idea became. Eventually, I began giving attention to her for as many other things (her classes, ideas, and friends) as I could, which only sort of worked. She went to find others who would react in the way she wanted them to.

In both these examples, there is a need to be more and more outrageous. Two things happen here. The first is, these people got lots of attention for being outrageous, which was the purpose of the behavior. But the second thing that happens is the reason this is a warning sign. When the focus is on your newest piercing or newest tattoo, people are focused on superficial aspects of you. The outrageousness creates a situation in which people, including yourself, are focusing on your behavior, and not on who you are. In order to find the path that will bring you Meaning and Fulfillment, you have to focus on the Real You.

Beyond the Barriers

The goal of Your Launch Pad is for you to connect to the Real You and feel the passion inside you that will be the basis for you to *Launch Your Life*. Without that connection and that passion, your results will be shaky. Remember, the target of *Launch Your Life* is creating a life of Meaning and Fulfillment. If you are getting stopped by any of these barriers, or if you are engaged in any of the activities I have called warning signs, I strongly suggest you take a courageous action right now and talk to someone who can help you break the pattern you are in.

It takes tremendous courage to make your life happen. If Launching Your Life were easy and obvious, then everyone would be doing it. Connecting to who you really are, and expressing it in the world, takes courage, perseverance, humility, and community. It's About People! And it's about passionately fulfilling the potential of the Real You. You have picked up this book and made it this far. I acknowledge your courage and your commitment to yourself!

HUGE OUTCOMES—YOUR LAUNCH PAD

I am beginning to realize I am **NOT CRAZY** and I am **NOT ALONE**. Everybody deals with doubts, Silly Self-Talk, and lack of motivation.

I also realize that things that don't seem possible, or that I don't know how to get, is perfectly okay. Actually, **IT IS EXCITING**.

Aha. Life is a **JOURNEY**, not a **DESTINATION**. What will get me what I want is starting the journey, **NOT WAITING AROUND** for something to happen to me.

JAMIE

I feel like I am **WAKING UP**. I now understand that that strange feeling is not something wrong with me, but is my **REAL YOU**.

I want to pay more **ATTENTION** to my deep desires. I want to learn about them, and I am ready to **START LIVING** with passion.

Oh crap. I am definitely caught up in behaviors that are not getting me **WHAT I WANT**. **WHAT WILL IT TAKE** for me to get out of it? I know deep down I want to get out of it—phew—does it feel like a **LONG JOURNEY**.

I now know, in my honest moments, there is **SOMETHING MORE** that I want. It is now just a matter of figuring out **HOW TO GET IT**.

It is a **RELIEF** that I don't have to have everything figured out. I certainly have **QUESTIONS** about what I want to do and how to do it, but now I realize the answers I want are not going to **MAGICALLY APPEAR** one day. I have the ability and desire to figure them out!

It is **AWESOME** knowing that I want it!

I am willing to do **SOMETHING** about it.

I want a life of **MEANING** and **FULFILLMENT**.

Ah! **MY REAL YOU**. Silly Self-Talk. My Play Huge Notebook. Gnawing Feeling.

It is great having **SOMETHING** to call these things!

Now I can **START NOTICING** what they are saying and when they are around.

Huge Outcomes: Text Version

And what is the importance of getting in the game? How will being connected to my Real You show up in my life?

AWARE OF THE REAL YOU

There is a Real You. You are in there, despite all the messages about who you should be and what you should do, and being intimidated by your Silly Self-Talk. You have that Gnawing Feeling, and, now that you recognize it, you are able to observe it when it shows up. As you observe it, you are able to listen to the messages the Gnawing Feeling has for you.

At this stage, the messages might not be clear, and you might still be wondering what being aware of the Real You does for you, but acknowledging its presence and giving it a name is the place to start.

YOU ARE NOT CRAZY...

When you get connected to the Real You, you realize you are not crazy. You realize that feeling confused, being disappointed, and wondering what is wrong with you, are all a waste of time. You realize that you care about yourself, and you want to do something powerful about all the confusion, disappointment, and harsh Silly Self-Talk.

...AND YOU ARE NOT ALONE!

Part of realizing you are not crazy is understanding you are not all alone in having the Gnawing Feeling that there is more to life. You previously thought other people could not possibly be feeling the same way, but now you realize they are wrapped up with their own Silly Self-Talks and their own challenges to connect with their Real Yous.

WAKE-UP CALL

The warning signs are real, and they are confirmation that some of the behavior(s) you are engaged in indicate you are struggling. Stop pretending everything is just fine. Figure out how to get more in line with what you really want from your life, now that you understand that the path to what the Real You wants is possible, you are not alone on that journey, and the journey is a lot of fun.

OUT OF THE TRANCE AND INTO YOUR PASSION

You have made it this far. You are listening to the voice inside you saying, "Yes! I want to begin living, and I want to begin, or continue, my journey toward Meaning and Fulfillment." You are beginning to remember that you are passionate!

You realize you have the ability to honor the Real You and live passionately.

When you realize you are at this point, be certain to acknowledge yourself. It takes commitment to yourself. It takes courage. And you have gotten to the place where you are by saying Yes!

This. Is. Huge! Congratulations!

Foundational Terms

Your Launch Pad introduced several ideas that appear again and again in *Launch Your Life*. You will continue to use your **Gnawing Feeling** as motivation to learn about the **Real You**; you will be challenged to quiet your **Silly Self-Talk** and resist the pressures of the **Test Score Culture**; you will have the opportunity to build your **Play Huge Notebook**, including the **Powerful Portfolio**; and you will figure out how to make your life full of **Meaning and Fulfillment**.

WRAP-UP

You are blasted awake by your alarm clock. But, instead of the sounds that usually come out of your alarm, there is a voice that repeats:

Your journey begins in the moment you decide to act.
And you can act.

In your confusion, you listen many times, and then you hit snooze. But, instead of the voice stopping as usually happens when you hit snooze, the message changes:

It will take connecting with the Real You,
awakening your passion, and then remembering
that you have the ability to make a difference.

Irritated and now awake, you get up and get yourself ready for the day. When you get around to checking your computer, your screen has another unusual message:

How ready are you for the journey? (click to continue)

You click and a presentation begins:

The goal of this presentation is to coach you to establish your commitment to get to the Play Huge Stage, because that is the place where your life has a clear destination and a clear way of getting to that destination.

On the Play Huge Stage, you will have a life full of Meaning and Fulfillment. You will be connected to the people you want to be connected to. You will deal with complexity and discomfort. You will honor the Real You. Everything you do will feel like it is on-target.

The commitment and desire is in you. It might be that it is quiet or uncertain. You may not feel confident that anything you want or believe is worthwhile. Your Silly Self-Talk may be strong and loud. You might think it will take something extraordinary to make your life happen in the way you want it to happen.

At this point you begin to stand up, thinking, "Enough of this craziness." But, as soon as you turn to walk away, you hear a song that shakes you into believing the Real You is in there and has something to say.

So you begin by inviting the Real You to speak up and share. You sense there is more to your life, so you also work to quiet your Silly Self-Talk, to clear time and energy to explore the possibilities.

At this point you have to get to school, so you leave the house.

As you make your way through your day, you notice yourself exploring possibilities of what the Real You wants, and you begin to realize what you want your life to become. You also notice what you don't like about your current activities, and think they are the source of the Gnawing Feeling you have.

And, just as you begin to get excited about going to the Play Huge Stage this evening to begin to make your life what you want it to be, your phone rings.

It's some person you barely know, inviting you to a party later.

You may find it very easy to say, "I am already doing something tonight. I'll catch you later," because you know you are ready and excited about the journey on the Play Huge Stage. Or, it may take a huge amount of courage to even consider the trip to the Play Huge Stage, and the invitation might give you an easy out. In either case, there are, and will continue to be, barriers on your journey. That is the nature of life, and confronting barriers is one of the many situations in which Meaning and Fulfillment happen.

Now, you may believe you are already on the journey; so, going to the party later is just fine for you. You may not believe you need the Play Huge Stage, and that may be the case. But, if on your journey there are signs that are confusing (what I call warning signs) and problem behaviors you are involved in, you need to be careful about accepting this person's invitation.

Substance abuse does not make for a Sustainable journey; self-harm has no chance of leading to Meaning and Fulfillment; overindulgence is not Sustainable; don't bet on your odds of gambling your way to Meaning or Fulfillment; beware of the "more outrageous" path; not everything is someone else's fault. These signs on your journey indicate that some self-discovery and self-exploration are necessary (and sooner is better than later).

Most of you will be completely capable of staying committed to the excitement you felt about what is possible for you, and of avoiding the warning signs. After the person's phone call, you get directions to the Play

Huge Stage, and begin to imagine what it will be like for you. As you are walking to class, your phone rings again.

This time it is your mom or dad. You tell them about your exciting day and what you plan to do tonight, but they are not as excited as you. If fact, they discourage you from going. You begin to feel that everyone and everything in your life is sending a message that you should stay the course, do what you are supposed to do, do what everyone else does, and be smart. You may even feel you have no choice and that all the variables are against you.

But, after you hang up, that Gnawing Feeling persists. You think you are crazy.

Just as you are about to bail on the idea of going to the Play Huge Stage, a friend sends you a text message:

I have had the strangest day! You would not believe the things that have happened. It started with my alarm clock...

You text back:

I have the directions to the Play Huge Stage.
Let's meet at six, and we will go over there.

Before you meet your friend, you go home and, by chance, check your computer again. There is another message:

Congratulations to you for connecting to the Gnawing Feeling and being curious about the Real You.

And be proud of your commitment to yourself. This journey will make all the difference you are looking for in your life!

The Real You knows you want more from your life,
so, right here and right now is the opportunity
for the Real You to make a choice.

Play Huge!

SECRET #1

SECRET #1

Believe in the Upward Spiral

Life is a series of steps forward.

You will never arrive at some place in your life where you have "made it." Life is a process, not an event. Nothing magical will happen when you graduate from high school. There is not a path paved from getting into college to living the life you want. Getting a job does not guarantee a life of happiness. Things don't happen that way.

Living the life you want happens on the Upward Spiral—by taking small confident and committed steps forward.

The Upward Spiral begins modestly and with humility. The beginning stages are not flashy and glamorous; they are dirty and challenging. But they are also massively rewarding and important. Getting a solid foundation will make all the difference.

This secret sits between Your Launch Pad and Play Huge for a reason. You are preparing to *Launch Your Life*. You know you have the Gnawing Feeling and you want to do something about it, but you may not feel certainty about what to act on. So, Believe in the Upward Spiral.

The Upward Spiral will both help you identify and get connected to the Real You, and the Upward Spiral will help you take that connection and make your life everything you want.

A HIKING TRIP

Imagine you are on a hiking trip headed to a campsite. You come to a fork in the path. Which path will get you to your destination? Perhaps you have a map; perhaps not. Perhaps you have prior experience; perhaps not. Perhaps you have a gut feeling; perhaps not. Perhaps there is a sign; perhaps not.

166

You have to choose a path. The sooner you are able to figure out which path goes to your destination, the better off you will be. You choose a path, and, the whole time, you are reflecting upon and evaluating whether you are on the path you want to be on. You realize that the farther you get from the fork in the path, the riskier your journey becomes, but you also realize you might be right in the middle of an important learning experience for yourself. No matter when you figure out which path is the one that will get you to your destination, you can make it a learning experience.

This experience is the same as connecting to the Real You on the Upward Spiral. The sooner you connect to the Real You, the sooner you can get on your way to your desired destination. But, it might be that you have to go far down lots of wrong paths in order to figure out what the Real You wants. The risk is getting too far down a path where the consequences are significant. For example, it is dark, you have nowhere to camp, and you haven't eaten. Or, you are now a college senior, your loans are running out, and it is time to find a job. In this case, you are still on the Upward Spiral, but you have created a big challenge for yourself.

A SOLID FOUNDATION

89

The solid foundation makes a difference because, when you get your path going on the Upward Spiral, amazing things will happen—things you cannot yet imagine. When those things begin happening, being grounded with a foundational connection to the Real You will allow you to keep the forward steps going.

Without that foundation, you will get thrown off the spiral and end up back at the beginning, bruised, poor, and with less energy.

Imagine you are at college and need to choose a major. You are uncertain, but the deadline is approaching. Then, one day in a class, you get excited about a project you are working on. You get caught up in your excitement and decide you want to major in that subject. You begin taking more classes in that subject, but they are not as exciting as the one you originally took. You figure it will get better when you get to the more advanced classes, but, when you are a senior, the advanced classes are no better. You are disheartened because you really don't like your major. But now you have invested time, money, and energy in this major, and to go back would be really difficult. It feels like being thrown off the spiral.

Now, if you think you need to have "it" all figured out before you begin your journey, you are wrong! You need three things. The first is willingness and courage to take the first step. The second is humility and a willingness to dig in and learn. The third is a seat belt. The Upward Spiral begins right where you are, right now, and, when it goes, it goes, so you have to be ready.

UPWARD SPIRAL CYCLE

The Upward Spiral builds on your foundation, and works by your beginning today to make an effort. You take courageous steps and you learn something small. Then, tomorrow, you take another courageous step and you learn a little more. Then, the next day, you make a mistake, fail, or have to deal with a challenge, but you work through it, and take another courageous step, and you learn a little more.

Each courageous step makes the next step more of a possibility. You gain momentum through your learning and expanding of who you are. But the mistakes keep getting bigger and more frustrating. Initially, you keep making an effort, but, with time, your effort gets harder and harder. As your frustration increases, it is harder to remember your foundation. When you forget your motivation and don't feel inspired, then you do something to remember the Real You. This will reconnect you with your foundation and help you feel reenergized to keep making an effort and creating learning experiences.

120 Once you understand the Upward Spiral Cycle, your learning increases, you feel good, things start going well. And they keep going well, and you keep learning and feeling good. And it keeps going. And, the whole time, you are learning and enhancing your abilities. You expand your self-knowledge. You trust yourself more and more easily. Things you used to think were challenging and/or were mistakes are now easy to handle, and you find new challenges to keep you on your Learning Edge (see page 86). Opportunities you used to think were impossible, become possible.

Launching Your Life is not superficial. It will not happen all of a sudden. You cannot say, "I want to be an expert at communication," and expect to wake up tomorrow and be an expert. The way it happens is that you learn a little bit today, more tomorrow and the next day, and then, a month from now, you have made some progress and your knowledge expertise is at a different level, and it keeps going. When you are in the momentum of the Upward Spiral, you will be amazed at how your life shifts in a positive way.

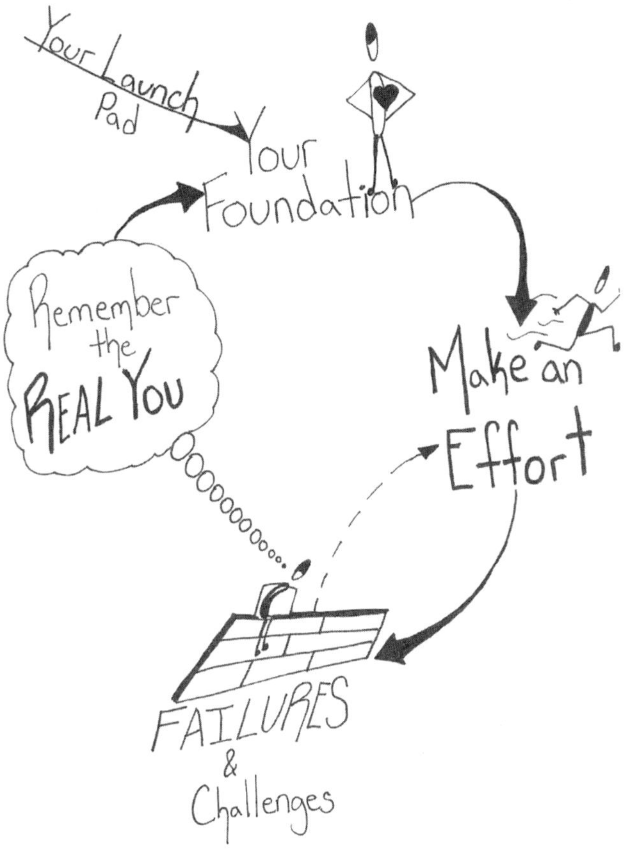

Next are more details on the four steps of the Upward Spiral Cycle: your foundation, making an effort, failures and challenges, and remembering the Real You.

More on Your Foundation

When considering a long-term relationship, it is easy to get swept up in superficial aspects of how someone looks, the clothes they wear, and how cool they are, and miss some important qualities. Do they treat people well? Do they listen? Do they have healthy habits? Are they respectful? Do they feel good about themselves for who they are (not the car they drive)?

Building your foundation on the Upward Spiral is similar. It is so tempting to get caught up in looking good and in image, but they do not create what you want in the long term.

Unless you are massively superficial—and you probably would not be reading this if that were the case—when you think about spending your life with someone, you want a foundational quality in that person. You don't want someone who is not connected to who they are but is good at being flashy; you will be more attracted to a good person who has strong values, is passionate, and is respectful.

You will constantly come back to your foundation, the Real You, as you take steps forward on your journey, because the journey is not a straight line and is full of struggles, challenges, mistakes, failures, and getting dirty. It will be frustrating and will test your perseverance. The way to stay on the Upward Spiral is to remember your foundation when these challenges arise.

Connecting to the Real You allows you to take the next courageous step forward.

Making an Effort

Once you have some foundation established, all you need is the willingness and the courage to make an effort. When you learn to Play Huge in the next chapter, you will be challenged to make an effort and get in action. And it is absolutely, 100% essential that you make an effort. Commitment, persistence, and action are the only things that will keep you forwarding the action and deepening your learning.

Failures and Challenges

But, making an effort will not be enough. When you make an effort, you make mistakes, create failures, and face challenges. The question becomes, what do you do when this happens?

You will learn strategies throughout *Launch Your Life* that will help you with these challenges. You have already learned a strategy for dealing with your Silly Self-Talk; you will learn to Play

Above the Line; you will get to learn on the Play Huge Stage; and much more. You will become more and more powerful in using these mistakes as learning experiences, and in dealing with the challenges. But, as you make your way and push your Learning Edge, none of these strategies will work unless you are connected to a solid foundation.

Remember the Real You

When these challenges arise, undirected action will not produce a solution.

An Upward Spiral is the journey to Meaning and Fulfillment. It is a life of courageous steps. But, if you are anything like me, at these challenging (and many other) times, I am ready for courageous action, but I lose the connection with my Real You. I know I want to be doing something productive and effective, but I cannot remember what productive and effective thing I want to be doing.

At these moments, it is critical to take action to remember the Real You! Pull out your Play Huge Notebook and do something that inspires you. 21

Remembering the Real You at challenging times will keep you on track during these times. Otherwise, you get caught in a dangerous loop that will eventually throw you off the Upward Spiral. Staying on the Upward Spiral will take a commitment to honor the Real You. 76

Here is a visual rendering of the Upward Spiral:

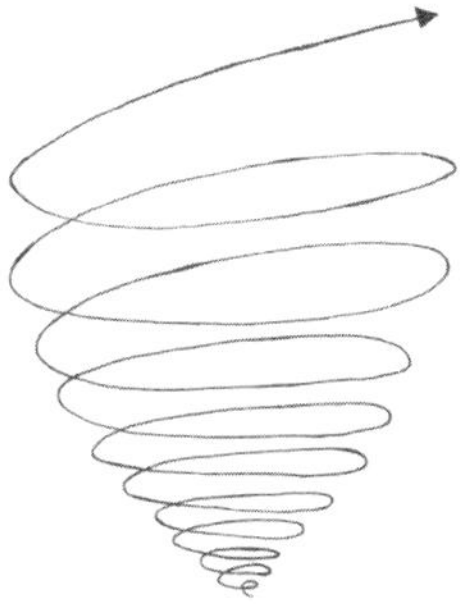

Your journey on the Upward Spiral will be filled with acknowledgment, the discomfort of being challenged, positive energy, and learning. It is absolutely amazing what will happen to your life, your relationships, and your commitment to Meaning and Fulfillment when you are connected to the Real You and believe in the Upward Spiral.

You know that, when you are on a downward spiral, bad things lead to bad things and to more bad things, and it can feel out of control. The same dynamic can happen on the Upward Spiral: when you work the cycle, good things lead to more good things, which lead to more and bigger good things. Believe in the Upward Spiral.

ONWARD TO PLAY HUGE

Enough of the explanation and ideas. Being true to the spirit of Play Huge, it is time to get in action. To get the Upward Spiral working, you have got to act. Whenever you face a challenge in your life, you can't make a decision, or don't know where to start, or whatever your chicken-and-egg scenario is (what comes first?), the answer is to Play Huge.

Ready? Let's go!

WHAT WILL IT TAKE?

HEY JAMIE! SEE YOU AT HOME!
YEAH, SEE YOU GUYS LATER ON.
MORGAN PARK
"OH, THEY DON'T KNOW ME. SOMEDAY THEY'LL SEE ME."
COOL. NOW LET'S GO HANG OUT AND PLAY SOME GAMES.
WE JUST GOT HERE AND NOW IS THE ONLY TIME I'VE GOT TO PLAY FOR A WHILE.
EVERYBODY ON MA ROUTE IS TALKIN' BOUT' SKYWRITIN'.
JOHN'S
IN HERE TOO, BUT I SAY ANYTHING TO LIVEN THINGS UP AROUND HERE IS GOOD THOUGH.

WHAT WILL IT TAKE?

...AND BE INSPIRED TO BE CREATIVE!
THAT'S "AWESOME"
I'LL BE THERE IF I CAN CONVINCE MY PARENTS.
I HOPE TO SEE YOU THERE.
AROUND THE DINNER TABLE
THEY SAY IT'S GOING TO BE FUN.
HE NEEDS TO PULL UP HIS GRADES FIRST.
I'M SURE. IT'S JUST THE KIND OF THING YOUR BROTHER WOULD LIKE.
SORRY I'M LATE EVERYONE, WHAT'S UP?
LATE AGAIN? DON'T MAKE ANY PLANS FOR THIS WEEKEND. YOU'LL BE AT HOME.
DON'T WORRY I PICKED UP SOME GREAT MOVIES ABOUT MODERN ART FOR MOVIE NIGHT!

WHAT WILL IT TAKE?

YEAH, I SAW IT.
I HEARD IT'S AN AD FOR A BAND.
NAW, IT'S FOR SOME COMMUNITY CENTER.
IT'S LIKE A COFFEE SHOP WITHOUT COFFEE.
I GOT BETTER THINGS TO DO.
WATCHING TV ISN'T "BETTER THINGS TO DO".
EAST HIGH
HAVE YOU GUYS SEEN THOSE POSTERS AROUND?
YEAH, I THINK I'M GONNA CHECK IT OUT.
I HEARD IT'S SOME KIND OF DUMB PRANK, I'M OUT.
HEY JIM AND COREY, YOU GUYS GOING TO THAT THING ON FRIDAY?
UM, WE'VE GOT A GAME ON FRIDAY AND THEN, UM...
YEAH MAN. THEN THE PLAN IS TO HANG AT SCOTT'S AND PLAY FOG.

WHAT WILL IT TAKE?

ECHH... MOVIE NIGHT.
READY TO LEARN ABOUT ART?
I'VE GOT A NEW LITERARY DOCUMENTARY TOO!
AAP
HELLO? IS IT COOL IF I COME IN OR AM I TOO EARLY?
NO! PLEASE COME ON IN AND ENJOY YOURSELF!

WHAT WILL IT TAKE?

WAIT... WHAT WERE YOU SAYING? SOME-THING ABOUT A SHOW?
WELL... I COULD DO A CONCERT HERE.
REALLY? YOU WOULD DO THAT? WE COULD DO IT NEXT FRIDAY!
OK, I HAVE A GOOD FRIEND WHO CAN DRAW. SHE'D PROBABLY MAKE A FLYER FOR US IF I ASKED HER.
YES! IT'S REALLY HAP-PENING!
THANKS SO MUCH FOR ALL OF YOUR HELP.
YEAH, THIS COULD BE GOOD, THANKS.
I HOPE THIS PLACE IS AT LEAST 1/2 AS COOL AS I THINK.

PLAY HUGE!

Huge means spending every day
in zestful expression of one's highest self.

Patch Adams

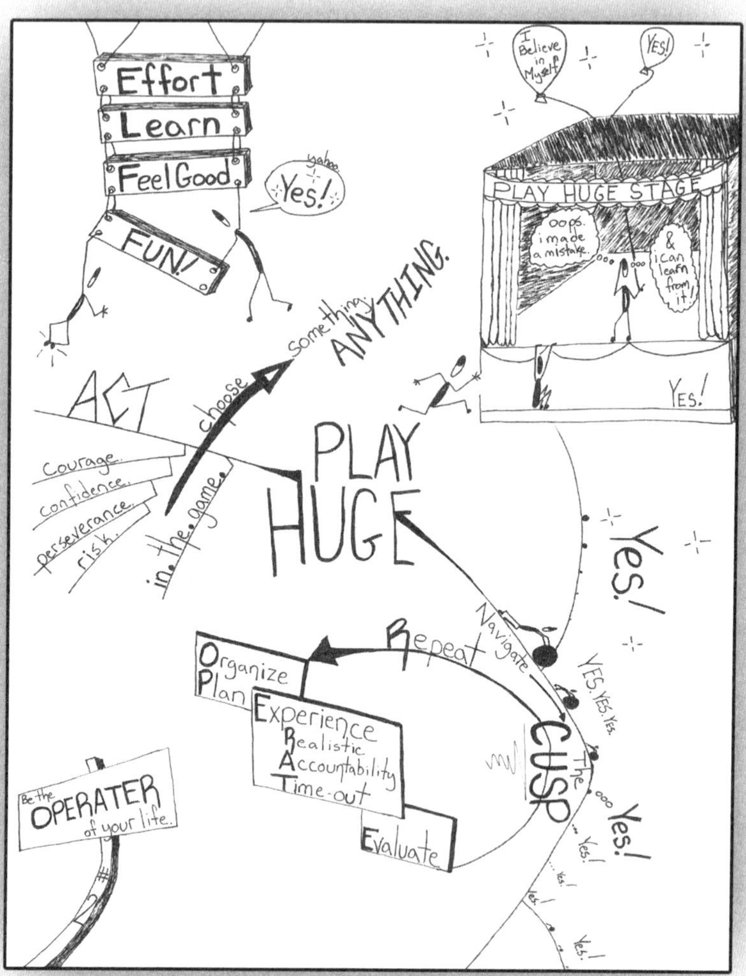
Effort
Learn
Feel Good
FUN!
yahoo
Yes!
I Believe in Myself
YES!
PLAY HUGE STAGE
oops. i made a mistake
& i can learn from it!
YES!
ACT
choose
something
ANYTHING.
courage.
confidence.
perseverance.
risk.
in.the.game.
PLAY HUGE
Yes!
Navigate
Repeat
Organize
Plan
Experience
Realistic
Accountability
Time-out
Evaluate
The CUSP
YES. YES. YES.
Yes!
Yes!
Yes!
Yes!
Yes!
Be the OPERATER of your life.

YOUR SIMPLE PLAY HUGE

283

When you Play Huge, you believe in yourself, take courageous action, and treat people with dignity and respect.

In the last chapter, you learned to connect to your passion and the Real You, and you continued forward because you are ready to figure out your life. Playing Huge is acting with confidence and courage. You take that passion and put it in action.

At any moment you ask yourself if you should go work out...if you should ask him out...if you should listen to what is in your heart, the Play Huge answer is Yes!

The way you live a life of Meaning and Fulfillment is by consistently, all the time, every day, in all your relationships, without question, absolutely, again and again, and with confidence, winning the simple moments of your life by saying Yes!

And, when you do, you will discover the opportunity to work the Upward Spiral Cycle, because you will make mistakes. When you make mistakes, you generate learning opportunities. Saying Yes! to those learning opportunities generates a commitment to excellence, and fills up your life with fun and enjoyment.

Play Huge is the commitment to Yes!

PLAY HUGE EXPLAINED

To set yourself up to Play Huge, you have decided you want to move beyond your Gnawing Feeling because you sense there is more to your life. When you Play Huge and say Yes!, you honor your journey toward Meaning and Fulfillment. You honor the desire to laugh and love. You honor your Real You!

In the moments you say Yes!, there are typically three Playing Huge stages:

STAGE 1—MAKE AN EFFORT

64

Playing Huge can be a tiny "Yes!" that gets you off the couch, it can be world-class exuberance, or it can be the decision to pursue what is in your heart. But, at its most basic level, Playing Huge is conscious action forward. When you act and move toward something you care about, you are creating the life you want.

STAGE 2—FAILURES AND CHALLENGES

Once in conscientious action, Playing Huge becomes learning from your experience, constantly. When you Play Huge, you create opportunities to step into your power and discover your potential. In other words, you will make mistakes. These opportunities happen along your Learning Edge. But—remember—as with all learning, it happens on the other side of risks, mistakes, failures, and reengagement.

STAGE 3—FUN AND FEELING GOOD

Finally, on top of conscious action and learning from experience, Playing Huge is all about having fun and loving life. Playing Huge is all about being connected to people and making a difference by filling up your life, and the lives of others, with laughter, joy, playfulness, and having a blast. When you Play Huge, you feel good.

In each of the following sections explaining Play Huge, you can see the stages woven throughout.

The Cusp

The Cusp is the edge between Yes! and no, the decisive moment of commitment. Sometimes I think of it as the specific, precise, second of transition when a ball goes from being rolled uphill to rolling downhill. It is the instant your momentum shifts, when it moves forward or it stops. In these moments, you are faced with a choice/decision to navigate what I call the Cusp. Life is made up of constant opportunities to navigate the Cusp. Navigating the Cusp with gracefulness, power, and respect of the Real You is Playing Huge.

Your expression of Play Huge will continue to grow and grow and grow, and will become Huge with conscious engagement and effort. But, even at the highest Upward Spiral level of Play Huge, the engagement at the Cusp is the same. It is the choice to say Yes! It is the choice to honor the Real You. It is the choice to match your actions to what the Real You wants.

Some Cusp Moments...

- When you are debating about being positive and seeing the possibilities in a situation, Yes! will make you feel great.
- When you are considering getting up in the morning at the time you committed to, Yes! will honor your word to yourself.
- When you are debating whether to execute your plan to work out, Yes! will make you feel good about your choice.
- When it is time to have that difficult conversation with your boss, your friend, your partner, or your kid—Yes! You have something you want to say, and it will only get more challenging the longer you avoid it. (And, by the way, it is usually much less difficult than your Silly Self-Talk tries to get you to believe.)
- When you are deciding whether to ride your bike in the rain, or to compromise your commitment to the environment by getting in your car, Yes! will feel great. You will only get wet, and it may inspire others to make the same choice.
- When you are afraid of saying something to a friend, Yes! is an expression of how you really feel.
- When someone expresses dissatisfaction with your work or your effort (maybe your baseball coach yells at you), this might shut you down (no) or it might motivate you (Yes!). The road to learning is to not let criticism shut you down, but to use the criticism as motivation to improve.

Navigating the Cusp in a way congruent with the Real You is what will fill up your life with Meaning and Fulfillment.

Navigating the Cusp is all the little, constant, daily moments in which you have the opportunity to say Yes! Eventually your Cusp may expand to include a grand, public, outrageous display of courage, like doing a presentation in front of five hundred high school students, or standing up to your boss, or powerfully requesting time to rejuvenate, or changing your career. But, even when you get to this level of the Upward Spiral, Play Huge must also include all the little moments of life. Playing Huge is taking a stand to say Yes!

PENALTY KILLING

My junior year of high school, I made the varsity hockey team, despite most of the other players being bigger and more talented, and we were favored to win the state championship.

During practice, we would spend time working on the power play, during which the other team has a player in the penalty box and we have a great chance to score a goal because we have one extra player on the ice. We would put our best players on the ice to try to score a goal, but Coach needed guys to pretend to be the other team and prevent our good players from scoring that goal.

In hockey, when your team is down a player and you try to prevent the other team from scoring, it is called "penalty killing." Because I was not one of the best players on our team, in practice I became one of our penalty killers. I always got that role, along with a teammate, Paul.

Usually, players in our role wouldn't make much of an effort, both because it was a clear statement about our inability to be in on the power play, but also because the coaches and good players wanted to be successful, so we were expected to be nice. Well, Paul and I were not nice. We both worked really hard to mess up their plays and make it difficult for them to score goals.

We got really good at penalty killing. In fact, when we practiced, Paul and I worked on taking the puck away and scoring goals for ourselves. Because of our hard work, we became the best penalty killers on the team, and, during games, instead of using our best players to kill penalties, the coach always put Paul and me on the ice.

> Instead of facing the situation and saying, "No, I don't want to do this" or "I will do it, but not try very hard," we faced a choice, the Cusp, and both said, "Yes! We will do it, and we will do it with lots of energy."
>
> We were competitors and wanted to be on the ice. We took a situation in which we were not going to be on the ice, and, because we worked so hard in practice and got so good, the coaches gave us the ice time we craved. And we helped the team win.

All of You Saying Yes!

When you have a moment in which you don't want to do some-
thing, and you do it, you are Playing Huge. You have certainly 374
seen people Play Huge. It comes in moments when you see some-
one do something and you say to yourself, "Wow, they are really
going for it. That takes a lot of courage. I wish I could do that."

Here are some quick examples of Play Huge moments, followed by a Play Huge story:

- Someone in your class offers an original idea during discussion.
- A friend asks out the person he has a crush on.
- You take your energy up a notch to make a good performance a great performance.
- You shake off an ouch and get back in the game.
- You say the thing you have been avoiding saying.
- You refuse to get sucked into the negative attitude of others.

There are many, many more examples. When do you remember Playing Huge?

A MUSICIAN SAYING YES!

Jeff is a musician playing a gig. The gig went quite well, and he felt good about his performance. People clapped. Some were really impressed and told him so afterwards. The positive feedback boosted his confidence.

After the music was done and he was getting his equipment together, he heard a voice say, "Not all of you was saying Yes!"

He looked around and saw an older man. He was not certain he had heard correctly, that the man had said anything, or even that it was directed toward him. He asked, "Did you say something to me?"

The man looked at him, smiled, and repeated, "Not all of you was saying Yes!"

The man was a musician who had spent significant time studying musical traditions from around the world. He had become very adept at reading people's body language and energy, especially the body language and energy of performers.

I too had seen the performance and had sensed Jeff was holding back. He is a talented musician and his performance was good. But it wasn't great.

When all of you says Yes!, you go for it with a huge amount of energy and confidence. You feel a profound level of confidence, self-expression, calmness, exuberance, and power.

It shows up in classrooms, musical performances, parenting moments, presentations, time with friends, athletic contests, work you produce, traveling adventures, and many, many more situations.

People who are the 3 out of 100 in life have a very high percentage of Yes! in everything they do. They make the most of all their opportunities—and they see everything as an opportunity. Their life is full of Meaning and Fulfillment.

A commitment to Play Huge is a commitment to the journey toward all of you saying Yes!

Playing Huge is not being at the place where you are constantly 100% Yes! because it is not about results. Playing Huge is the journey of discovering, learning, and enjoying what it will take to be a 100% Yes.

Have Courage and Confidence

228

Playing Huge is a connection with your Real You. You begin to live in the zestful expression of your Real You so that each of your actions becomes saturated with an honest expression of yourself.

It takes outrageous courage to constantly say Yes! It takes perseverance. It takes faith in yourself. It takes constant effort. It takes the willingness to enjoy your life, to laugh, to be silly, and to find joy in the simple moments.

In your zestful expression, you may look silly sometimes. People may laugh. You may fail at what you are trying to do (give a poor presentation, bad-mouth someone, try a joke that doesn't work, eat an extra chocolate chip cookie). But, when you are willing to express the Real You and learn from your experiences, you will begin to feel the power and the possibilities of Play Huge.

Once you get beyond the fear of your image and of how people perceive you, you are able to enjoy life a great deal more. I recently went to a performance of a children's pirate band with my kids. I love the music, but at first was hesitant to dance. Then my little boy, Ezra, got me up and dancing, and I began to play along with him and the kids. At first I felt a bit silly and wondered what other parents were thinking. Then I realized I was having lots of fun. After the performance, a parent came up to me and said, "That was fun watching you dance. I wish I could do that."

My response was, "You can. All you have to do is Play Huge."

And, when you do, there may be someone watching who says, "All of you is saying Yes! I wish I could do that."

You can.

Your Learning Edge

Your Learning Edge is the balance between taking risks and taking care of yourself, the boundary of your discovery zone and your comfort zone. In your comfort zone, you don't learn anything. When you take risks and move beyond where you are comfortable, you enter a discovery zone where there is opportunity to learn. Learning happens by creating new experiences and failures in your discovery zone, and then reflecting upon and evaluating them in your comfort zone. You will not learn anything by spending all your time in either zone, and the dance back and forth is what I call your Learning Edge.

The Play Huge Stage

The Play Huge Stage is another way to understand Play Huge. Watch for it throughout the rest of *Launch Your Life*, to remind you of the importance of this idea.

GETTING ON THE PLAY HUGE STAGE

Imagine a stage. The stage is a dynamic place. There are lights. There is music—instruments and players. There are several large lumps of a claylike material that looks like you can sculpt it. There are as many other materials as you can imagine, all ready for use. Above the stage is a banner that says, "The Play Huge Stage." And it is a place of opportunity, where you can create whatever you want to create, and you are in control of what you want to have happen on the stage.

When you decided to honor the Real You, you walked into the auditorium and saw the Play Huge Stage. Now it is time to act on your passion.

The place where life happens is on the Play Huge Stage, so Play Huge is about being on the stage.

You have got to get on the stage. Some of you certainly will jump onto the stage because you are ready to play. Others of you may crawl toward the stage, struggling with your Silly Self-Talk, which is saying, "You are going to look bad and probably make a fool of yourself."

4:44

When I was in a ninth-grade drama class, I had to perform a lip sync on stage with all my friends watching. I remember that just about every girl I wanted to go out with was in the class (or so it seemed).

At first, I was terrified to get on stage. What I remember is sitting in the audience with a wrenching feeling in my stomach, watching my friends perform, and waiting for the horrible moment: "Morgan, you are next."

Then it felt like that creature called my Silly Self-Talk began pulling me back into my seat as I struggled against myself to get on stage. It was this confused, painfully slow-motion, running-in-quicksand, kind of feeling. But what was worse than getting up onto the stage, was when I began my strumming and I realized how pitiful my effort was. My "performance" was standing on stage strumming an air guitar for four minutes and forty-four seconds to John Cougar Mellancamp's "Pink Houses."

It was very likely the longest 4:44 of my life. The whole time my Silly Self-Talk was in the front row laughing, to make sure I knew that everyone—including all the girls—thought I was lame.

The teacher thought I could do better, so asked that I do it again the next week.

Ugh.

There was no way I was going to air guitar for 4:44 again, so I began to practice. I practiced all week. I figured out a way to act out all the lyrics. When the time came, I was still nervous. My Silly Self-Talk still tried to convince me I should decline and take the failing grade, but I fought through the voice and performed.

It was by no means an award-winning performance. Nor did I get any dates from my effort. But I was still alive. I did persevere. I stepped into and through my fear, and I learned that it felt better to get up on the stage and make an effort than it did to sit in the audience.

You don't Play Huge sitting in the audience. By getting up on the stage, you make a choice about how you want to live your life. On the stage, you have the opportunity to create your life, to take (and learn from) risks, and to meet new people. And a great thing about the Play Huge Stage is that you don't need to know anything! The only requirements are your effort and your willingness to learn.

When you start Playing Huge, it is not about getting things right. You don't even need a specific idea of where you are going. You simply have to start, because action triggers possibilities and learning experiences.

Further, when you go for it 100%, you run into these things called mistakes and failures. When you make a mistake or fail at something, it is an opportunity to believe in yourself and take courageous action.

And Play Huge is all about believing in yourself and taking courageous action. As you continue onward (Yes!), you will learn that the difference between just a performance and an outstanding performance is your zestful expression and your powerfully standing for the Real You. You will learn more about what works for you and what does not. You will begin to see a direction for yourself.

The learning in life happens on the Play Huge Stage. It does not happen sitting in the audience watching others, and wishing you were up there.

Bringing Launch Your Life All Together

Play Huge will take all the elements of *Launch Your Life*. When you Play Huge, you will believe in your Know Yourself. When you Play Huge, you will Trust Yourself and take courageous action. When you Play Huge, you will Empathize and live It's About People by treating people with dignity and respect.

As you continue along the Upward Spiral of these concepts, the level at which you Play Huge will come along the Upward Spiral with you—just as when you are the OPERATER of your life, you gain clarity on the most powerful actions for you. The powerful actions include always honoring the Real You and taking ownership of your actions as you Play Above the Line.

Finally, the only way to Always Honor Sustainability and make *Launch Your Life* create the difference in your life you want it to, is to navigate each Cusp moment with Yes! The Cusp moments will get bigger and will always be challenging, and Always Honoring Sustainability is being certain that you constantly execute the small, simple, daily things with Yes!

THE PATH TO PLAY HUGE

The basis of the path to get to Play Huge is your commitment. You have connected to the Real You and you feel some level of passion inside you. Now it is time for the next step, which is Play Huge, and it is all based on taking your commitment into action.

Choose Something to Work On

CHOOSE SOMETHING. ANYTHING.

In the early stages of Play Huge, the most important thing is to act! It is not significant what action you choose to commit to, but that you commit to *something* and go for it. Choose something...anything...to take a Stand for.

You want to break a pattern of being ineffective, and you want to create a pattern of making a commitment to yourself and following through. Choose something that, when you wake up in the morning, you can remember and be able to execute. Some examples of what you can say to yourself include, "I absolutely will eat five healthy things today!" or "I will go to all my classes" or "I will say something nice to three people today."

You want to choose something you will be successful executing. You want to begin to accumulate in your Powerful Portfolio, actions in which you navigate the Cusp. Accumulating a pattern of successful Cusp moments is crucial in breaking through the barriers that are holding you back, and then in being able to Sustain the new and effective patterns.

You may be clear on actions that honor the Real You, and, if so, be certain to capture them in your Play Huge Notebook. You can begin to be the OPERATER of your life as soon as you have specific ideas of things you want to work on.

You may also be in a place where you are uncertain what to do. If this is the case, choose *something*. And when you choose something, make a commitment to it for at least seven days. Only then can you change it, as you will want to avoid jumping from thing to thing. Choosing something different every day can be frustrating, difficult to remember, and sends a message that you are not in control. Remember, you *are* in control, so choose something and begin to establish a routine around it. By doing this, you will give yourself a good chance to honor the Real You.

140

MAKE THE EFFORT

Choose something to work on because doing so will engage your consciousness. It is much easier to *keep* energy going than it is to *get* energy going. Once you make the effort to express the Real You, your energy is going. Keep it going by choosing something.

I say to my kids all the time, "The results are not important to me. What matters is that you are making an effort." They are in the Upward Spiral Cycle, so I know that, when they make an effort, they have the opportunity to learn something, especially when they feel confident and one of us is ready to help them learn from their mistakes.

The critical aspect of your choice is that you engage your consciousness and challenge yourself to negotiate the Cusp. To Play Huge, begin to be conscious of your commitment to yourself. You cannot continue to go through the motions in your life. When you engage your consciousness, you make an active decision and commitment to yourself that you remember constantly.

Intention is essential, but not sufficient. Action is where your intention becomes your reality.

LIKE, YA KNOW

I have a friend who was trying to stop saying "like, ya know" when he was speaking to friends. He asked me to help him.

If you have ever made an effort to change your language (or any habit), you know you must make an active decision to do it if you want it to work. It is not just going to happen by chance. And, asking people to help and creating a supportive community, as with everything you do, will make it more likely you will succeed in your effort.

My friend eventually realized he went through stages. He realized the first thing he did was begin to notice when he was saying "like, ya know." He kept saying it, but he began to notice when he was saying it, and, as he did, he began to catch himself—the second stage. Sometimes he was able to stop saying it, and sometimes he was not. In the third stage, he began to notice before he was going to say it and was able to stop himself. Finally, once he was consistently aware enough to stop himself, he kept making a conscious effort to not say "like, ya know," and eventually eliminated it from his communication.

Here, then, are the stages of changing a pattern:

- Notice the pattern.
- Catch yourself when you do it.
- Catch yourself before you do it.
- Reinforce your success by maintaining your focus.

Even if you are not successful accomplishing the task, you must begin to act and make an effort. In fact, it is almost guaranteed that before you begin successfully to navigate the Cusp, you will have some false starts during which you are not successful. But remember: Playing Huge is not about being 100% successful; it is about being 100% in the game. Playing Huge is perseverance in your actions and engagement of your consciousness in these moments!

Conquer the Cusp Moments

You know the Cusp is the edge between Yes! and no, the moment you face a decision. When you are navigating the Cusp with gracefulness, power, and respect of the Real You, you are Playing Huge.

All of You Saying Yes!

We have all seen someone when all of her was saying Yes! Perhaps you have experienced it yourself at times. It is a profound level of confidence, self-expression, calmness, exuberance, and power.

It shows up in musical performances, parenting moments, presentations, time with friends, athletic contests, traveling adventures, and many, many more situations.

People who are successful in life have a high percentage of Yes! in everything they do.

Perseverance

The way you learned to walk is through perseverance. Everyone knew you were going to learn how to walk, so you kept on going. You fell. You got up. You fell. You got up. People encouraged you. You fell again. They got excited. You got up. They told you that you were doing great. They videotaped your effort. You kept trying. And kept trying. And, eventually, you were successful.

By applying the same idea to making your life what you want it to be, you can create success for yourself.

You will make mistakes. You will fall down. But, if you keep trying, you will learn. Eventually, as you accumulate experience and continue to make an effort, you will reach further, perhaps going from walking to running. I say to my clients, "The bigger the mistakes you make, the more huge you are playing, because, if you are out there making big mistakes, then you are out there making a big effort."

What matters most is to keep on trying. If what you are doing is not working, then try new and different ways to act. If what you are doing is working, then keep doing it! It takes courage and commitment to continue stepping up.

POWER THROUGH

There will be times when it is necessary to power through whatever tough feelings are around. You may not be motivated, you may not have energy, you may feel sick, or you may think you want to hang out on the couch, or take a nap, or lots of other possibilities.

There are times when the way to get what you want is simply to Play Huge. Say Yes! Act! Fight through the resistance. Persevere, and honor the Real You.

It gets easier and easier to power through if you keep it up. The biggest challenge is getting your momentum going.

Keep Your Word

When you commit to do something, follow through and do it. Successful people are accountable for their actions. It is a very simple thing, but few people do it effectively.

Your word is your honor. It is your power. It is what you offer to other people. When you give your word to do something, do what it takes to make that thing happen.

If you cannot do what you promised, take the responsibility to tell the person to whom you made the promise that you couldn't follow through. Then apologize and accept the fallout.

And, remember, you make the most commitments to yourself. Keep your word to yourself, as well as keeping your word to other people.

One of the secrets to Knowing Yourself is to Play Above the Line. And Playing Above the Line is taking ownership and responsibility for yourself. Keeping your word is the most significant way to make this happen.

CONTRACTS—HIGH-LEVEL

Sometimes you will make a choice not to execute what you have committed to. When you do this, you make a contract with yourself. You either say something like, "Well, that is not that important anyway," or you say, "I will do it later."

Often, when you bail out on something, you make a low-level contract with yourself.

MAKING A HIGH-LEVEL CONTRACT

Let's say you make a commitment to go to all your classes. You do well for a week, but then comes that class you don't like. Instead of honoring your word and going to class, while lying in bed you convince yourself, "That class is not that important anyway. No one will notice if I am not there, and it will not affect my grade," and you go back to sleep.

The Play Huge way to renegotiate a contract is to make a high-level contract. This allows you the opportunity to make a specific plan to get done what you said you would get done.

The day before the class you don't like, you feel like you could use the time more effectively than by going to class. But, you remember that you made a commitment to yourself that you would go to all your classes, so, despite not feeling excited about it, you keep your word to yourself and decide to go to class.

Or, the day before the class you don't like, you feel like you could use the time more effectively than by going to class. You decide to create a new contract for yourself. Instead of going to class, you will read the chapter today and then go to the teacher's office hours to discuss an idea you have. Then, if your grade dips below a B, you will go to all the classes (and office hours).

Going the route of "that is not important" while lying in bed is giving up your power by making excuses. You are negotiating a low-level contract. If you find yourself doing this often, then perhaps you ought to be more careful what you are giving your word to.

A high-level contract is one in which you make a specific plan to get done what you said you would get done. Then, when the time comes, you execute it. If you give your word to someone or yourself, follow through. Honor the Real You and treat people (including yourself) with dignity and respect.

QUIET YOUR SILLY SELF-TALK

Once you establish a pattern of making an effort, navigating the Cusp, powering through, and making high-level contracts, your Silly Self-Talk gets quieter and less powerful. Eventually, self-acknowledgment even replaces it. In other words, you get on the Upward Spiral, not a downward spiral.

As you learn to Play Huge, your Silly Self-Talk will be loud. Your Silly Self-Talk does not like it when you Play Huge because it currently has a lot of influence on what you do (or, more likely, don't do). It is fighting to keep a strong influence over you, so it will likely be critical, offer excuses, compare you to others, and/or doubt your ability to execute your intended action. In other words, it will suggest that you stay in bed.

A key part of Playing Huge is learning to get past your Silly Self-Talk and get into action.

Remember that you—not your Silly Self-Talk—are in control of your choices. You can jam your Silly Self-Talk by saying, "Yes.

Yes. Yes. Yes." Or, "I am in control and I am in action. Here I go!" Or anything else that will get you thinking and feeling positive about yourself. Some people make up a mantra to say again and again and again to themselves whenever they are not feeling the energy and they notice their Silly Self-Talk: "Yes, I can" or "I am ready to Play Huge."

Whatever method works best for you, use it, because, while your Silly Self-Talk will get quieter, it will always be along for the journey. Learning to be in control, and even occasionally asking for input from your Silly Self-Talk, can be powerful, but all unsolicited negativity is not a productive part of your Playing Huge.

Learn from Experience

BE OKAY WITH MISTAKES AND UNCERTAINTY

Many of the possible barriers to choosing something, making an effort, persevering, and saying Yes!, go away when you are committed to learning. You will not learn anything by sitting on your couch. You have done that (either literally or metaphorically) and you want something different. The reason you are reading *Launch Your Life* is because you are ready to break your ineffective patterns.

The way to learn is through being in action. You may not know exactly what to do. You may not be very good at what you want to do. There may be lots of other reasons your Silly Self-Talk brings up for you to remain complacent and inactive. But, the most effective way to get beyond all these challenges is to do something and learn from it.

You will definitely make mistakes. You definitely will not follow through on commitments you make. You will possibly make someone mad.

This is called learning. Remember that this is how you learned to walk. You were in action. No one learns to walk by thinking about it or by sitting around doing nothing. When you learned to walk, you fell over, again and again. And, each time, you learned a little more, until, eventually, you figured it out.

The way you will figure out exactly what the Real You wants to be doing is to try out lots of things you want to do and get real experience doing them. The way to get really good at what the Real You wants is to keep taking risks and pushing the edge—believe in the Upward Spiral.

Again, I tell my clients that, the bigger the mistakes they are making, the bigger effort they are making. Mistakes are learning opportunities, and, when you make them, you learn to do it differently next time.

Once you get momentum going, you will begin to crave mistakes and learning opportunities in your life. The Meaning and Fulfillment you are searching for come from the complexity and challenges you encounter. As you get to the point where you crave opportunities created by mistakes and complexity, you will realize that life is a process, not an event. It is these daily interactions and moments that make up our lives. There is no trophy for getting what you want in life. The enjoyment of the process is where you find the Meaning and Fulfillment.

BIKE SHOW

My friend who builds custom bikes was going to show his bikes at a handmade bike show. He knew he wanted to accomplish certain tasks before the show. He knew how he wanted it all to go. They had to design some things, organize the materials they were showing, prepare the booth, and more.

He knew he wanted to do it differently than he had done it previously. When he had prepared for the same event before, it was unorganized, stressful, and no fun.

This time, he made a plan, shared the plan, and then executed the plan. At the show, we talked, and he said, "I got 98% there, but realized I did not leave enough time for myself to rest so that I would be ready for the show. I am the most important thing on display here and I am tired. I am thrilled with how everything went, but, next time, I will remember to build in buffer time for me to rejuvenate."

GET THE LEARNING ATTITUDE GOING

When you begin to live life with the attitude that everything is a learning opportunity, life becomes really fun. The possibilities for your life become much bigger, and, along with them, comes the opportunity to extract bigger learnings.

As you get the learning attitude going, your original "choose something…anything" can shift to be more than anything. It can now gain focus and direction. When your learning attitude is going, you are on the Upward Spiral! If you choose, you can start to take on more challenging actions, and ones more connected to the Real You.

EDISON CREATING THE LIGHT BLUB

The story goes that Thomas Edison tried more than nine thousand ways to make a light bulb work. He failed all those times. He is quoted as saying, "I have not failed. I have figured out nine thousand ways it will not work."

Obviously, each time he failed, he learned something else about how it would or would not work.

Imagine the first light bulb he tried to create. He probably did not know what he was doing. He probably did not have an idea of how it was going to work out. He probably knew it was going to take a lot of effort. He probably had many of the same challenges you face with your Silly Self-Talk and navigating the Cusp.

He learned from his mistakes and his failures, and he took on his uncertainty; he persevered and made something amazing happen. You can do this too.

Ask for Help

GET THE SUPPORT YOU NEED

When you connect to the Real You, you know you want to have a meaningful and fulfilling life. The challenge of making it happen hinges on your effort to Play Huge. Perhaps the core of Play Huge—the most critical and challenging aspect of Playing Huge—is asking for help. The journey the Real You wants to go on will be much, much easier if you ask for help. Creating a supportive community will significantly enhance your journey.

Some very common Silly Self-Talk discourages you from asking for help:

- How big a failure are you that you can't do it on your own?
- What is wrong with you?
- You are absolutely crazy.
- Wuss.
- Everyone is going to think you are weak and crazy and dumb.

This is a time to remember that you are making a commitment to yourself to get what you want in your life. There are lots of people out there who will be supportive of, and quite possibly inspired by, your efforts! Begin to talk, with pride, about your search and your desire to connect to the Real You.

One of the things that helps me remember to ask for help is my absolute belief that everyone wants to get what their Real You wants in life. If you are courageous enough to be taking steps to do something about it, your action here will be inspiring to others. And, if not, it's their loss.

BEKY AND WENDY, RUNNING PARTNERS

My neighbor and a friend of hers get up three or four mornings a week and go running together. Beky said it would be really hard for her to get up and run unless she had her friend to go with her. When it is cold and rainy and she is in her warm bed, she often doesn't want to go. But, because she knows her friend will be waiting for her on the corner at 6:00 a.m., she gets up. By making that commitment, she has the additional motivation of supporting her friend and keeping her word. All this makes it much easier for her to honor her commitment to her Real You.

Finding someone to join you or support your commitment to yourself is all about being courageous enough to ask, and willing to be inspiring. The more people you ask and the more powerful your request, the more positive your results will be.

HEIDI AND THE MARATHON

A client of mine was struggling with a number of things in her life. She was out of shape and wanted to be working out. She reported she was dealing with several challenging relationships, including those with her daughter, husband, and mother. All these relationships meant a great deal to her.

She had known for a long time that these relationships needed attention in order to get better, but she had no idea what to do about it. She also knew she needed to begin exercising because she was getting more and more unhealthy. But, again, she did not know what to do or how to do it.

She decided to join a marathon club and begin walking. By doing this, she was asking for help and creating accountability for herself, just like my friends Beky and Wendy. She began taking steps forward, literally and figuratively.

The success she began to experience with her health made her feel great. Her training was also a great metaphor for her relationship situations.

She could not solve all the challenges with one event, just like she could not get up one day and walk a marathon. The training and consistent attention were what would make a difference.

As she worked on her weekly goals in her marathon training, she drafted goals to take small steps forward in her relationships. She began to listen more, and that allowed her anger and frustration to dissipate. She began to feel better about herself, and that has allowed her to bring more understanding and empathy to the relationships.

She has walked her real marathon and is taking significant steps in her relationship events as well.

Asking for help by finding a buddy or a partner will help you be accountable for executing on the actions to which the Real You has committed.

POSSIBLE BARRIERS

What follows are possible barriers to your Playing Huge. Some certainly came up when you were connecting to the Real You and awakening your passion, but—now that it is time to act—their strength may increase. Many of these can be handled by the ideas just covered.

You may find you get to deal with all these barriers, or you may find the barriers you face are not even mentioned here. Whatever the case, it is essential to remember that the path to Meaning and Fulfillment is all about dealing with these kinds of barriers. That is where the learning happens. If you choose to not deal with these things, then the Gnawing Feeling will reemerge.

IT IS NOT THE RIGHT MESSAGE

When it comes time to act, you may find yourself feeling that the message you got from the Real You is not the right message. This might sound something like, "I really do want to try that, but it isn't what I most want to do in the world," or "I have an idea, but it is not a very good one." This is your Silly Self-Talk. And you have learned how to jam it, so do it here.

The way to know whether an idea is or isn't a powerful one for you is to put it into practice and learn from the experience of trying it.

IT'S NOT GRAND ENOUGH

You might find yourself thinking something like, "Darn, I am supposed to save the planet, or become president, or make a bazillion dollars."

Your Silly Self-Talk might even make up the story that everyone else's dreams are much bigger and grander than yours. It is easy to believe there is something wrong with you, and that other people are able to do something you are not.

Again, in cases such as this, the safest thing to do is to jam your Silly Self-Talk. Don't play the game of comparing your ideas with others. Allow your ideas to be your ideas, and know they come from the Real You. You know how to get onto the Upward Spiral and make your ideas amazing.

I DON'T DESERVE THIS

This would sound something like, "Who am I to deserve something like that? I am not ________ (smart, talented, good, deserving, etc.) enough to get that."

This is again your Silly Self-Talk, so jam it. Also, pay attention to this excerpt from the book **Return To Love** by Marianne Williamson:

We ask ourselves, Who am I to be brilliant,
gorgeous, talented, fabulous?
Actually, who are you not to be?...
Your playing small does not serve the world.

Stand in your power. Act.

WHOA, THAT IS SCARY!

You may know exactly what you want to go for, but it may be really scary to go for it. You may spend time contemplating the possible outcomes, and then get paralyzed by the fear of what happens if it doesn't work out.

Yes! It is good to be scared. If you are not scared, then you are not taking a big enough risk. If you keep getting stuck here, go back to the beginning of The Path to Play Huge and work through it.

Playing Huge takes confidence and courage.

OTHER PEOPLE MY AGE ARE...

You might find yourself comparing yourself to other people your age. Jam your Silly Self-Talk. The only way to make this different is to act.

If you buy into this idea and get stopped, then you just fall farther behind. The only way to catch up is to act. Now.

I DON'T KNOW HOW TO DO IT

You may be entering new territory with new actions, and, when you do, you may not be good at what you want to be doing. It is possible you don't know how to do it (whatever it is), and so it is likely you will not be good at it.

The opportunity you have is to make it a learning opportunity. Go back and read the story about Thomas Edison and how he invented the light bulb.

I'LL LOOK BAD

You might have a fear about the image other people will have of you if you go out, try something new, and look bad doing it. You are worried about how other people will perceive your actions and your efforts.

By asking for help, you are admitting you cannot handle the situation by yourself. You are afraid of being judged by others; you are afraid they will think there is something wrong with you.

It is true: when you make a mistake, you might look bad. But ask yourself, is honoring the Real You worth someone maybe thinking I look bad?

223

Remember my story about my ninth-grade drama class. Remember that the way you learn is by making mistakes. And, if you are really stuck here, look ahead to the Trust Yourself chapter. A one-sentence summary of that chapter is, when you Trust Yourself, your self-esteem is not determined by the approval of others.

IT'S EASIER TO KEEP DOING WHAT I'M DOING

It may be easier to keep doing what you are doing than take action and create a new pattern. You might think that keeping your current patterns going will certainly be easier than shifting to new patterns. If you are stuck in this place, make room for the Gnawing Feeling, because it will never go away just because. You will have to do something.

Your Silly Self-Talk might work the interesting-idea-you-have-there-but-it-is-not-worth-getting-off-the-couch-for angle. And, by this point, you have a good idea what to do with your Silly Self-Talk.

I CAN'T GET IT RIGHT

You may be clear that the way to learn is to take action, but you might not believe you have what it takes to understand the learning opportunities that come from your actions. Or, you might worry that by making an effort and failing (again), things will get worse for you rather than better.

A good thing to remember is that there is nothing "right" to learn. Your Silly Self-Talk may be running the you-are-not-smart-enough line, which you know what to do with. Play Huge takes confidence. As with looking bad and getting judged, if you are really stuck here, look back through The Path to Play Huge and/or look ahead to Trust Yourself.

NO ONE WILL WANT TO HELP

You might think you are all alone and there is no one you know who will understand your situation. And, even if they do, you might think they will not want to help you.

My experience tells me that everyone wants to be doing the work of honoring his or her Real You. The more courageous and confidently you stand, the more people will be drawn to you. If you sense you are annoying people with your persistence or courage, then look ahead to the Empathize chapter. It may be time for you to spend awhile standing in other people's shoes.

You can also check out the web site at www.themeaningrevolution.com/launchyourlife to see other resources to help you build your community.

Beyond the Barriers

I heard a leader of people say the other day, "I will not be perfect. I will make mistakes. But I will always be honest; I will always listen; I will always keep on trying and keep on learning." Before you Play Huge and, then, when you Play Huge, you will run into barriers, and, like this leader, you can take powerful control of your life.

Playing Huge is about learning by being in action; it is about turning over rocks, taking risks, trying new things, and learning. When you are challenged by someone's perspective or opinion, Playing Huge is not about being stopped, but about taking it as a challenge to step up your effort. As Marianne Williamson said, "Your playing small does not serve the world."

You might be scared that you will be all alone without anyone to coach you, or you might think it is easier for you to keep doing what you are currently doing, but, as with all the elements of *Launch Your Life*, the opposite is true. The bigger the effort you make, and the more you Play Huge, the more people you will draw to you!

You are completely capable of making Play Huge happen in your life.

HUGE OUTCOMES—PLAY HUGE!

I feel a lot of **SUPPORT** from my family and friends!

My **LIFE** has begun—and I **LOVE** it! Yahoo! What took me so long? I am **HAVING FUN**. I am doing things that I never would have done before. I am learning a ton. I notice that I **LAUGH** more and **ENJOY LIFE**.

I don't feel like this **PATH** is a "one-hit wonder" or a moment of **INSPIRATION**. This feels like a journey I can sustain, and like it is my path—or will, at least, lead to a path of **MEANING** and **FULFILLMENT**.

LESLIE

I feel more **COURAGEOUS**. I feel more confident. I feel **INSPIRED**.

I am **CONNECTED** to my Real You, and I am **LEARNING** what that means every day by **LIVING IT**!

I have figured out that the **WAY TO LEARN** is through **EXPERIENCE**. So, now when I have a question about whether to try something, my answer is **YES**!

I am **IN THE GAME**! No more sitting on the sideline wishing I were in the game, or **THINKING** about how to get there. I am **TAKING THE RISK** to play the game called "My Life."

While I don't feel like I'm there yet, I feel **WAY CLOSER** to living the life **I WANT TO BE LIVING**. It feels like I'm on the path I want to be on, and I'm making the effort I want to be making.

It feels so much better when I engage and say **YES!** and take action on something I **CARE** about, than when I don't.

Huge Outcomes: Text Version

And what do you get from all your efforts? What's in it for you if you Play Huge?

SIMPLE AND COMMITTED STEPS

You realize that to honor the Real You and live passionately does not take a superhuman and extraordinary effort.

Knowing you are capable of making it happen is powerful in itself. But, even though you may not have figured everything out, taking any step that honors the Real You is Playing Huge.

YOU ARE IN THE GAME

The only way to create a life of Meaning and Fulfillment is by being in the game. When you Play Huge, you are in the game.

In the game, you take risks (just being willing to play is taking a risk), and, in the process, you create experiences for yourself, some of which will feel successful and some of which will feel like failures. But you now know this is the way to learn.

You don't learn by reading about experiences. You don't learn by watching others have experiences. You learn through your own experiences. You learn by being in the game.

Don't underestimate the significance of this step. For many, it takes as much energy engaging and getting in the game as it does to Sustain their momentum. Be certain to acknowledge yourself for the effort to Play Huge.

YOU HONOR THE REAL YOU

There is a Real You. The Real You likes to act. Despite all the intimidating messages from your Silly Self-Talk—how bad you will look, what people will think, doubting your credibility, etc.—you are making a difference.

By being in action, you are sending a powerful message to yourself and others that you care about yourself. It is an indication that you are whole, capable, and resourceful.

YOU ARE FIGURING OUT WHAT YOU WANT

It might be you are ready to take your experiences and learn from them, or it might be you need to build up your Trust Yourself in order to begin to reflect and extract the learning.

You will either find yourself creating plans and setting yourself up for your next steps (jumping onto the Upward Spiral and going for it), or you will find yourself with an increased amount of information to evaluate your next steps. You can consider this getting closer to the journey the Real You wants to travel.

Regardless of where you find yourself, when you Play Huge at this stage, you are on your journey toward Meaning and Fulfillment.

STRATEGIES FOR DEALING WITH BARRIERS

By Playing Huge, you get good at using the *Launch Your Life* tools to deal with potential barriers. When you are afraid of what people will think or that you will look bad, you know it is your Silly Self-Talk, and work to jam it. You know when you face a Cusp moment, you say Yes! and honor the Real You. You know if you are feeling funky and not wanting to do your work, you power through because it will feel good.

There are many more such strategies, and, by Playing Huge, you identify the ones you like and that work for you.

ASKING FOR HELP

Asking for help becomes very different when you Play Huge. Instead of being seen as a weakness or admission that something is wrong, asking for help becomes a strength.

When you ask for help, you are saying, "I care enough about myself that I am willing to do whatever it takes to make it happen."

That is a powerful change.

YOU BECOME INSPIRING

You will find that the courage and commitment it takes to Play Huge will draw people to you.

You will also be more courageous in engaging other people. It's the difference between sitting back and waiting for something to happen, and making it happen. You make life happen, and, when you want to talk with someone, you go talk to that person.

Instead of always having shallow conversations with people, you'll find yourself engaged in more meaningful conversations. You will also notice that people who always want to live in the shallow place become much less interesting to you.

Besides asking for help becoming a strength, there is another shift when you Play Huge. Instead of thinking that, when you put the Real You out into the world, you are going to get a negative response, you realize it inspires people.

Everyone is hungry to honor his or her Real You. People want to live passionate lives, but there are not enough examples of others doing it. When you do it, you will find that people are intrigued and inspired.

In the younger generation, the intrigue and inspiration might still come off as teasing or ridicule, but pay close attention, listen carefully, and Trust Yourself, because, beneath these simple negative responses, is pure curiosity. The pure curiosity comes in the form of these kinds of questions:

- Can they really get away with being that courageous?
- Are they going to Sustain in the face of some challenges?
- Could I do that?

LIFE IS FUN!

Playing Huge is fun. The Gnawing Feeling is like carrying an anchor around with you; so is not feeling confident or courageous. When you act in your life, it creates freedom from those challenges and opens you up to playfulness and freedom.

All of this Launching Your Life stuff ought not to be work. It will not be easy, but it should be fun. The game of making your life everything you want it to be will bring joy to you.

Foundational Terms

Play Huge introduced several more ideas that will appear again and again in *Launch Your Life*, some of which carry over from Secret #1—Believe in the Upward Spiral. In order to *Launch Your Life*, you will have to *make an effort*, and one way to do that is to *navigate the Cusp*, which you can do by saying *Yes!* constantly. Saying Yes! will get you in action, and, when you do that, you make mistakes, just as the *Upward Spiral Cycle* says you will. The Play Huge way to handle them is to *learn from the experience* and make a *high-level contract* with yourself to handle it differently next time.

WRAP-UP

You decided to honor your Real You by getting in action. The place where life happens is on the Play Huge Stage.

The first scene you'll be a part of on the Play Huge Stage is called Momentum—Getting Your Upward Spiral Cycle in Motion.

You have been cast in the leading role. It is time for all of you to say Yes!, to go for it, and to look forward to the learning.

Whether you are an experienced performer or brand-new to the stage, there are opportunities for you to learn.

And there are challenges.

Some challenges provide the opportunity to remember the Real You and get back to your solid foundation before making your next effort. Other challenges show up as Cusp moments, at which you get to make a decision.

The first challenge is whether to accept the lead role or to go sit and watch. Remember the Real You and say Yes!

Another challenge will come when the director of the play criticizes your performance. It may be an unpleasant feeling, but it's an opportunity to show up. Will someone else's negative reaction stop you, or will you use it as motivation to do better?

Presuming that you continued onward (Yes!), you will learn that the difference between just a performance and an outstanding performance is zestful expression.

You will learn that to Play Huge is the very simple (yet profound) choice to get on the stage, but it is also the huge, zestful, expressive, playful, joyful, choice to completely, 100% go for it.

But, when you go for it 100%, you run into these things called failures. Failures create Cusp moments and opportunities to use the Upward Spiral Cycle, where you get to choose whether to exit stage left or stay home and figure out what to do.

Let's say that the Play Huge Stage director gives you an assignment to do a lip sync. As soon as you get the assignment, your Silly Self-Talk kicks in and you begin to sing a song in your head (to the tune of "Happy Birthday to You"):

An assignment for you—
You'll blow it, you shrew.
They'll laugh at your effort,
And you'll stink like dog poo.

The faster you jam your Silly Self-Talk and get back to your Play Huge, the better for you. Along with the Silly Self-Talk, you may have doubts about your ability to complete the assignment, but, when you Play Huge, you persevere. No matter how small the effort, when you keep on moving forward and saying Yes! to the Real You, you are Playing Huge.

However, sometimes, you will not be able to complete the assignment. When that happens, what is the way to continue to Play Huge? (Hint: it is not to give up, blame the director for giving the assignment, or feel sorry for yourself.)

One tool you have is a high-level contract. When you make a high-level contract with yourself or someone else, you stay in your power, you come up with a solution, and you give your word to follow through with Play Huge energy.

A couple of other tools when you get to a Cusp moment are to remember that, when you Play Huge, everything is a learning experience (especially when you are the OPERATER of your life), and you can always ask for help.

On the Play Huge Stage, an amazing transformation often happens. Things you used to consider failures and try to avoid, you now crave. On the Play Huge Stage, failures become powerful opportunities to advance on the Upward Spiral.

Perhaps it all feels easy, but, unfortunately, the pressure of the Test Score Culture, your grade point average, and SAT/ACT high-stakes tests are still around. Under that pressure, it feels like your Play Huge Stage script has been replaced with a script where your roles are very different.

In a play called "My Silly Self-Talk," you play the following roles:

- The Bully
- The Your-Idea-Is-Not-Grand-Enough Gremlin
- The Evil Twins: There-Is-No-Message and It-Is-Not-The-Right-Message
- Mr. Stage Fright (I am going to look silly; people are going to judge me; this is scary; I don't know how to do it; I'm not good at it.)

In a play called "I Can't Do That," you play several roles, including:

- Mrs. Inertia
- Who-Am-I-To-Have-That?

- I-Can't-Figure-Out-What-I-Am-Supposed-To-Learn

But, remember: Playing Huge is about perseverance and quieting your Silly Self-Talk. And, when you are the OPERATER of your life, you will quickly notice if you are trapped in one of the wrong scripts and be able to put it down and get back on track.

You can do it. Play Huge.

SECRET #2

Be the *OPERATER* of Your Life

The second secret to *Launch Your Life* is to be the OPERATER of your life. When you are the OPERATER, you pay attention to the big picture so that, when you are "in the experiences" of your life, you have an easier time understanding them.

Here is a metaphor to explain what "in the experiences" means.

IN THE EXPERIENCES

Imagine you wanted to get through a maze in a cornfield in which the corn was ten feet tall. If you just run into the maze and try to find your way through, you would have a hard time. But, if you had a chance to look at the maze from a bird's-eye view to find the way through, then, when you got into the maze, it would be easier to navigate your way.

Here is another metaphor to illustrate the importance of being an OPERATER:

COAT RACK

Imagine you have a coat rack. Your coat rack has many hooks and, hanging on those hooks, are different kinds of coats for different activities, different seasons, and different weather.

Before you leave the house in the morning, you choose the coat(s) you will need for the activities of the day. When you have some information about the day—your plans, the weather, the day of the week, etc.—it is more likely you will choose a coat or coats that will get you through the day. Whereas, if you don't have a coat rack and just grab whatever and run out of the house, the likelihood you will be able to handle the circumstances of the day is significantly less.

When something unexpected happens, it offers an opportunity to make a choice—a Cusp moment. You can react emotionally, make do, and deal with the stress of figuring out what to do.

Or, you can say Yes! because you have anticipated the challenge and brought the right coat. Or you might choose to run home because you know exactly where you'll find the coat you need.

Being the OPERATER of your life is making sure you have an idea of where you are going and what you need, so that, when you are inside experiences, you have a better understanding of where you are, what to expect, and where you want to go.

OPERATER

OPERATER is an acronym for the steps within the four stages of being the OPERATER of your life:

PLANNING STAGE

O—Organize
P—Plan

EXPERIENCE STAGE

E—Experience
R—Realistic
A—Accountability
T—Time-out

POST-EXPERIENCE STAGE

E – Evaluate

UPWARD SPIRAL STAGE

R – Repeat

THE STAGES

Planning Stage

The "OP" is a coat rack for your life. A coat rack gives you something to hang your coat on to prevent your house from getting messy. An OP gives you something to hang your experiences on so your life does not get messy.

In the OP stage, you remember the Real You, reconnect with your Stands, get yourself ready to Play Huge, and create real-life actions to move you forward. It is where you set your strategy for forwarding your action and deepening your learning.

The OP sets the stage for your experience. OPs create meaning. OPs provide focus for your experience. You are able to see any upcoming challenge as part of a larger learning process and not just a random event. The actions, intentions, and goals you create in the OP stage will provide the context for your experiences. The OP helps you create success by working through the challenges. The OP helps remind you that you are working on something, thus giving you a reason to persevere.

Experience Stage

When you are in an experience, you will have available to you the tools of being Realistic, taking Accountability, and calling Time-out; these tools help you make sense of your life while you are living it. When an event is understood as part of a larger process you have created, you can control your reactions and stay in your power, instead of getting sucked into behaviors and feelings that get you off track.

Individual and random experiences can easily be considered failures or negative events, and, depending on how you are feeling, they could really kick you into a downward spiral. The context you create with your OP allows all the thoughts and feelings of the learning experience to be understood as part of a bigger picture.

But, being Realistic, taking Accountability, and calling Time-out is not just about avoiding a downward spiral and making sense of what you are doing. It will have a bigger impact than that.

When you are realistic and you connect with your sense of accountability, you are more likely to remember to call Time-out than if you are randomly proceeding down a path based on emotion and laziness. When you call Time-out, you revisit your OP, which allows you to reconnect with your larger purpose and get back on track. Being back on track allows you to get back to Playing Above the Line.

Post-Experience Stage

The third step when you are the OPERATER of your life is Evaluate. This is a chance to look at your whole process to this point. When you Evaluate, you get a chance to look back and learn from your experience. You get to see how your OP has worked. You get to assess how well you took Accountability, whether you were Realistic, and how effectively you have been using your Time-outs. This is the time you see the whole process, and learn from it. Then, you also look ahead and think about what choice you will make next time you have an opportunity to be the OPERATER of your life.

Upward Spiral Stage

And, finally, after all the evaluation, it is time to get back in action. You already know that the Upward Spiral is a key component of getting what you want, so you have to Repeat the OPERATER process. Again and again and again. Being the OPERATER is a constant process in your life.

GOING BACK TO SCHOOL

When you can get a bird's-eye view of your life by calling Timeout, you can step out of the emotional and intense moments in life. Then you can evaluate the situation, work the Upward Spiral Cycle by remembering the Real You, and work to determine what effort is best for you and what is Sustainable over time.

RALPH'S GOING BACK TO SCHOOL

A client, Ralph, was beginning graduate school in the fall. He knew he was going to be busy with school, work, and family. Because he knew what was coming, he was able to set up a plan for handling what he thought was going to happen—stress, projects to complete during family time, loss of some focus at work, and being tired, among other things. We did what we could to anticipate the challenges and opportunities of the coming months. He was calm, thoughtful, and able to think clearly about the big picture.

Then the fall came, and he attended coaching sessions week after week. He was dealing with not being able to give an assignment enough time, a decision about whether to pursue a great opportunity at work, not working out enough, and other similar things. It was all exactly as he had anticipated. He was emotional, excited, challenged, and focused on the tasks at hand.

He had planned the trip and now he was on his trip. So, we spent our coaching sessions working through specifics, but doing so while remembering the ideas (and structures) we had created in the summer when he was calm, thoughtful, and thinking clearly.

At the end of the semester, we had several coaching sessions during which we talked about how things had gone while he was in school, what he wished had been different, and what he wanted to do differently next semester. We spent time both evaluating and planning, while he was reflective, recuperating, and able to evaluate.

Then the whole process began again, and we got to repeat what we had done in the fall.

Ralph's experience illustrates the stages of being the OPERATER of your life.

But it also provides insight into the reason that being the OPERATER of your life is as powerful as it is.

DIFFERENT KINDS OF THINKING

As this story illustrates, we think and feel differently during different experiences in our lives. There is a different kind of thinking that happens at each stage, as well as a different emotional response. Some kinds of thinking are better for the planning stage, just as some kinds of thinking are better for the experience stage, the post-experience stage, and the Upward Spiral stage.

All these offer very different experiences, and it is challenging to switch quickly into and out of the different feeling and thinking modes.

The human brain works like this: the core of our brain is made to react—fight or flight. The outside of our brain is made to think—consider possibilities, plan, and organize. In order to think, you need to feel safe. It does not make sense to sit and plan when you are in a dark alley with lots of threatening people. It makes sense to get out of there, and quickly. But, you will be much better off if you have a plan in place that you created when you did not feel the immediate threat. You anticipated this situation, and now you have an idea of where to go.

It is challenging, if not impossible, to switch your thinking and feeling quickly. The consequences of not doing so can be significant, and provide the reason to be a good OPERATER.

MANAGING STRESS

When you are the OPERATER of your life, that provides an understanding that the thoughts and feelings you are experiencing are part of a process. They are not isolated. They did not come out of nowhere. They are an expected part of learning from experience; despite being difficult and yucky, you have got to go through them.

Knowing this eliminates stress and makes your life easier to understand.

Because you have an idea of what is going to happen, when it happens you realize there is nothing wrong with you. You are not in trouble. You are not crazy. You simply are in the middle of a learning experience. The middles of learning experiences can be challenging (and you want them to be challenging to push your Learning Edge). But, when they are challenging, a way to learn is to call Time-out.

When you call Time-out during an experience, you are giving yourself an opportunity to remember the Real You, reconnect with what you Stand for, and revisit your plan.

HEATHER AND HER DESIGN

Heather is designing a travel book. She has lots of experience as a clothes designer. She worked for many very successful clothing companies as a designer. She knows her creative process well. It includes phases of excitement, of struggle, and of breakthrough. She could clearly outline the stages of design, and she could easily identify some thoughts and feelings she was going to have in the process of designing anything.

This time, however, she was designing a book, not clothing, and it was for herself, not her company.

In the middle of the process of creating her book, she came to me for coaching. She said she was having a really tough time, and she spent the first ten minutes of the session talking about how she was never going to finish her book project. She said she thought her book project was too ambitious, she had to figure out what to do next with her life, and she felt like she was crazy.

My evaluation was that she was in the Experience stage of her project and she had lost touch with what she had created in her Organize and Plan work. After acknowledging her feelings and letting them settle, she called Time-out. She was in an emotional and intense moment and needed some perspective. When she called Time-out, she went back to the coat rack and remembered the Organize and the Plan for the project. She had not considered this project in the same way she did her design projects, but, as soon as she thought about it, she realized she was in one of the stuck times of her design process.

Second, she got Realistic. She knew that if she had planned the process of creating her book, she would have anticipated exactly what was happening because it had happened every time she designed something. The emotions of frustration, self-doubt, lack of motivation, and feeling crappy, became familiar, and, while she did not like it, she knew from all her design experience that part of the creative process is working through the times when she felt stuck and the ideas were not flowing.

With this perspective, she was able to understand where she was in her book design process. She took Accountability for the process and was able to get back on track. She remembered that her emotional response was an essential aspect of the process, and she knew to persevere and be ready for the creative breakthrough.

By taking the time to see the whole process, Heather remembered that the thoughts and feelings she was experiencing were part of her design process. They were not isolated. They did not come out of nowhere. They were an expected part of learning from experience, and, despite being difficult and yucky, she has to go through them.

Notice how easy it is to get off track and doubt yourself as Heather did. It doesn't take much. Her Silly Self-Talk was all over her—she thought she was crazy, there was something wrong with her—and she was considering abandoning her project.

The perspective made her realize there was nothing wrong with her at all. She was not in trouble. She was not crazy. She simply was in the middle of a learning experience. By calling Time-out, she remembered her Real You, reenergized for the learning part of her project, and jumped back into the Experience with a different perspective.

ONWARD TO KNOW YOURSELF AND PART II

Because you can get a bird's-eye view of your life, you can step out of the emotional and intense moments in life and evaluate the situation to determine what action is best for you and what is Sustainable over time. But, to be able to do this effectively, you will need to know who you are and what you Stand for. And this is the work of Know Yourself.

HAPPY BIRTHDAY PITT!

Ye' old Chap.

Yer nearly a fullon Brit by now,
ye Pond crossing fellow.
What a courageous &
adventuresome
Spirit!

PLAY HUGE™

I wish for you a
year full of
creativity, ♪♪,
♥, imagination,
learning & health.

Playing Huge.
[illegible]

WHAT WILL IT TAKE?

HEY, NICE OFFICE D!
WOW... NO ONE'S CALLED ME 'D' IN A REALLY LONG TIME AND ONLY ONE PERSON USED IT...
...ONLY ONE PERSON WHO DRESSES LIKE A LIBRARIAN ANYWAY.
I BROUGHT A LITTLE PHOTO-GRAPHIC PROOF JUST IN CASE WE HAD TROUBLE.
WOW, IT'S GREAT TO SEE YOU LESLIE.
HEY DEREK, IS YOUR FRIEND COMING TO THE MEETING?
I THINK I'LL PASS ON THE MEETING FUN. STOP BY MY PLACE ON FRIDAY AND WE'LL CATCH UP.
OH, AND BRING YOUR PORTFOLIO TO SHOW OFF.
SAME OLD LESLIE ALWAYS UP TO SOMETHING.

WHAT WILL IT TAKE?

DAMIE!
WHAT DO YOU THINK YOU'RE DOING UP THERE?
DAD?
IS THAT A TRICK QUESTION?
WHOA DAD!
YOU ARE COMING HOME RIGHT NOW!

WHAT WILL IT TAKE?

ON STAGE
WOO WOO W
GOODNESS, WHAT IS HAPPENING?
YOU WILL NOT BE SEEING MY SON AGAIN MA'AM.
I'LL MAKE SURE TO LET OTHER PARENTS KNOW WHAT YOU DO HERE.

WHAT WILL IT TAKE?

LATER THAT WEEK
IT'S NICE TO HAVE A COUSIN WHO HAS HIS LIFE TOGETHER.
I CAN'T EVEN MANAGE TO PICK A MAJOR... IT MUST BE NICE TO HAVE A GOOD JOB AND SOME SECURITY.
HONESTLY I'D RATHER BE SAILING... I HAVEN'T BEEN HAPPY AT MY JOB FOR A LONG TIME.
...SECURITY IS NICE BUT IT'S NOT EVERYTHING.
FUNNY, D. THE WHOLE FAMILY IS PROUD OF YOU.
YEAH, I GET STUCK ON THAT. BUT THAT'S NOT WHAT IT'S ABOUT. I'M MISERABLE DOING WHAT I "SHOULD" BE DOING.

WHAT WILL IT TAKE?

WHAT-EVER, LOOK AT THIS.
THOSE RULES ONLY SOUND **STUPID** TO STONERS LIKE YOU AND JAMIE.
AAP
JOIN US IF YOU ARE:
COURAGEOUS, CURIOUS, FRIENDLY
RISK TAKING, HEALTHY, WILLING
TO LEARN, APPLAUDING EFFORT
FUN, OPEN MINDED AND NICE.
A
MOVE ALONG IF YOU ARE:
B
JAMIE GET HIGH? HA! YOU AND HIM ARE LIKE THE SAME PERSON WITH DIFFERENT CLOTHES. HE'S NOT EVEN COMING TO SCOTT'S ANYMORE.
WAIT? JAMIE DOESN'T DO DRUGS WITH HIS FRIENDS?
... WHAT ELSE HAVE I BEEN WRONG ABOUT?

— PART TWO —

PERSONAL TRAINING

KNOW YOURSELF

How are you smart?

Learning Forum/SuperCamp Question
(adapted from the work of Howard Gardner)

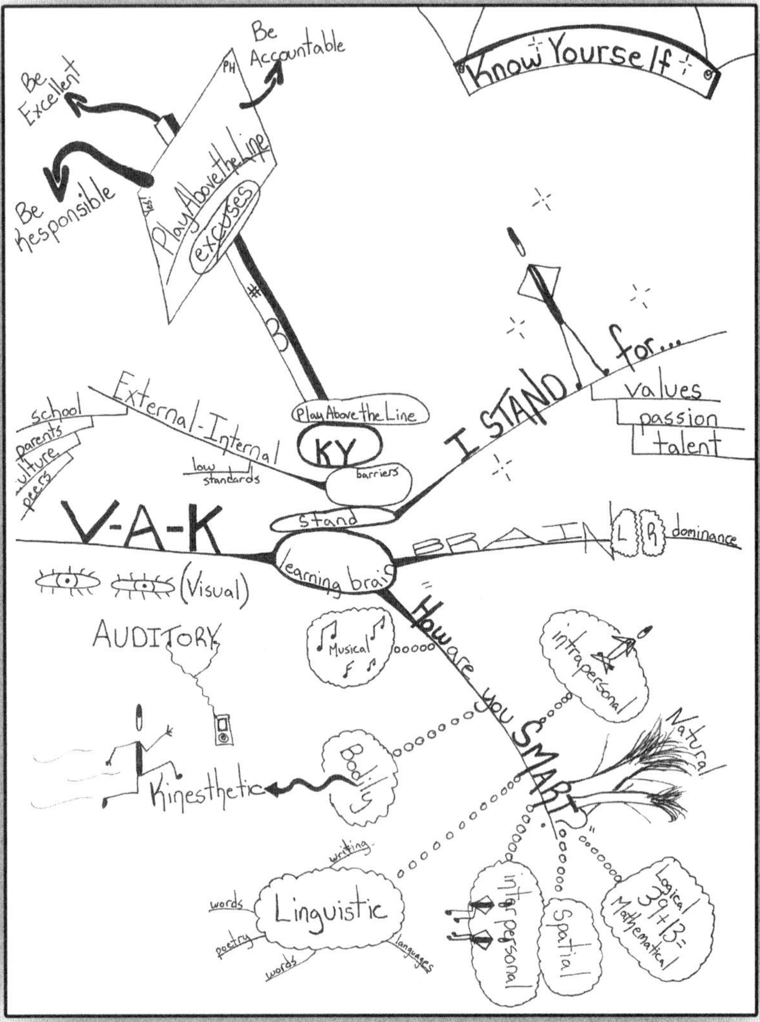
Know Yourself
Be Accountable
Be Excellent
Be Responsible
Play Above the Line
excuses
#3
I STAND for...
values
passion
talent
External-Internal
school
parents
culture
peers
low standards
Play Above the Line
KY
barriers
stand
V-A-K
learning brain
BRAIN
L R dominance
(Visual)
AUDITORY
How are you SMART?
Musical
intrapersonal
Natural
Bodily
Kinesthetic
Linguistic
writing
words
poetry
words
languages
inter personal
Spatial
Logical
39+13=
Mathematical

YOUR SIMPLE KNOW YOURSELF

Who you are is a combination of how your brain works and what is in your heart and your body. When you Know Yourself, you understand that you are okay just the way you are. You will always continue to expand who you are and what you know, and you get to decide what is best for you and what you care about. No one can tell you how you learn, what you care about, and that who you are is not okay. You are who you are, and it is important for you to Know Yourself because it is a key component of the foundation of Launching Your Life.

Knowing Yourself is made up of two elements—your learning brain and what you Stand for.

Your Learning Brain

Your way of understanding information is unique to you. The ways you are smart are unique to you. There is no right way you should be; there is simply the way you are. And it is important to understand the way you are.

In *Launch Your Life*, your learning brain consists of:

- how you like to learn,
- how you are smart, and
- which side of your brain you like using.

When you Know Yourself, you have a solid foundation in how you learn, how you are smart, and the way you tend to think. This knowledge sets you up to create wonderful, exciting, and meaningful learning experiences for yourself.

Your ability to create these learning experiences is further enhanced as you identify what you Stand for.

What You Stand For

152

You want to make a difference in the world and passionately fulfill your potential. Your Stand is what the Real You wants to do; it is the answer to how you want to make a difference and what you are passionate about.

You move beyond the "choose something…anything" stage here and learn, or expand, your focus by identifying what you Stand for.

Your Stand is what is in your heart, and the feelings in your body. It's an expression of what you love doing, how you want to impact life, and your commitment to make it happen. It is a connection to the Real You and what you want to express to the outside world.

By connecting your learning style with your Stand, you begin to Know Yourself, and you set yourself up to become as powerful and fulfilled as you want to be in your life, because you create your own internal validation of who you are and what you want to become.

KNOW YOURSELF EXPLAINED

A cairn is a balanced pile of stacked rocks. You would find a cairn when following a walking, hiking, or backpacking path.

The intention of a cairn is to mark the path so those who follow will be able to find their way. Making a cairn is a considerate and thoughtful act.

In building a cairn, there are several steps, all equally important. Finding rocks that will work for the structure of the cairn—in terms of size, shape, weight, and unique features—is critical to making your cairn what you want it to be. Then, when balancing your rocks, you've got to know the rocks and how they can fit together. You can make a cairn that barely balances, or you can make one that is solid.

Here is what a cairn looks like.

Creating your Know Yourself is much like the process of building a cairn.

The human brain is the most powerful learning entity in the world. In fact, it is incredibly powerful. But, until you know how your brain works, it will not be as powerful as it can be.

Identifying the pieces that make up your learning brain and your Stand is essential. Figuring out how they fit together is also critical in the process. Your Know Yourself can be captured and expressed in many ways, and it will certainly grow with time as you travel the Upward Spiral, but, having an understanding that you Know Yourself will allow you to travel powerfully throughout Launching Your Life.

LEARNING HOW MY BRAIN WORKS

I had no idea how my brain worked until the summer after I was done with college. School was always a struggle for me; it was always hard for me to make sense of the information teachers were conveying.

I remember three experiences when I did well in eighteen years of school (not counting gym class and recess).

In fifth grade, we went to a place called Loredo Taft, where we got to spend two days walking around the woods, reading a compass, and searching for scavenger hunt clues.

After my dad died, I studied philosophy. In my classes, we were talking about death and living life with honor. Because of my recent experience, I was able to contribute significantly to the conversations.

Then, my senior year of college, I traveled around the world on a ship, studying and visiting ten different countries. I got to talk with people in those countries, visit their schools, have dinner with them, ride their buses and trains. And then I got to write papers about my experiences.

When I returned to college, I almost flunked out in the last month of my senior year. I did survive, but not until after I was all done with school did I learn information that explained why I had spend the last eighteen years of my life in school feeling stupid.

I learned how my brain works. My primary learning style is as a kinesthetic learner. I am spatially, intrapersonally, interpersonally, and kinesthetically smart, and I favor my right brain.

In other words, I am the kind of learner who needs to be in an experience to understand it. I don't process facts. I love interacting with people and am able to communicate with them. I am excellent at navigating around places I have been and places I have not been. I like being in action. I am more inclined to have a sense about something than I am to know lots of data about it.

Knowing this about myself changed my life. I hope Knowing Yourself does the same for you.

THE CHALLENGE OF SCHOOLS

The power of Know Yourself is that it provides a nontraditional and nonacademic look at how you learn and who you are. What I see happening more and more often in schools particularly, but also in the general population, is reliance on medication to fix conditions. In some cases, it is a good decision.

But, too many times, I have seen someone who is simply a kinesthetic learner being diagnosed as ADD, or someone who has a set of intelligences that don't match her learning environment being diagnosed with a learning disorder. When there is a mismatch between how your brain learns and the environment in which you are expected to learn (e.g., school, work, relationships), it can be massively challenging and lead to low self-esteem, behavior challenges, and bad performance in school.

Increasingly, there are very limited sets of intelligences that work in schools. Drama, art, music, and physical education are being cut from schools, and, with them, recognition of a whole set of intelligences of young people. And, at the same time, in most schools and in the minds of most parents, significant energy, money, time, and credibility are being given to high-stakes testing that focuses on only two intelligences, and an ability to test in a high-pressure environment. The combination of these issues pushes the idea that the most important intelligences are linguistic and logical/mathematical, and that you had better be able to sit for long periods of time without physical activity and focus (an advantage to visual and auditory learners).

But what happens if those are not your strengths?

Currently, the conclusion is, if you don't do well in school...if you act out...if you don't perform well on high-stakes tests, there is something wrong with you. Now, if you would just take this medication...

When you Know Yourself, you have information to dispute any feelings or evaluations that there is something wrong with you. Instead of thinking you learn wrong, you can be confident in the conclusion that you learn *differently*.

Your Learning Brain

It is time to uncover the way your brain naturally works and how you understand the world. Every person on the planet has a different brain and, therefore, a unique way of understanding the world and a unique way of learning.

Life is filled with experiences and opportunities to learn. When you identify your natural learning styles, it is easier to create meaningful and fulfilling experiences for yourself. The rocks of your cairn simply provide a way for you to understand how your brain learns. And, again, how you experience the world is unique to you, and how you go about understanding what you have experienced is unique to you.

What follows are comprehensive explanations of three theories that will help you understand your learning brain—Learning Styles, Multiple Intelligences, and Brain Dominance Tendency. By going through and identifying this aspect of your Know Yourself, you will understand the simplicity of these concepts and, yet, the profound impact they can have on your life.

THE LEARNING STYLES: VISUAL, AUDITORY, KINESTHETIC

BIKE ASSEMBLY

Imagine you have just purchased a bike that needs to be assembled. How do you proceed?

Do you read all the directions and then begin assembly? Do you look at all the pictures and all the pieces, and then begin assembly? Do you dump out the box and begin putting pieces together? Do you call a bike shop to ask them how to proceed?

The learning style options are visual, auditory, and kinesthetic. They describe one way your brain works. Knowing your style will provide insight into why you like what you like. It explains why you care more about whether your clothes match or how they feel, why you love books but not music, or music but not books, and so much more.

Knowing your learning style may provide you insight into reasons that you struggle in school, or why you don't like gym class, or why you love summer camp as much as you do. It may explain your love of going to lectures or book readings, or why certain careers are very appealing while others are hard to imagine for yourself.

Everyone has a combination of visual, auditory, and kinesthetic learning abilities, but we each tend to have one that dominates how we like information to be presented to us. Here are lists of the three different styles and what they mean.

Visual Learners

- You like information to be represented visually.
- You want to look at information on the chalkboard.
- You like images and graphical representations.
- You use graphic organizers and make concept maps, so you can see information and link ideas and concepts together.
- You like to use symbols, images, and illustrations.
- You pay attention to your clothes and how they look. You care if they match, if they are wrinkled, and how people will perceive how you look.
- You like to watch videos.

Auditory Learners

- You like to hear the teacher speak.
- You like to listen to a lecture.
- You like to listen to audiotapes.
- You learn best when information is delivered by the spoken word.

- Having noise in the background when you read makes it easier for you to understand what you are reading.
- You like to listen to music.
- You think in words.
- You speak well and listen to people. You are unlikely to interrupt because you want to hear people's thoughts, and you want people to hear your thoughts.
- You have an ability to organize group activities.

Kinesthetic Learners

- You learn best when there is physical activity involved, as you have realizations while doing things with your body.
- You like the process of learning by doing, being in the experience, moving your body, and naturally discovering things through that process.
- Movement helps you focus.
- You are restless when you are understimulated in educational situations.
- You like wearing comfortable clothes.
- You have very good balance, timing, coordination, and natural body movement.
- You like doing manual tasks.

You may already be identifying the above statements that apply to you, and that is perfect. Or, you may have trouble reading a list like this and applying it to yourself, which is also perfect. The idea is, you begin to realize that however you understand information is unique to you, and it is not wrong or bad or anything other than your style. It is like choosing rocks for your cairn. You choose your rocks and use them to build a structure that works for you.

But, you cannot build a one-rock cairn and you are more dynamic than just your learning style. The first rock is one part of your learning brain, and the next piece to add is how you are smart.

THE MULTIPLE INTELLIGENCES

Howard Gardner, a professor of education at Harvard University, developed a theory that human beings have multiple types of intelligences. Some people are naturally able to understand and play music, while others are naturally able to do math. Others are good at relating to people in social situations, and others enjoy quieter settings. And so on. One use of Gardner's theory is to help you understand that you have skills and abilities that are most natural for you.

Are you smart?

When you are asked this question, you will respond either "Yes" or "No," depending on the perspective you have of your abilities and how you feel about your performance at school. Multiple Intelligences theory allows that question to become,

How are you smart?

And the possible answers are many. You can be smart in playing baseball. You may be smart in finding your way around a place you have never been before. You may be smart in math class, but not English. Or you might be smart in gym class, but not in music. You might be a great friend. The possibilities are endless, and it is essential to know how you are smart. 296

While building your Know Yourself, identifying "how you are smart" is a component to help you navigate your way successfully in the world.

Gardner has identified eight intelligences:

- *Interpersonal*—This means you are good at relating to other people; you have good communication skills; you are understanding of other people. You might be someone people really trust and be a good friend. You may be comfortable speaking up in class, or the one who volunteers to give your group presentation.
- *Intrapersonal*—This means you have a good knowledge of yourself and are able to be self-reflective. You may journal

and you may be quiet. You may come across as shy. You are likely to be able to explain your reasons for doing something.

- *Logical/Mathematical*—This means you are strong with numbers and logic. You can solve problems both with numbers and in the real world. You are able to think through situations. You might be recognized by your ability in math class, or your comfort talking about numbers and statistics. You might be someone who always figures out solutions that seem to make sense.
- *Linguistic*—This means you are strong with languages, whether it be foreign languages or native languages. You like words, writing, and playing language games. You may be easily able to pick up foreign languages or have a strong knowledge of English. You may love Scrabble or crossword puzzles.
- *Musical*—This means you like music, play music, or are able to orient your thoughts around music. You have a sense of rhythm and can follow a beat.
- *Bodily/Kinesthetic*—This means you are coordinated in your body movements, able to understand things through experience, learn by doing, and are comfortable in your body. You may be an athlete, dancer, other kind of performer, and/or fine artist.
- *Natural*—This means you have a knowledge and love of the natural world. You like being outdoors and exploring nature. You might love camping and going to summer camp, or perhaps you know a lot about flowers, animals, and the environment. You find bugs when you are outdoors and want to keep them as pets.
- *Spatial*—This means you have a sense of your surroundings. You are able to interpret and navigate in the physical world with grace. You may be an artist or an excellent parallel-parker, or you can estimate the right size of a container to use for leftovers and/or are able to see how things fit together.

MY FRIEND, BEN

Ben did all the illustrations for *Launch Your Life*. He is an incredibly talented visual artist. He also is a musician. His intelligences are spatial, kinesthetic, and musical.

When we talk, he often sits and doodles. I often wonder if he is paying attention, but then he will show me his "doodle," and it will be a visual representation of what we have been talking about.

Check out the comic book if you haven't already, because those are the kinds of images he came up with as I was describing Launch Your Life. He has fully embraced his talents, and continues to learn and explore the possibilities of his capabilities in exciting ways.

But things were not always easy for him. Because the way his brain learns is not conducive to sitting still in a classroom, when Ben was in fourth grade, his teacher told his parents she thought he was mentally retarded.

As you did with the learning styles, as you read these lists and the story about Ben, you may have begun to identify how you are smart. As you do, remember that you have some degree of each of these intelligences. You will have some in which you are stronger than others, and some in which you might be really strong or weak. Everyone has a unique arrangement of how they are smart, and you can always expand how you are smart by learning new skills. But, for the purpose of understanding your learning brain, the focus is on how you are smart now, and the answer is the second rock for your cairn.

BRAIN DOMINANCE

Human brains are absolutely amazing. Your brain is the most powerful learning device on the planet, and the understanding of how the brain works continues to increase dramatically. Like everyone, you have two sides to your brain. You use both sides of your brain for everything you do.

But there is an elegant division of labor in the brain. The left side deals with one set of tasks, and the right side deals with another. While there is some debate about the specifics of this idea, for the purposes of *Launch Your Life* I have found that the idea that each side of the brain handles information differently is very helpful. It will give you a sense of your way of interpreting information, which will be in line with the tasks of one side of your brain or the other.

The set of tasks that your left brain likes is work with numbers, charts, spreadsheets, graphs, and text. The left brain analyzes data, does linear thinking, is organized, likes step-by-step procedures, processes information sequentially, wants to zero in on an answer, and is logical and linear.

The set of tasks that the right brain likes is dealing with feelings, creating art, and putting things in context. The right brain likes big-picture understanding, abstract thinking, imagery, simultaneous processing, synthesizing experiences, and empathizing.

Just as with each part of your learning brain, it is critical—*critical*—to understand that neither of these set of tasks is correct, better, worse, or exclusive. Everybody does all these tasks, but, as with your learning style and intelligences, you have a natural bias.

QUESTIONS	LEFT BRAIN RESPONSE	RIGHT BRAIN RESPONSE
How many people are there in the world?	6,849,612,545 as of August 2008	A lot
What is wrong with the sentence structure?	The verb is in the wrong tense, and there is no direct object.	It doesn't feel right.
What is the test going to be like?	Mr. Rich said there would be twenty questions–ten multiple choice, seven short answer, and three essays. The facts will be easy, and he said you could use charts and data for the longer answers.	It is going to be pretty hard; you need to know the facts.
What is the weather going to be like?	The Weather Channel is reporting that it will be about eighty degrees this morning and then there is a 70% chance of rain beginning at noon.	It's warm out–shorts weather. It looks like it might rain later.

The chart indicates some stereotypical differences between a left-brain thinker and a right-brain thinker. There are many levels of nuance and possibilities here, so, while this gives you an idea of the kind of differences you might find, there are also more subtle differences and tendencies. But, having an idea which side of the brain is your natural tendency will help you know the third rock to add to your Know Yourself cairn.

WRAP-UP OF YOUR LEARNING BRAIN

When you have an idea of how your brain learns, you will be able to understand and see your world differently. When you struggle with something, you will understand why you are struggling, instead of criticizing yourself. When you love doing something, you may have a new appreciation of why you like it so much.

As you progress on the Upward Spiral, you can expand how your brain learns, but, when you know your learning style, how you are smart, and which side of your brain dominates, you will have a greater capacity to make sense of your world. You will also have a clearer picture of who you are, and will have established a cairn on your path.

All three of these theories provide labels for the way your learning brain works. If you prefer other ways to label and identify your learning brain, use those. The theories I have presented happen to be the ones I have found most beneficial in my experience. The most critical aspect of this section is that you find some way of understanding how your brain learns, so you stop any Silly Self-Talk telling you that you are not smart. In other words, it does not matter what labels you use, but *that* you use labels.

What You Stand For

Through understanding your learning brain, you are building your knowledge of how you most naturally learn about the world. The next step of building your Know Yourself is identifying the rocks that represent what you care most about in the world, your gifts and talents, how you take care of yourself, and who you are not. When you put all these together, the combination is what I refer to as your Stand(s). Your Stand is an expression of the Real You and helps you make powerful decisions and choices. By taking a Stand for something you believe in, you clear a path for yourself to live a life of Meaning and Fulfillment.

WORKING WITH A POSITIVE ATTITUDE

My friend really cares about people. She treats people well and expects to be treated well by others. She was working at a place where people were not nice. They were critical of each other and talked behind each other's backs all the time. She tried to say something sometimes, but got ridiculed for it.

Eventually, she did an evaluation of her situation and realized that she Stands for treating people well. In her heart, she believes that being mean and disrespectful to other people does not solve any problems; it just creates them. With her renewed commitment to herself, she again began Standing up for herself. Then, when her co-workers talked back to her, instead of getting stopped by it, it increased her resolve to be positive.

The impact was tremendous in the organization, but, for her, the impact was that she felt good about her life again.

RIDING MY BIKE

5,16

I ride my bike all over Portland. I do so because I have several Stands that bike riding supports.

I Stand for living a lifestyle that is Sustainable—meaning that, if everyone on the planet lived as I do, there would be enough resources for everyone for many, many generations.

I Stand for taking care of my health.

One day, it was raining and cold, so I didn't want to ride. I started to think about not riding, but immediately dismissed the idea because of my Stands. I know if I don't ride, I get frustrated at myself and feel like I am compromising my values and what I care about. If I don't ride, I let the rain and cold be more powerful than my commitment to Sustainability and my health.

> But, if I was not as clear in what I Stand for, the ambiguity in my commitment could make it easy to compromise my values. If there was nothing compelling that I was committed to, the presence of the rain and cold would dictate my decision. I would let myself off the hook, on some level feel crappy about it, and let the weather be more powerful than I am.

Stands keep you in your power. Without a Stand, my friend allows the negative energy and meanness of people to control the situation. Without my Stand, the rain and the cold become more powerful than I am. Taking a Stand for who you are connects you to the Real You. Your values, your passion, your talents, get to emerge on the Play Huge Stage when you begin to Stand in your power.

219

VALUES

Values are the guides you use for your standards of behavior. They are what you deeply believe. They are the rocks that make up the foundation of your cairn. They are your determination of what is important in life. They provide a guide for you to follow when going through each day.

Knowing your values is a vital aspect of living a life of integrity. When your actions match the things you care about, then you are in integrity. When your actions are not consistent with your values—whether because you don't know them or because you are not honoring them—you are out of integrity and compromising the Real You.

Below is a list of some values. There are many more than this, but this will give you an idea of what values are. (For a more comprehensive list, go to page 170.)

Originality	Curiosity	Orderliness	Perseverance
Personal growth	Peacefulness	Movement	Nature
Nurture	Kindness	Choice	Love
Honesty	Freedom	Integrity	Responsibility
Excellence	Spontaneity	Partnership	Forgiveness

PASSIONS

A passion is an activity you do that really excites you. It is something you have an intense desire to do, and that you feel very enthusiastic about doing.

The things you are passionate about usually have a close relationship to how you are smart and what the Real You wants. You will also find you are good at doing the things you are passionate about, although you can be passionate about learning something new. A passion might be lifelong, or it might be shorter term. When you find something you are passionate about, making an effort to be engaged in that activity is easy and joyful.

You have certainly seen someone who is passionate about what they are doing. Maybe it was a dancer doing his favorite dance, a friend talking about a presentation she gave, a teacher who loves his subject, a parent who loves her job, or someone watching a sunset. You will absolutely love doing what you are passionate about.

TALENTS

A talent is something you do that you have a natural aptitude for doing. When you are engaged in an activity in which you are talented, it comes easily for you, and you find great joy in doing it, and you are usually willing to work hard to improve your ability.

You may be a gifted musician. You may be talented in reading, writing, or math skills. Perhaps you are gifted at performing or are a gifted athlete. You may find it easy talking with people or listening to people. Drawing, being creative, singing may be things that come easily to you.

As with your passions, there are no right or wrong rocks when it comes to your talents. They are simply who are you and what you are great at. You can make your cairn with the rocks that are for you.

REJUVENATION

Rejuvenation is doing an activity that makes you feel healthier, makes you feel alive, helps you to feel rested, or gets you reenergized. You choose the activity because you know that, after doing it, you feel energized and ready to Play Huge.

It may be a place you go in order to feel completely alive. It might be engaging in a physical activity—doing yoga, going for a bike ride or on a run, playing hockey or Ultimate Frisbee. Perhaps going for a hike in the woods rejuvenates you, or sitting by a stream. For you, it might be listening to music, writing poetry, exploring the city, designing your room. You will discover you have your own ways to rejuvenate yourself.

WHO YOU ARE NOT

Part of the exploration of discovering your values, what you're passionate about, what your talents are, how you rejuvenate, and even your learning styles, is also learning who you are not. What are the rocks that will not work in your cairn?

Identifying experiences that are the opposite of all the items focused on above—thus allowing you to understand who you are not—will be helpful in creating your Powerful Portfolio and in getting you tied into your Know Yourself.

You might discover that sitting in a classroom isn't a powerful way to learn. You may not care about deforestation or endangered species. It might be that you are not a talented athlete. It might be that you are not good at playing or listening to music. It might be that traveling or risk taking does not rejuvenate you. As with all the steps of building your Know Yourself, the possibilities here are endless. So take what you come up with, realizing that the information is important in finding the rocks for your cairn, and recognizing that some will not be right for you.

WRAP UP ALL THIS INTO YOUR STAND

In general terms, a Stand is adopting a particular attitude toward an issue. But, when you *Launch Your Life*, your Stand is more powerful than this because the foundation of your Stand comes from the Real You.

Your Stand is what you are willing to fight for, what you care most about, the way you believe things should be done, the way you want to be treated. It is a powerful assertion that broadcasts to the world, "Here I am, and here is what I am about."

When you have a significant decision to make or someone asks you what you care most about in the world, having a clear Stand makes it easy for you to be decisive and assertive. It allows you to take powerful action and doubt yourself less. Having a Stand is a statement to your Silly Self-Talk that you are in charge and will accept input only on your terms.

Your ability to create these outcomes increases on the Upward Spiral and is further enhanced the more specifically you identify what you Stand for.

- What do you care about?
- What do you love doing?
- What gets you fired up?
- What does your Real You love doing?
- What does your Real You want to make your life about?
- What does your Real You want to say to the world?
- What does your Real You want to say to other people?
- What is the expression your body wants to share?
- What is in your heart?

Your Stand is an expression of what you love doing, and how you want to make a difference, and your commitment to make it happen.

In Launching Your Life, your Stand becomes a statement of what you are willing to commit your life to. It is your foundational cairn, and, because it is an expression of what is in your heart and what you feel in your body, it is the beginning of all your actions. It is a connection to your Real You and what you want to express to the outside world.

Your Know Yourself

You've now been exposed to all the elements of Know Yourself. You are ready to take each of these ideas, put them all together, and create an understanding of who you are and how you understand the world.

You will have to figure out which of these ideas work best for you and which don't work at all. The whole concept of Know Yourself is that you figure out a way you understand the world so you can powerfully create the life you want.

When you Play Huge, you act with courage and confidence, and you learn. Learning requires perseverance and commitment. The only way to Sustain a high level of perseverance and commitment is to be Playing Huge with things that matter to you—what you know about yourself. If you are compromising who you are, you will never be able to Sustain and create Meaning and Fulfillment. Playing Huge based on your Know Yourself is a step beyond "choose something…anything." It is an announcement to yourself and the world: "Here I come!"

THE PATH TO KNOW YOURSELF

As you *Launch Your Life*, you will constantly return to your Know Yourself. As you journey on the Upward Spiral, you will realize that you want to expand your Know Yourself. Once I began to build my Trust Yourself, and accepted that I am a highly kinesthetic learner, I returned to my Know Yourself and used the power of the Upward Spiral to develop my auditory and visual skills. I also wanted to learn to play the guitar despite my low musical intelligence. And I wanted to learn how to be more "left-brained," so that I could appreciate and learn to do research more effectively.

But, first things first, and the task your first time through *Launch Your Life* is to establish your foundational cairn(s). This section will provide steps to determine your natural Know Yourself.

NATURAL LEARNING

I have a friend who builds custom bikes. The bikes he makes are absolutely beautiful. He absolutely loves the design and crafting of bicycles.

As he has gotten more successful in making a business for himself, he has had to do things at which he is not as naturally gifted. He is writing stories for his customers on his web site and is having to manage his customers and co-workers.

In working on solutions to how to make the non-bicycle-creating activities more fun and high quality, he explored his natural process. He does not need to contemplate his process for creating a bicycle. When he crafts a bike, he is engaged, focused, challenging himself to learn, and "in the zone." He loves the hands-on metal work, the creative decisions, and the exploration of how to make his ideas come to life.

When he shares about his process, it is easy to imagine him in his workshop making his magic happen.

But, for some reason, when he sits down to write a story about creating his bikes, it becomes a painful, difficult endeavor that he avoids, finding other things to distract him. He wants to write the stories and have them available for his customers, but, when the time comes to make it happen, it is a massive struggle.

He began to identify the way that his process for creating a bike works. That became part of his Powerful Portfolio, and he then was able to more easily identify the strengths he brought to the writing process and the challenges he was going to face.

This section will outline steps for you to take to build your Know Yourself. These are but a sample of the possible activities; the way to take full advantage of these is to Play Huge.

POWERFUL PORTFOLIO

While you build your Know Yourself, it will help to capture the things you learn about yourself in the Powerful Portfolio part of your Play Huge Notebook. This can be a collection of pictures, words, poems, quotes, music, or whatever else will keep you connected to your Know Yourself and on the path of the Real You.

Discover Your Learning Brain

IDENTIFY YOUR TENDENCIES

In the resource section of the *Launch Your Life* web site, *www.themeaningrevolution.com/launchyourlife*, there are links to sites where you can take inventories to identify your learning style, how you are smart, and your brain dominance. I recommend checking out these inventories and beginning to assemble the way you naturally learn.

If you feel you don't need to take the inventories because you can figure out your tendencies in another way, make it happen. And know that creating an accurate Know Yourself will benefit you in the long run. If you feel confident in your ability to assess your learning brain, then make a high-level contract with yourself and complete the task with excellence.

RESEARCH YOUR RESULTS

Once you have taken the inventories and/or identified the natural way your brain works, learn about your identified styles. When you do the inventories they will (usually) provide information about your results. There will be separate information about the three different theories used in *Launch Your Life*, so you will get to integrate it. Reading about your results is one way to do research. You can also share your results with parents, friends, teachers, or someone at your school who would know something about these ideas.

Beware that some people might not know about these theories, or may not want to talk about this stuff. If this is the case, then keep looking for someone who can help you learn more about your learning brain.

However you learn/research these—whether by reading, talking, asking, or some other means—the important thing is that you begin to understand some details about your learning brain.

LEARN BY EXPERIENCE

The inventories and your research will provide you an idea of your learning brain, but it will only be part of the picture. As with all assessments, these inventories are limited. Once you have your results, use your daily experience to test what you have discovered.

By beginning to understand what it means to be a left-brained visual learner with high spatial and musical intelligence (for example), you will begin to understand how to make sense of your world. You will begin to observe how and whether your experiences match up with what you have discovered through your inventories and research. You will be able to measure whether your interpretations of your experiences match your learning styles and intelligences.

THE BACK TWO LEGS OF MY CHAIR

I was—actually I still am—the kid who leans back in my chair. I love trying to balance on the back two legs of a chair. I was also a pencil-tapper. I drove my teachers crazy. But I did not have any information about my learning brain.

If I had known, I would have realized I was a kinesthetic learner and my teachers were not. I am completely able to focus—in fact it helps me focus—when I am playing with that balance, but, to them, I was distracting.

Not only was I leaning back in my chair, not at all interested in sentence structure ("linguistic" is not one of my strong intelligences), but when I was asked what is wrong with the sentence on the board, I was inclined to say, "It doesn't feel right" (a right-brain answer), rather than "The verb is the wrong tense and there is no direct object" (a left-brain response from someone with "linguistic" intelligence).

Then, after I got the wrong answer, I would lean over to ask my friend (my "interpersonal" intelligence) to try to understand what just happened, but that, too, was distracting to my teacher.

Finally, it would be time for recess and I could go run (my kinesthetic abilities thriving), create new games to play (right brain), and deal with conflicts (right brain and interpersonal intelligence). But, I never got graded for recess.

You can begin to notice that it is easier for you to learn from your teacher who uses lots of visual aids than from your teacher who talks the whole class. Or, you may notice that the teacher who talks during the whole class is easier to learn from than the one who uses visual aids. You may notice that you really like to go to museums. Or you may find that museums are not your thing, but musical performances inspire you. As you Know Yourself in this way, the world around you begins to make sense as viewed through the lens of your natural way. For me, when I realized how my brain learns, I realized that classrooms are really challenging places for me to learn, and that the world makes much more sense to me when I am learning my natural way, by doing.

What is it like for you?

PLAY ABOVE THE LINE

200

Knowing Yourself does not justify your actions, and it is not an excuse to play small. Actually, it increases your accountability. For example, just because I am a right-brained kinesthetic learner who does not like English class, that does not mean I can goof around, not try, not care, annoy the teacher and other students, and then say, "Well, I know myself and this class does not work for the way my brain works." Secret #3 is Play Above the Line. When you Play Above the Line, you take ownership for your actions. By Knowing Yourself, you have more ability to take responsibility for your learning.

What that means for me, as a right-brained kinesthetic learner who does not like English class, is that I have to figure out a way to make it work for me. It might be talking with the teacher after class to figure out a strategy, or getting a tutor, or, if I have a choice (in college, for example), not taking classes that don't work for me, or taking them as a step on the Upward Spiral to expand my learning brain.

OTHER MEASURES

Remember that the metrics I have chosen—learning styles, the multiple intelligences, and brain dominance—are ones I have found to be useful and meaningful over my years of working with people. If you have other measures that you find to be congruent with your way of being, then use those. The whole point here is for you to Know Yourself and get in touch with the Real You. If you know ways to make that happen, go for it!

Also know that there are many sophisticated systems that will give you similar, but different, assessments of how you understand the world. I have found that these can be useful at a later stage of the Upward Spiral. I suggest learning styles, the multiple intelligences, and brain dominance because they provide a solid foundation in Knowing Yourself, so, when (or if) you decide at some point to do one of the more sophisticated assessments, you will have an easier time understanding it.

22

Finally, as you discover aspects of your Know Yourself, be certain to capture your learning style, your intelligences, and your brain dominance, in your Powerful Portfolio.

Create What You Stand For

152

When you have a clear understanding of what you Stand for, it eliminates a tremendous amount of ambiguity and creates a tremendous amount of clarity. Your Stand is based on what you care about in the world and is a reflection of your values, your passion, and your talents, among other things. It is a valuable piece of your Know Yourself cairn.

The most important element of creating what you Stand for is learning to reflect upon and evaluate your experiences. In all the exercises that follow, whether it be determining your values or connecting to your passion, you will have to increase your ability to connect to the Real You and honestly determine who you are and who you want to be.

EZRA AND SYLVIE AT THE DINNER TABLE

Marcy and I want our kids to be responsible and respectful. We place a high value on family time, and eating dinner together is a commitment we all make to our family.

Our kids are active. When we sit at dinner, they move all over the place, up, down, around and round. They spill food everywhere. Marcy and I go back and forth about our expectations of them. Sometimes we think they should sit still. Sometimes we remember how I was as a kid and think, "Give them a break; they are active kids just like I was." We go back and forth with our expectations. We also go back and forth with our reactions. Sometimes we are calm; other times we get angry and frustrated.

It has got to be confusing for our kids. There is no clarity. The expectations change constantly. Our reactions change constantly. From their perspective, they don't know how to act. They have no way to win.

What we have not done is take a Stand. Finally, we took a Stand and made it clear to ourselves and the kids:

We will all sit up at the table. Your first plate has a small amount of food and you have to eat it all. When you finish it all, you can ask for more of what you want. When you are done eating and talking, we will all clean up together.

Our Stand eliminated the ambiguity in the situation. The expectations become clear. The ability to be successful was simple. We were prepared for our Stand to need to be adjusted, but we decided we would try out these ideas for a month. Then we would reevaluate our Stand.

This is the opportunity that exists when you take a Stand. You are able to focus on your actions and not debate whether you should or you shouldn't. You are able to act on your principles more easily because your Stand is clear.

How do you figure out what you want to Stand for? As the following sections explain, it begins with your effort to Play Huge; then you learn to do high-level evaluation and reflection; then you can do some exercises that may help you clarify your values, passion, talents, way to rejuvenate, and more. You may also have other ways to figure it out, which you are welcome to explore.

PLAY HUGE—BEYOND SOMETHING...ANYTHING

You have been in action from the moment you decided to Play 89
Huge. You might be taking classes you like, volunteering for causes, doing an apprenticeship, or doing a self-study. You

might be realizing that what is happening at school is driving you crazy or the environment at work is dragging you down.

Whether what you Stand for jumps into your head, or you are having trouble identifying it, when you put time and energy into something, you will quickly determine whether it is something that matters to you, especially when you can step back and get a bird's-eye view of the situation, and evaluate and reflect.

What are you finding that you have strong feelings about and care about? Are you willing to make the extra effort? Are you willing to do whatever it takes to create a different outcome in your daily life? Will you be able to Sustain your effort to make a lasting difference?

Whatever experiences you are creating in your effort to Play Huge, you have got to be able to reflect on these kinds of experiences, and evaluate whether they are connected to the Real You.

PAY ATTENTION TO THINGS THAT MATTER TO YOU

In the Play Huge energy that leads to your evaluation and reflection, you want to be looking for things that you love doing and make you feel great. But, you also want to pay attention to when things are frustrating, because that indicates you have an idea of a different way to do things. The frustration is based on a vision of how things could be different, and you want to capture that vision because it may be an expression of the Real You.

The difference between living with that frustration and doing something about it is taking a Stand. It is not a powerful way of being to continue to get frustrated about something when taking action could do something about it. And the first thing to do with it is some evaluation and reflection.

EVALUATION AND REFLECTION

On the path to Play Huge, I encouraged you to "choose something...anything." The point of this was to get you Playing Huge. Now it is time for the next level of Play Huge, which is honestly reflecting upon and evaluating your experience.

You will know you have found something to Stand for when you enjoy what you are doing. It will feel good and be easy for you to pay attention to. You will be interested in learning more about it. You will be intrigued by the challenge and feel good at it. You will consciously choose it, and you will find it easy to continue.

Your reflection and evaluation will be based on your answers to these criteria. There are two different lists of questions to cover different types of situations and different types of learning brain.

My friend working in the place where everyone was being really negative and mean and talking behind people's backs, could use questions like these to connect to her Real You. Here is the list of questions from page 157, applied to a specific scenario:

- What do you care about?
- What do you love doing?
- What gets you fired up?
- What does your Real You love doing?
- What does your Real You want to make your life about?
- What does your Real You want to say to the world?
- What does your Real You want to say to other people?
- What is the expression your body wants to share?
- What is in your heart?

If you have chosen to do an activity to Play Huge, but you are wondering whether this activity is something you Stand for, you might use this list of questions to reflect upon and evaluate the activity:

- How much do I like this activity?
- Does it make my Real You feel good?
- What do I want to learn about the activity? How motivated am I to learn about it?
- What doubts do I have about the activity? What questions do I need answered?
- What are the challenges? Am I intrigued by the challenges?
- How easy will it be for me to overcome the challenges?
- What are the best parts of it? What opportunities exist for me to assert myself and Stand for my Real You?
- How committed am I to creating a successful outcome?
- Will I continue to do it because I love it? Do I feel powerful in my choice to do it?

In your effort to get in touch with the Real You, you may be choosing to volunteer for causes, take a class, do an apprenticeship, or create a culture change at your school or work. Perhaps you are focusing on taking classes that you like and following your interests in other choices you are making. Or, you may already be in touch with the Real You and on track to create your Stands.

Wherever you find yourself, it is time to get good at reflecting upon and evaluating your experiences. This is the difference between the beginning stages of the Upward Spiral and the stages of the Upward Spiral at which you begin to enhance your abilities and make powerful Stands. Whether it is creating your first Stand or honing a Stand you already have, keep on learning to reflect upon and evaluate your experiences.

Value, Passion, and Talent Exercises

Now, building on the above lists and all the ideas from *Launch Your Life* up to this point, here are some exercises to continue to enhance your Know Yourself. Remember to use your newly found information about the way your brain learns, because, as you go through these exercises, you will want to lean on your learning style, how you are smart, and your brain dominance. All these exercises are intended to be fun, meaningful, and informative. There is no right way to do them, so, if you want to write a song or a poem, draw something, record the answers as you talk, create a performance, or anything else, please do. Finally, I suggest you make a page (or pouch) in your Play Huge Notebook to keep track of what you create as you do these exercises.

VALUES CLARIFICATION EXERCISE

Please read the following list of qualities (adding any other qualities important to you, but not on the list), and circle any that feel particularly important to you. Then go back through those you've circled and identify the five that best express who you are.

Abundance	Contribution	Guidance	Originality	Self-expression
Acceptance	Control	Harmony	Partnership	Sensation
Accomplishment	Courage	Health	Patience	Sensuality
Accuracy	Creativity	Holistic	Peacefulness	Serenity
Achievement	Dedication	Honesty	Perception	Service
Action	Delight	Honor	Perfection	Sincerity
Adventure	Dependable	Hope	Performance	Solitude
Aesthetics	Devotion	Humor	Perseverance	Space
Alignment	Direct	Image	Personal growth	Spirit
Altruism	Discernment	Imagination	Persuasion	Spirituality
Artistic	Discovery	Improvement	Planning	Spontaneity
Assistance	Divinity	Independence	Playfulness	Stimulation
Attainment	Drama	Influence	Pleasure	Strength
Authenticity	Dream	Information	Power	Superiority
Autonomy	Educate	Ingenuity	Preparation	Synthesis
Awareness	Elegance	Inquisitive	Privacy	Tenderness
Awe	Empowerment	Inspiration	Process	Thinking
Balance	Encouragement	Integration	Professionalism	Thoughtfulness
Beauty	Energy	Integrity	Prosperity	Thrill
Bliss	Enjoyment	Intimacy	Quest	Touch
Bravery	Enlightenment	Intuition	Question	Transformation
Calm	Entertainment	Invention	Radiance	Trust
Candor	Excellence	Judgment	Realization	Truth
Choice	Exhilaration	Justice	Recognition	Understanding
Clarity	Expansion	Laughter	Refinement	Uniqueness
Comfort	Faith	Leadership	Reflection	Unity
Commitment	Family	Learning	Relationship	Vision
Community	Feeling	Love	Religious	Vitality
Compassion	Flexibility	Loyalty	Resilience	Vulnerability
Competition	Focus	Magnificence	Responsibility	Wealth
Completion	Forgiveness	Mastery	Reverence	Wholeness
Conformity	Freedom	Movement	Risk taking	Will
Congruent	Fun	Nature	Romance	
Connection	Glamour	Nurture	Safety	
Contemplation	Grace	Openness	Satisfaction	
Contentment	Gratitude	Orderliness	Security	

PASSIONS EXERCISE

- What do you care most about?
- What are the issues in the world you pay attention to?
- What are you passionate about?
- What do you think about when you think about being able to do anything?

TALENTS EXERCISE

- List the things you are best at.
- List the things you enjoy the most.
- From each of these lists, choose the top three.

REJUVENATION

- Where do you feel most alive? Where do you love being? (Be specific, even to noting the temperature.)
- What are you doing when you feel most alive?
- Who are you with when you feel most alive?

LITTLE KID QUESTION

- What do you want to be when you grow up?
- Who do you want to be when you grow up?

These are questions you have probably answered many times during your school career. When you actually are a little kid, there is often a free and easy response. Then you can easily dream, and all the doubts or questions about whether things are really possible don't interfere.

As you search for the Real You and your Know Yourself, these questions come back into play. Answering them in the same way you did in first grade, without your Silly Self-Talk, will give you the cleanest view of the Real You.

YOUR REFLECTIVE MOMENTS

Listen whenever reflective moments arise. They may come when you're showering, exercising, dreaming, or talking with a friend. Really, they may show up anywhere and any time. They are messages from the Real You. When they do show up, listen to what the Real You has to say.

Find a place in your Powerful Portfolio, or some other place you will remember, to capture these reflective moments.

LISTENING TO OTHERS' STORIES

Stories are profoundly powerful. Listening to other people's stories will enhance your Know Yourself, and your ability to Trust Yourself, on a number of levels. When you hear a story, you naturally put yourself into the story and begin to explore.

Sometimes you learn along with the person telling the story. Sometimes you realize how different you are, or how similar you are. Sometimes you are able to explore possibilities you would not have considered otherwise.

Listening to stories engages your creativity and opens possibilities for you. Listening to stories also normalizes what you are experiencing and allows you to understand that you are not alone. You spend so much time in your head chatting with your Silly Self-Talk, that to hear other people's experiences and their interpretations of those experiences gives you new perspectives.

PUTTING YOUR STAND ALL TOGETHER

When you identify what you Stand for, you take your values, what you are passionate about, the kinds of things you dreamed of as a little kid, the moments in classes where you feel absolute frustration that things in your school are not different, and all the other moments and feelings, and put them together to create what you are willing to commit your life to, today. Your first statement does not have to be THE statement (you never have to have THE statement); it simply needs to be something that matters to you and that you are willing to commit to for the next seven days. Here are some examples:

- I Stand for honest communication.
- I Stand for being positive and energetic at school/work.
- I Stand for staying in touch with my friends.
- I Stand for making eye contact with my kids each day.
- I Stand for learning to play soccer.
- I Stand for being on time.
- I Stand for exercising.
- I Stand for volunteering two times a week to help people less fortunate than I am.

When you have made this decision, capture it, whether in words, an image, a song, or whatever. Capture it, because you will "put it up on the wall" so you can be reminded constantly of what you Stand for. My Stand is hanging next to my computer. It's been revised again and again, because I did not capture it the way I wanted to the first ten times. Now it's getting closer.

What you Stand for is a combination of what is in your heart and what you feel in your body. Make it joyful and challenging. You deserve to be powerful and share your connection to the Real You and what you want to express to the outside world.

PUTTING IT ALL TOGETHER

Your Stand is an expression of what you love doing and how you want to make a difference, and your commitment to making it happen. You now have a lot of information and many exercises to help you get connected to the Real You.

When you have all this positive and exciting information about yourself swirling around, you are living on your Upward Spiral, and, when you get to this place, you create powerful things.

In the song "Endless Night" from *The Lion King*, a young lion is missing his dead father. He feels alone and is searching for who he is. (Sound familiar?) He is looking deep inside, wanting to hear what he thinks is his dad's voice, but, really, he is looking for his inner conviction that he will be okay. He is searching for what he Stands for. He wants confirmation that he is okay, and he thinks it will happen when he hears just a single word...some acknowledgment...something...from his father. But it's got to come from himself; he will only find his voice and confidence when he connects with his Real You.

The work now is to keep on practicing Secret #1—Believe in the Upward Spiral. No matter at what stage you are of putting your Know Yourself together, keep working the process. And what is the process? It's continuing to take the next step, more action, generating failures and mistakes, sharing how your brain learns, getting frustrated, feeling powerful, getting a vision of what is possible, doing more reflection and evaluation, feeling the glimmer of connection, choosing something to Stand for—and then beginning all over again, at the next level of the Upward Spiral.

POSSIBLE BARRIERS

You will face two different kinds of challenges as you begin to assemble your Know Yourself. In the true spirit of Know Yourself, you will have your own unique way of confronting these challenges. The way you have interpreted your experience will dictate how your challenges show up. The first variable in the creation of your challenges is internal, having to do with your Silly Self-Talk. The second variable is external, having to do with challenges that show up in our culture.

YOUR CHALLENGES

Just as your combination of learning styles, intelligences, brain dominance, and Stands is unique, the challenges you face are unique to you and are based on your interpretation of your own experience.

The last component of your Know Yourself is your understanding the specific obstacles that make your journey challenging for you. In the same way that you have different learning styles, intelligences, values, passions, talents, and ways to rejuvenate, you will have a different combination of challenges to deal with. So, you will have your own combination of Silly Self-Talk, cultural influences, challenging habits, connections with people, vulnerability, ego, and more. Further, the impact you feel from each of these challenges will shift as you *Launch Your Life*. So, it may be that your Silly Self-Talk is currently really loud, but you have a handle on your challenging habits. In three months, however, you might have gotten a handle on your Silly Self-Talk but are now challenged by your ego. It does tend to be true, though, that those you can identify today will continue to challenge you over time, and identifying them now will enhance how you Know Yourself.

Internal Challenges

There are challenges you will face when you make an effort to Know Yourself. They will put you in a vulnerable position and make it tempting and easy to compromise the Real You. By knowing the challenges, and having the tools to connect to the Real You and trust your Know Yourself, you can make a conscious effort to avoid slipping onto a downward spiral.

WE ALL WANT TO BE LIKED—SO WATCH OUT

What I have learned in my years of working with people is that all of us desperately want to be liked. We want to have friends, we want to be included, we want people to be thinking about us, we want people to do special things for us, we want to be part of groups. We all want to be liked.

This desire creates a place of vulnerability. When you feel like you aren't liked, you get scared and you search for ways to feel included, to feel part of groups where you are liked and known. You try to figure out ways to get people to notice you. You explore ways to get liked in order to create friendships. We are really—all of us—constantly trying to figure out ways to navigate this space so we feel included and liked.

While you search and explore, you are in a vulnerable place.

MIKE AND RENEE

I went to boarding school when I was fourteen. It was my choice. I wanted to pursue my dream of playing professional hockey and baseball.

The first several months were really challenging. I didn't have any friends, and my hockey tryouts were not going very well. Finally, I started hanging out with a guy from my mom's hometown. His name was Mike. It felt like he was the only guy who would talk to me. However, he liked drinking beer and smoking pot. I resisted.

But then we were hanging out with some girls, and one of them told Mike that she liked me but I was too straitlaced. I had never been very good at talking with girls, so I was very excited and this broke my resistance to drinking.

I had some crazy adventures and, soon enough, I was kissing Renee, but our "relationship" did not last. I was not being crazy enough, and, thankfully, just when she challenged me to be more outrageous, I made the hockey team.

The first thing the coach said to me was that, if I wanted to play hockey, I should pay attention to who I hung out with.

xxxii One of the challenges to Know Yourself comes in this place of vulnerability. In this place, you may feel you are all alone and you want to be included, and, because of those thoughts, it is easy to compromise the Real You. There is the potential for Knowing Yourself out of desperation vs. Knowing Yourself in authenticity. And you might be really good at deceiving yourself, which is a short-term gain and a long-term loss.

I AM ALL ALONE

Secret: everyone wants to be liked. Everyone feels vulnerable!

Even those you perceive who seem to have it all together...well, they, too, feel the same way you do. They also want to connect. They want to feel that people like them. They want to feel like they're understood.

You may perceive them as the leaders, or as the cool people, or as confident, but they are people, too, and they are dealing with challenges just as you are.

The challenge of Knowing Yourself is realizing that, because everyone wants to be liked, there's a real temptation to try to be like someone else because you think they have it all together, they feel really good about themselves, and they know themselves. So you compromise, and give up the Real You, in order to match your perceived idea of what you have to be to feel liked.

The opportunity here is to connect to the Real You and build a community of people who support you. The opportunity is to Play Huge and choose the path going to Meaning and Fulfillment, not to a short-term solution.

BEING INCLUDED

Once you choose a group, it often happens that it's not as wonderful as you expected it to be (because of the perception that things are better "out there"). When you are not included and accepted in the way that you want to be, there is a temptation for your behavior to get more and more outrageous. You certainly have seen this before, or perhaps done it yourself. The clothes become more outrageous. The dancing becomes more provocative. The activities become more dangerous. The stunts become more excessive, and so on.

The message: Notice me. Notice me.

TONGUE SPLITTING

One summer, a camper had lots of piercings, and she got lots of attention. The next year she came back with more, and got more attention, and then kept on getting a reaction. Some thought it was cool. Others thought it was crazy. But, as the summer moved on, the reaction became less. So she began talking about her next adventure, tongue splitting, and that brought another round of attention.

ADRENALINE JUNKIE

One of my students loved outrageous adventures. Over the four years of high school, his adventures continued to get more and more risky. The cycle was obvious. He would get attention for his latest adventure, and then the attention would tail off. As soon as it did, the next risk was launched; after a time of anticipation and attention getting, the event would happen, there would be the reaction, it would fade and...here goes the cycle.

We all want to be liked. And we will do what it takes to get attention.

HIGH STANDARDS

You know you want to be successful. When you are honest with yourself, you know you want to have a good life. If you could choose to fill your life with the things in the following boxes, which box would you choose?

BOX A	BOX B
Fun	Substance Abuse
Play	Debt
Joy	Loneliness
Friends	Lame Work
Love	Laziness
Connection with people	Poor Health
Laughter	Boredom
Meaningful Work	Apathy
Savings Account	Sickness
Health	

When you have the chance to explore Know Yourself, you could come to the conclusion that Knowing Yourself means knowing that you like to be lazy, smoke pot, skip class, play video games all day, etc. You and I can both imagine someone we know saying something like this:

- I like to hang out, play video games, and get high. I don't want to exercise or eat healthy.
- All my friends are hanging out and getting by. I think it's cool to do that all day.
- Yeah, I choose Box B because it's easier, and you would have to be a geek to choose Box A.

Perhaps there is some truth to parts of that in some people, but that is Knowing Yourself at a low level. If you play that game, you play the game of compromising the Real You.

I simply don't believe that you want to play at that level. You want more from your life.

My challenge to you is to have high standards. Don't rip yourself off. Connect with the part of you that knows how to answer the question of which box you would choose.

If you feel compelled to push this issue, and to Know Yourself with low standards, this book is not for you—yet. There will be a day when you look back and say, "Dang, I wish I had jumped on that opportunity then and not now. It would have saved me a lot of time and energy (and, quite probably, money)." But this is your choice. You *can* hang out on your couch while the rest of us go out and make a difference in our lives and in the world.

When you get to your Know Yourself, have high standards and stand up for the Real You.

SILLY SELF-TALK

If the Real You is there but is still small and quiet, you likely recognize the voice of your Silly Self-Talk. That voice is persistent and will continue to show up. Remember the image of the big hairy monster intimidating the Real You? (See page 17.) Here it is again, up to its old tricks.

You know how to jam your Silly Self-Talk. If you are still having trouble connecting with the Real You, now is the time to keep practicing.

EGO

Being Perfect

You might try too hard here to find your perfect Know Yourself. If you spend too much time searching for your ideal learning style, the perfect balance of your intelligences, the thing you are most passionate about, or the exact words to use for your values, you might miss out on your everyday, natural way of being, and the entire point of this exercise is capturing your authentic self. Developing your Know Yourself is a constantly evolving process. It is not an event you will get in an hour of reflection. The Upward Spiral never ends, so enjoy the process.

With time—weeks, months, years—you will discover more and more distinctions and possibilities for your Know Yourself. As you travel the Upward Spiral, you will realize the learning opportunities are endless, and the development of your Know Yourself is an ongoing process.

Too Basic

You might be working to dismiss the early stages of getting to Know Yourself as too basic. The temptation to get into other levels of Know Yourself may be great. Your ego wants to move forward. You will naturally want to move beyond this foundational step and get into other aspects of Know Yourself. But, creating a solid foundation in your Know Yourself is crucial for long-term and Sustainable success. If you skip this stage, eventually you will "injure yourself," and that may come in the form of taking off down a path in your life toward your destination and then realizing it is not what you really wanted.

Without a solid foundation of Know Yourself and a connection to the Real You, your ventures will be risky and in danger of never getting off the ground to fulfillment. There will be a temptation to say to yourself (or others), "I know how I learn and all that stuff; I don't need to take those inventories."

You've probably heard a story like this one:

CHOOSING A MAJOR

A friend of mine chose a major she was told would be good for her. She took lots of classes, and then, in her senior year, she finally admitted to herself that she didn't like it. But, by this point, she was too far along to change unless she wanted to spend another year (or more) in school. She couldn't because it was too expensive, so she ended up completing the major she did not like. Now, years later, she is still regretting her decision.

The ego of your Silly Self-Talk will push you toward more "advanced" levels of Know Yourself. Whether it be choosing a major, completing a project at work, writing a paper for a class, building a relationship, or your Know Yourself work, time spent at the foundational stages—while it may seem basic and perhaps a waste of time—will greatly accelerate your long-term success, and save you time, money, energy, and aliveness.

YOGA CLASS

When I go to a yoga class, I notice my urge to do the poses just like the teacher and the more experienced students. My ego gets engaged, and I completely disregard that others have been practicing far longer than I have, and they have different body types.

In yoga, the pose is never finished. There is always more to learn and new ways to refine the pose. I have learned that, to get to the more challenging poses, you must have a really solid foundation in the basic poses or you will end up injured. And, when you get injured, you usually end up farther behind even than where you started.

It might be that you think you look bad and others will perceive you as dumb for not Knowing Yourself. I urge you to take seriously this step and build yourself a solid understanding of your learning brain and what you Stand for. Creating a solid Know Yourself is crucial for long-term and Sustainable success (Secret #5). Even if you think you know, it is worth learning more. There is always another level of distinction to understand. Further, when you begin to expand your Know Yourself, knowing the specific areas where you can grow is very helpful.

LACK OF CONFIDENCE

Building your Know Yourself and being willing to put your ego aside help you build confidence. There is a profound sense of taking care of yourself when you know you handle the basics really well.

LEARNING TO PLAY THE PIANO

A friend of mine told me about when he took music lessons as a kid. His parents really wanted him to be a musician, but he didn't like the lessons and he didn't practice between the lessons. He said his parents hoped the lessons would boost his confidence and give him another skill.

But, as my friend reflected back on his experience, he said that he did not have a strong enough foundation of confidence to take on another skill. He didn't have a good sense of what he was good at, so, when he was asked to do something else new and he wasn't successful, it further diminished his self-confidence.

Once you feel solid in your Know Yourself and you are honoring the Real You, it makes a lot of sense to enhance your natural abilities to include other ways of learning and being. But trying to jump up onto the Upward Spiral, instead of taking care of all the steps, will eventually send you backward.

WRAP-UP OF INTERNAL CHALLENGES

The secret that follows this chapter is Play Above the Line. The reason it is there is because all the challenges as you develop your Know Yourself have to do with how big you want to play. If you are ready to face the challenges of people giving you a hard time when you Stand for yourself, and you are ready to quiet the challenges your Silly Self-Talk will create (including battling your own ego), then you are ready to Play Huge. Even if you are willing simply to make an honest effort with high-level contracts while battling these things, you are ready to Play Huge. But, if you are willing to compromise the Real You because it is scary, or you think you have it figured out, or your ego is too strong, then you are going to get sucked into one of these challenges (or those coming next).

You can deal with the challenges. Take ownership, and be responsible for yourself and your actions, by taking a Stand that matters to you. You can do it.

External Challenges

You have your own internal challenges to deal with, but, unfortunately, there is a lot of support for those challenges and there are many reasons they exist. So, in addition to handling your own challenges, you get to try to handle external messages, too.

You get messages from society about who you should be, in the form of advertising, television, movies, the Internet, and technology, among other places. You also get messages about who you should be from your peers, from your parents, and from schools.

You are inundated by these external messages, and they usually come with flashing neon lights.

And all the messages really convey the same message:

- Who you are is not okay.
- You should do things differently.
- You should be different.
- If you did ________________, you would be okay; in fact, you would be much happier, cooler, and smarter.

What goes in the blank? Choose one of the following: buy these jeans, use this shampoo, do well on this test, get into this college, smoke this, drink this, say this, pay attention to this, etc.

Society, peers, parents, and schools are all challenges to Know Yourself.

SOCIETY

In American culture, you are inundated every single day with messages that imply "who you are is not okay." If only you used this shampoo, if only you had this phone, wore these shoes or jeans, if you drove this car, then you'd be okay. You are not attractive, smart, cool, as you are, but, if you had our product, you'd feel much better about yourself.

Our society is based on your buying stuff. A great way to get you to buy stuff is to make you feel insecure about who you are, and then encourage you to feel more secure by buying things.

This constant barrage of messages compromises and eats away at your Know Yourself. It makes it challenging to know the Real You. It makes it challenging to know who you want to be in the world, what gifts you bring to the world, and how you want to make a difference in the world.

PEERS

The advertising and marketing world is not the only influence. Your peers are also conduits for messages of who you should be. You perceive that friends and people who are older than you and people who are younger than you are all cool. They're wearing the right clothes; they have all the right friends; they're really secure about themselves; they're dating; they're hanging out with girls or they're hanging out with boys. Certainly, they feel great about themselves.

You want to be like them, because you perceive they've got it all together—and you don't.

YOU HAD IT ALL TOGETHER

Since I've been out of high school, I've communicated with a lot of my friends from those teenage years. They're still friends of mine. One time recently, I said to two of them, "You know, it's amazing. When you were in school, you were so cool, you were so confident, you did well in school, and you were so good at communicating with girls/boys." They just looked at me with the "are you crazy?" look.

They looked at me, and each one took a turn saying, "No, no. I didn't have it all together. You had it all together. You were the one that was so good at all those things (except the talking to girls part), and you were a great athlete."

My interpretation of my experience was that I was in a place just wanting desperately to be liked by them, wanting to be their friend, wanting to be included in their group, and wanting to be part of what they were up to.

And the amazing thing I keep running into is, that they felt the same way I did. They wanted to be hanging out with me or someone else they thought was really cool.

You are influenced by that desire to be included, and so what you do is compromise who you are. It's a real challenge, because these messages start to influence your thinking about who you should be. They start forming your image of yourself and your identity, and, as they do, they pull you away from who you know you really are.

PARENTS

Parents, of course, have a big influence on your understanding of who you should be. Their impact is especially pronounced when they have their own challenges with launching their own lives.

Of course there are many parents who are fabulous. They really understand, and they try to value where you are; they really support your knowing yourself, and using your talents and your abilities to travel on the path that is best for you, not what will make them look and feel good.

But, when they're trying to establish their own identities and connect to their Real Yous ...when they're trying to Play Huge ...when they don't trust themselves, it is common for parents to use their kids to validate their lives.

They feel a sense of validation when they can say, "Oh, my kid goes to Harvard," "My kid graduated at the top of her class," or "My kid is studying to go to medical school." When the parents are working to feel good about themselves, they put pressure on you to be a certain way, whether they are aware of it or not.

This kind of statement makes you feel, "Oh well, I should be smart enough to get into Harvard; I should do well in the SAT; I should get good grades. That's the way to be successful, and, because my parents value and care about these things, that is who I should be."

Sometimes these messages are very obvious and, sometimes, very subtle. When they ask seemingly innocent questions—such as "How are your grades? Ready for me to help with your homework? What friends did you make at school today?"—they are subtly implying that grades, homework, and friends are the things that are valuable.

More obviously, when you're deciding what to do after you graduate and are thinking about applying to colleges, your parents say, "Oh, you should go to this school, or that school will look good on your résumé," "The business program there is very good," or "That will get you a good job when you graduate." When they make these comments, they are indicating the things they value. The implicit message is that these are the things you should value, too.

You start to do things that aren't really in line with who you are. You start to think, "I'm supposed to be a different way than I am."

SCHOOLS

Schools send similar messages. Both intentionally and unintentionally, schools make statements about information that is important, information that is valuable, information that is going to make you successful. The challenge in developing your Know Yourself is that you spend significant amounts of time in school. When you are in a vulnerable place, it is very easy to succumb to the messages and start to compromise yourself. It can be hard to develop your Know Yourself in an environment that consistently (relentlessly) defines the way to be successful.

Schools provide those messages about who you should be 36 through high-stakes testing. These tests begin, usually, in third grade, and they continue through high school and beyond.

Further, most schools put emphasis on sitting still and being quiet, the memorization of information, and the ability to recall it for a test. Schools are increasingly making statements that nonacademic abilities are not valuable, as indicated by the cuts in music, art, drama, and physical education.

The messages thus include: you should be good at math, reading, and literacy. You should be good at memorizing and then recalling in pressure situations. You should be able to sit still and listen for extended periods of time without talking. You don't need music, art, recess, listening skills, character development, or any life skills.

Some of you love school. You're excited about it, you're passionate about it, you're engaged by it, and it is authentically part of your Know Yourself. School works great for some people (about 5%), but that doesn't mean there is anything wrong with those of you for whom it doesn't work.

Connecting to something, not from a place of vulnerability, but from a place of excitement and engagement and congruence with the way your brain works, is exactly the hope of *Launch Your Life*. For some, school provides that environment, but, for the majority of you, school is a place that is a big challenge to your Know Yourself, because it does not work with your learning style, intelligences, and brain dominance. The message is, "Compromise who you are, because you are not okay the way you are, and, in order to be successful, you need to change."

WRAP-UP OF EXTERNAL CHALLENGES

Know Yourself is about identifying how you learn, how your brain works, and what you Stand for. It sounds easy, yet it continues to be a challenge. The reason is that you are inundated with messages that tell you that you are not okay. You get these messages constantly from society (including advertising, television, movies, etc.), from peers, from parents, and from schools.

The challenge that you face begins with Knowing Yourself, is enhanced by Playing Above the Line, and, after that, will be further enhanced when you learn to Trust Yourself.

The moral of the story of the possible barriers you face in Knowing Yourself is consistent with the spirit of Know Yourself. Your challenges with internal and external barriers will be unique to you. As you read and reread this last section, you certainly will realize where you have to be powerful and Stand up for yourself. Thankfully, at the beginning of this chapter, you gained some insight into ways you are, and things you believe, that will allow you to move powerfully forward in your life.

Beyond the Barriers

Hopefully, you are choosing to take powerful control of your life. When you Know Yourself, you are able to understand the world and the kinds of schools, people, jobs, travel, and experiences that will be the most meaningful for you. As you begin to use your learning styles and your intelligences, your Stand, how you rejuvenate, and your whole Know Yourself, you will gain new insights into your ways of interpreting information effectively.

You will find being in a classroom a much different experience. You will be able to relate to people and request projects at work in a far more effective way. You may not take on a project that you know doesn't cater to your strengths. You will be able to talk with people who are helping you find a job, choose a school or a major or any course of action, and leverage your knowledge about the way you experience the world into a choice that will be most beneficial to you. You will be able to leverage your strengths to find Meaning and Fulfillment in your life.

As you master being able to create a powerful state of mind and motivate yourself, you will find it easier and easier to get yourself motivated to act. You will get more done. You will be able to enjoy each moment of your life more because you will hear that voice inside you, the Real You, more often and with more confidence.

HUGE OUTCOMES—KNOW YOURSELF

I can **CONTROL** my Silly Self-Talk. It still shows up (and sometimes in a **NASTY MOOD**), but I am much better at noticing it and **DOING SOMETHING** about it.

I **CHOOSE** my life. I am not giving my **POWER** away anymore. I know that **BEING ME** makes a difference.

Life **FEELS GOOD**. I like myself.

I have much **BETTER ABILITY** to relate to people because I can **IDENTIFY** and understand their learning brains and **ADAPT** to them.

I used to make **DECISIONS** based on what I thought people would **THINK** of me, or what would be **COOL**. Now I know that decisions connected to my **REAL YOU** help me create the kind of life I **REALLY WANT**.

I have profound **UNDERSTANDING** of my way in the world and who I am. I have an entirely **DIFFERENT PERSPECTIVE** on the world.

And it makes me feel really **POWERFUL** and in control of **MY LIFE**.

When I face a **CHALLENGING SITUATION**, whether it be in a classroom or out in the world, I have some ideas about how to **USE MY STRENGTHS** to take on the challenge!

I **KNOW** what I Stand for! And I know that my Stand makes it **EASIER** to **TAKE RISKS** and make the kind of difference I want to in the **WORLD**.

Huge Outcomes: Text Version

And what is the impact of knowing how your brain works? What are the benefits from understanding your unique way in the world?

NEW PERSPECTIVE ON THE WORLD

There is nothing wrong with you. You learn the way you learn. You know how your brain learns and what you Stand for.

You take on the right kind of challenges. You see opportunities in the world that do or don't match your way of understanding. You will see the world through the lens that makes clear the things that will be easy for you and those that will be more challenging.

You create your interpretations. You know that your interpretation of events is your interpretation of events.

You Know Yourself and you are a learning machine. Your brain is the best learning machine in the entire world, and, as with a yoga pose, there is always the opportunity to learn more. All you have to do is Play Huge.

GAIN MORE CONTROL OVER SILLY SELF-TALK

Your Silly Self-Talk continues to show up, but, as you identify your Know Yourself, you become more adept at controlling when it shows up. The big giant monster that towers over the Real You is becoming more like a teddy bear as the Real You continues to grow, be more assertive, and get stronger.

FOUNDATIONAL CONFIDENCE

You already knew there was a Real You deep in there beyond the messages about who you should be and what you should do. Now you are getting more and more connected to what the Real You does for you and the power that comes when you honor it.

You may be beginning to feel the profound sense of integrity and confidence that comes when you honor the Real You. It feels like a foundational confidence in your being.

YOUR STAND

By taking a Stand, you are beginning to realize how much easier that makes decisions and choices, and you are learning how good it feels when you make decisions and choices from what is in your heart.

You feel the confidence to Stand for what you believe in, even when it is challenging and scary.

YOU STAND IN YOUR POWER

206

What a great feeling to know that you are more powerful than your circumstances. You make decisions about your life; you don't react to whatever is happening. If people are negative, you choose to do something about it. If your teacher lectures every day, you learn a way to take notes that helps you focus and engage your creativity. You stop giving away your power—because it feels really good to Stand in it!

EVERY EXPERIENCE IS A LEARNING OPPORTUNITY

You have begun to reflect on and evaluate your experiences in a way that makes every experience a learning opportunity. This includes relating to people. You now have a valuable tool that will help you understand other people. As you capture these learning experiences in your Powerful Portfolio, you build a constant reminder of how awesome you are.

BUILD A STRONG FOUNDATION

5, 16

You know all the potential barriers and the temptation to skip the foundational steps in order to look good and impress people (and your own ego). You know that doing the work to Know Yourself makes your future as promising as today is. As with your Stand, when you honor yourself at this deep level, you build credibility with yourself (and others) that you are okay, you are powerful, and you can fill up your life with Meaning and Fulfillment.

YOU MAKE A DIFFERENCE

Imagine what happens when everybody takes a Stand for what they believe in. Imagine what happens when everybody knows how they learn and who they are. When you Know Yourself, that offers an opportunity for other people to know you differently, but also for them to get to know themselves. When you Know Yourself, you make a difference.

Foundational Terms

Know Yourself continued to build on the foundational terms from Your Launch Pad and Play Huge. As happened with Play Huge terms, some of the terms come from a secret. In this case it is Secret #2—*Be the OPERATER of Your Life*. You learned what it feels like to be inside of *experiences*, and the advantage you gain by being able to call *Time-out* to return to your *Organize* and *Plan*. You also learned the importance of then *evaluating* your experience.

From Know Yourself, you began to understand your *learning brain*, which includes both how your brain works and what you *Stand* for. It is also very likely that you have dealt with some (maybe all) of the internal and external challenges. But you know that having high standards helps you deal with your *ego*, *Silly Self-Talk*, and the messages you get from the *Test Score Culture*.

WRAP-UP

You have negotiated around the Gnawing Feeling and connected to your Real You, and you have chosen to step onto the Play Huge Stage.

You have also discovered the first two secrets to a life of Meaning and Fulfillment—Be the OPERATER of Your Life and Believe in the Upward Spiral.

And, while on the Play Huge Stage, you notice a huge mound of clay with a flashing neon sign above it saying, "Build Your Know Yourself."

While you begin to sculpt your Know Yourself, you reflect that Know Yourself is a conceptual idea. There is no action in Knowing Yourself. The action comes when you Play Huge and when you Trust Yourself, but Know Yourself is creating an understanding of who you are, how you learn, what you Stand for, and who you want to become.

It is so, so tempting to want to sculpt something perfect, to do more than you are capable of, to feel like you should do something better than what you are creating, to skip the foundational step, but it is hugely important to establish a solid foundation. You know the audience is coming soon and you want to look good for them, so it is tempting to make something flashy that will impress people during the show, but will not last.

Just as you are beginning to listen to your Silly Self-Talk—which is making you feel inadequate because you don't have something flashy yet—you come across the directions to sculpt an award-winning self.

The directions begin with figuring out how your brain works and how you learn. Knowing whether you are a visual, auditory, or kinesthetic learner informs the size of your sculpture's eyes and ears, and whether your sculpture should be in motion. Further, knowing how you are smart will help you figure out what your sculpture can be doing.

There are many different award-winning possibilities for your sculpture depending on your particular combination of musical, spatial, linguistic, interpersonal, intrapersonal, bodily/kinesthetic, natural, logical/mathematical intelligences. And it might be fun to try to depict whether you are more a "left-brained" or "right-brained" person.

The directions continue by suggesting you create a banner for over your head that conveys your Stand. It might look something like this:

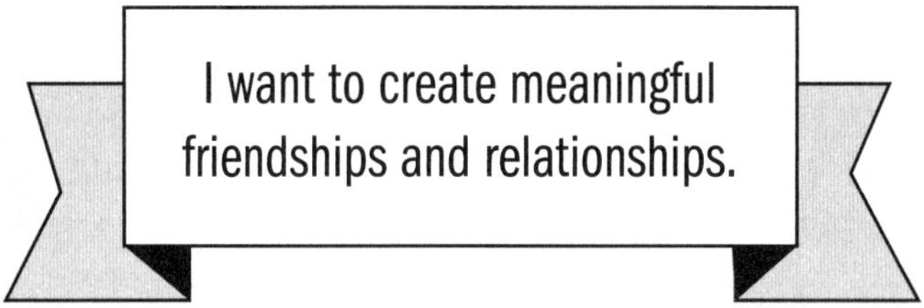

And because your Stand is based on your values, what you are passionate about, your talents, how you rejuvenate yourself, and the things you don't like and are not good at, you might find that you have several banners. And the beautiful thing about your Know Yourself is that it honors the Real You. There is no right way to be, and no one can tell you that your Know Yourself is wrong. It is yours.

But then a voice booms over the loud speakers that hang over the Play Huge Stage. The voice is accompanied by a shaking stage and flashing lights (to be certain to get the attention of all types of learners):

Don't play small.
There are some things to remember
about your statue and banner.

The shaking and light show continue as the voice says:

There is no place on the Play Huge stage for this:
"Duuuuuuude, my Know Yourself likes to sit
on the couch, play video games, smoke pot,
and get laid by any means possible."

There is also no room for justification,
like the temptation to go off on the path on
which you say, "I am perfect just the way I am;
my Know Yourself is all about being lame."

You hear the rumor that someone once did the "I want to be lame and apathetic" performance on the Play Huge Stage and got booed off. One thing everybody knows about the Play Huge Stage is that asserting your Know Yourself and Playing Huge significantly ratchet up your level of responsibility. There is no playing victim. On the contrary, there is only stepping into taking charge of your life and making it huge.

The reason (and this is posted on a backstage wall) is that you want more from your life than these kinds of responses. You choose "Box A." And you choose "Box A" despite the many challenges that surface when it is time to Know Yourself, some of which are a result of our wanting desperately to be liked. You want to make the effort to resist compromising the Real You; you want to maintain high standards.

After you recover from the loud voice and the light show, you continue reading the directions. They state a reminder that you don't have to be perfect or have a clear message from the Real You to make a powerful sculpture. If you are having trouble hearing the messages or understanding the messages about what you Stand for or what you care most about or what you want to create with your life, the way to figure it out is to create the best sculpture you can and present it to your audience. Dealing with this stuff means you are right on track. Keep on Playing Huge and you will get to your Know Yourself.

But, in presenting your sculpture, you always have to Play Above the Line. You have to take ownership and responsibility in order to get yourself where you want to be going, because as soon as the Test Score Culture, grade point average, parent/school status, and SAT audience members hear the "small you" grab the microphone, they seize the opportunity to agree with the small you. Your Silly Self-Talk reminds you that the perceived way to feel good about yourself is to wear the right clothes, get good grades, do well on the SAT, be quiet and fall in line, get into and/or go to a "good" college, do the right kind of work, and build an impressive résumé. You will get external validation when you do this.

The directions for your sculpture have one more section, which is another reminder. It reads:

Building and establishing your Know Yourself is where you are most vulnerable to the perception that there is a right way to be and right things to do. It is so easy to feel you are supposed to be good at school or a certain kind of work, but all the power of Know Yourself is about understanding that your brain works the way your brain works. It is perfect the way it is, and there is no reason to feel like something is wrong with you because of something someone else says is important. Play Above the Line and create your own internal validation!

SECRET #3

Play Above the Line

You get to choose how your life happens. You can choose to play at a low level, or you can play at a high level with excellence, passion, and commitment. My challenge to you is to start at a high level and keep on challenging yourself to go higher.

Playing at a low level is being a victim of circumstances. Playing at a low level is sitting around and pretending that you don't care. Playing at a low level is justifying your lameness by saying that's what the Real You wants. Playing at a low level is selling out what you know is the right thing to do because it will benefit you in the short term. That is all playing below the line, and it will get you nowhere in your life.

But, I flat out don't believe that is what you want for your life. You know you want to be powerful in the face of challenges. You know you want to be excellent at what you do. You want to feel successful. You want to play your life at a high level.

The benefits of playing life at a high level are that you are engaged, you care, you connect to other powerful people, you learn, you get really good at what you are doing, you learn to deal with adversity, and so much more. At its most basic level, you begin to fill your life with Meaning and Fulfillment.

Choosing to be powerful is what I call Playing Above the Line.

The line is the choices and decisions you face every day. When you Play Above the Line, you choose how you respond to your experiences.

SECRET #3

The way to make your life awesome is to Play Above the Line.

You now have the concept, and it is time to figure out what it takes to Play Above the Line.

RESPONSE-ABILITY

You have the ability to control your responses to events—Response-Ability.

When an event happens, that event has no control over how you will respond. The event is neutral. The question is whether you will give up your power and allow the event to dictate your reaction, or whether you will keep your power and choose your reaction.

The reason I am in such a bad mood today
is because it is raining.
If you were not so negative, I would like my job a lot more.

When you Play Above the Line, you choose to be more powerful than the rain, someone's bad attitude, something that does not go your way, etc. You choose to be powerful.

I got to use my new rain gear today.
I am learning so much about the difference between how I feel
when I am negative and when I choose to be positive.

TAKE CHARGE OF CHANGE

When you Play Above the Line, change is something you create. It does not happen to you; rather, you make it happen. Like our friend in the tollbooth, who chose to have a positive attitude about his work, or my friend who worked in a place where there was a bunch of negativity from her co-workers and supervisors, and she took a Stand to treat people with kindness and to be positive, we too can take charge of change and make each day a great day for ourselves. You can make the same choice to take charge of what happens in your life.

HAVE HIGH STANDARDS

One secret to *Launch Your Life* is to Play Above the Line at a higher and higher level. Just like everything in *Launch Your Life*, having high standards happens on an Upward Spiral. There is no finish line at which you have learned it all. Learning happens always and forever. The higher your standards for yourself, the more accountable and responsible you will be. One of the things that creates character—remember the 3 out of 100 people?—is holding yourself to a high level of expectation.

When you are in the game, you will make mistakes. You will make people angry. You will do things you probably could have done better. When you are playing at a high level, you take responsibility for your actions and you apologize or clean up your mess.

Play the game of taking ownership, being responsible, and taking accountability at a high level, and, regardless of the circumstances, playing this way will lead to a life of Meaning and Fulfillment. When you begin to see the world as in your control, you Stand in your power, and there is no limit to the amount of excellence you can create for yourself.

DO NOT RIP YOURSELF OFF

Don't even go to the place of "my Stand is to be the most apathetic person I know"or "my Stand is to sit in the audience of the Play Huge Stage longer than anyone ever has" or "my Stand is to be a bully."

Don't rip yourself off. If you told me that was your Stand, my response would be, "I don't believe you. I am not going to play the playing small game with you. I simply don't buy it."

I know you want to play at a higher level. And, on the higher level, you are getting ready to take what you have learned about your Know Yourself and put it into action as you begin to Trust Yourself. Wherever you are in the process, embrace it, Stand up in your power, and take ownership for your life.

Don't make excuses to justify your actions, deny that you did anything wrong, or simply quit.

When you Play Above the Line, you Stand tall and proud.

LEAVE NO TRACE

There is a camping ethic of leaving a place you come upon in better shape than when you arrived. It is called Leave No Trace, which makes the idea obvious. The intention is that when you leave a campsite, no one should be able tell you have been there.

368

Or, when you walk through a field, be conscious of the impact of your footstep.

The same idea applies to experiences in your life. Imagine a world in which you leave each situation throughout your day better off than you found it.

A kind word…creative solution…listening ear…hug …an apology…all are examples of what Leave No Trace could look like.

44 MAKING EXCUSES: PLAYING BELOW THE LINE

What follow are examples of playing below the line in the world of excuse making, in which you allow things that happen to you or other people dictate your decisions.

It is easy to make excuses for why things don't go your way in life. When you Play Above the Line, you don't make excuses.

You might think, "But there are lots of situations in which things that happen *are* other people's fault." Here is a list of examples:

- I was late because of traffic.
- I got a bad grade because the teacher does not like me.
- We lost because the referee made a bad call.
- I don't have to clean that up; it was already a mess when I got here.
- If it were important, I would do more.
- I don't like it anyway.

But, Playing Above the Line is all about rising above the excuses and taking ownership for the events that happen in your life. One way to avoid being late is to leave earlier. One way to avoid getting a bad grade is writing a good paper. And one way to win is to put yourself in a situation where the referee cannot decide the outcome.

Justify

The first kind of excuse you can make is to justify why things happen the way they happen. For example, you might say, "I wouldn't have done it, but everyone was doing it." When you justify something, you make it seem unimportant because it happens all the time, or because other people do it also, or because you tried.

In the above scenarios, when given options to avoid excuses, you might still say, "I did leave early, write a good paper, and put myself in a situation to win, but it didn't work. It was still their fault."

You might think, "I did everything I could, but there are circumstances beyond my control."

The question you get to answer is, on how high a level do you want to play?

Deny, Lay Blame, and Give Up

As you get down to these last three ways to play below the line, you are lower and lower. If you are hanging out down in these places, you are beyond the innocent mistakes and challenges; you are in the realm of warning signs from Your Launch Pad where some self-exploration and self-discovery are needed.

When you are involved in a situation that creates conflict or some disagreement, and you simply deny there is an issue by saying something like "I was not late" or "everyone is making a big deal out of nothing," you are lacking any ability to take responsibility.

You might think it's funny or clever to blame someone else for something you created or have a part in, but that is not a powerful way to live.

And, if you give up, well, hopefully you will figure out a way to engage in something that can restore your sense of hope and generosity of spirit.

STAND IN YOUR POWER

Don't give away what you believe in. Stand in your power.

If you constantly have the perspective that things are not fair, that things are not your fault, and that you are a victim of circumstances, then your journey to Meaning and Fulfillment will be very, very long and unfulfilling. You must shift your perspective. You can complain all you want, but your power comes from Playing Above the Line.

You get to choose: someone or something else controls what happens to you, or you control what happens to you. Someone or something else controls how you react, or you control how you react.

I challenge you to consistently make high-level contracts with yourself. Don't compromise your power and your Real You because it seems easier and convenient. If something happens that you feel is not fair, figure out your role in the event, exercise your ability to respond, do something about it (whether it be changing your attitude or getting in action), and learn from it so it doesn't happen again.

ONWARD TO TRUST YOURSELF

When you Play Above the Line, you take steps on the Upward Spiral. Because you are honoring your Real You by being truthful, responsible, and the OPERATER of your life, even if you disappoint someone else or yourself, your Trust Yourself grows because you are being honest about it. You learn that you can handle difficult situations and enter into the complexity and still be okay—even if you really screw up.

It is when you are not truthful, or you begin telling stories so things are "in your favor," that you compromise your Trust Yourself. Even if people believe you, or you end up looking good, *you* know. You know you are being deceitful and playing below the line. You will never find Meaning and Fulfillment if you are playing games with your word.

SECRET #3

As you move into Trust Yourself, you will see that learning to take responsibility allows you to increase your confidence and establish your Trust Yourself. With the perspective that everything is an opportunity for learning, and the shift in your actual desire to make mistakes, you will realize that, when you don't take responsibility and Play Above the Line, you give away your power. When you give away your power, it compromises your Trust Yourself and your ascension on the Upward Spiral.

WELL WHAT I CAN SAY IS THAT I'M SORRY THAT YOU FEEL THAT WAY.
I WISH WE COULD HAVE AVOIDED ALL OF THIS UNPLEAS-ANTNESS IN THE FIRST PLACE.
IF YOU INSIST ON CLOSING YOUR ACCOUNT SIGN HERE.
DEREK I WAS DISAPPOINTED TO SEE YOU AT THAT PLACE LAST FRIDAY. I THOUGHT YOU HAD BETTER JUDGEMENT.
MA'AM I REJECT YOUR DIS-APPOINTMENT. YOUR ACCOUNT IS YOUR BUSINESS BUT WHAT IS BEST FOR ME AND WHERE I DO IT IS MINE REGARDLESS OF YOUR APPROVAL.

WHAT WILL IT TAKE?

THE BOSS'S OFFICE
DEREK... THAT ACCOUNT WAS VERY IMPORTANT TO OUR COMPANY.
THE CLIENT MADE HER OWN DECISION FOR HER OWN REASONS...
I'M NOT SORRY ABOUT HOW I HANDLED THE ACCOUNT SIR, I WOULD DO IT AGAIN.
SIR, I'LL BE TAKING MY VACATION TIME THIS YEAR FOR ALL OF JULY & AUGUST.
WHAT? SUMMER IS OUR BUSY TIME!
I LIKE YOU SIR BUT THIS ISN'T A REQUEST. MY MIND'S MADE UP.
PLEASE COME TO THIS IF YOU CAN.
I'LL THINK ABOUT IT.

WHAT WILL IT TAKE?

THEN HE TOLD ME HE REJECTED MY DISAPPOINTMENT...
WELL I DON'T KNOW.
I THOUGHT HE HAD IT TOGETHER BUT TO FIND HIM AT THAT PLACE!
HEY JAMIE!
JAMIE HAS BEEN FOCUSING ON HIS MUSIC A LOT LATELY.
JAMIE NEEDS TO BE FOCUSED ON SCHOOL.

WHAT WILL IT TAKE?

COREY, WHAT ARE YOU DOING WITH THAT OLD THING?
I'M FIXING IT TO USE AT THE COMMUNITY CENTER.
DAD SAYS IT'S BROKEN.
DAD JUST DOESN'T LIKE TO MOW. IT NEEDED A NEW BELT.
I'LL BE.
RRRARRAZ

WHAT WILL IT TAKE?

SHOULD JUST TAKE A SEC.
YEAH, LET'S TRASH IT!
THAT PRACTICE WAS GREAT!
MAN! I FORGOT MY BACKPACK.
C'MON HURRY UP!
THESE CHAINS ARE TOUGH!
WHAT THE...!? HEY WHAT DO YOU GUYS THINK YOU'RE DOING?
DUDE! STEVE PUT THOSE DOWN. YOU COULD GET ARRESTED FOR THIS KIND OF STUFF.
JUST TURN AROUND AND GET OUT OF HERE COREY!
YEAH, MIND YOUR OWN BUSINESS!

WHAT WILL IT TAKE?

FIRST, THANK ELLY FOR THE FOOD.
SECOND, THANK ALL OF YOU FOR MAKING THINGS RUN SO GREAT HERE AT AAP.
I'VE GOT SOME IDEAS OF HOW WE CAN GROW.
I THINK WE SHOULD USE THIS BULLETIN BOARD TO POST THINGS THAT INSPIRE US AND GIVE US HOPE.
BUT WHAT IF THE THINGS THAT I POST INSPIRE ME BUT DON'T INSPIRE OTHER PEOPLE?
NO PROBLEM, AS LONG AS WE FOLLOW THE GUIDELINES YOU CAN POST ANYTHING THAT MAKES YOU FEEL GOOD.
SEEING THIS BOARD FILLED WITH OUR DREAMS WILL INSPIRE US ALL.

WHAT WILL IT TAKE?

TRUST YOURSELF

I feel shakeproof.

Former Client

What you do speaks so loud
that I cannot hear what you say.

Ralph Waldo Emerson

I have never been able to find out precisely what
a feminist is; I only know that people call me
a feminist whenever I express sentiments
that differentiate me from a doormat.

Rebecca West

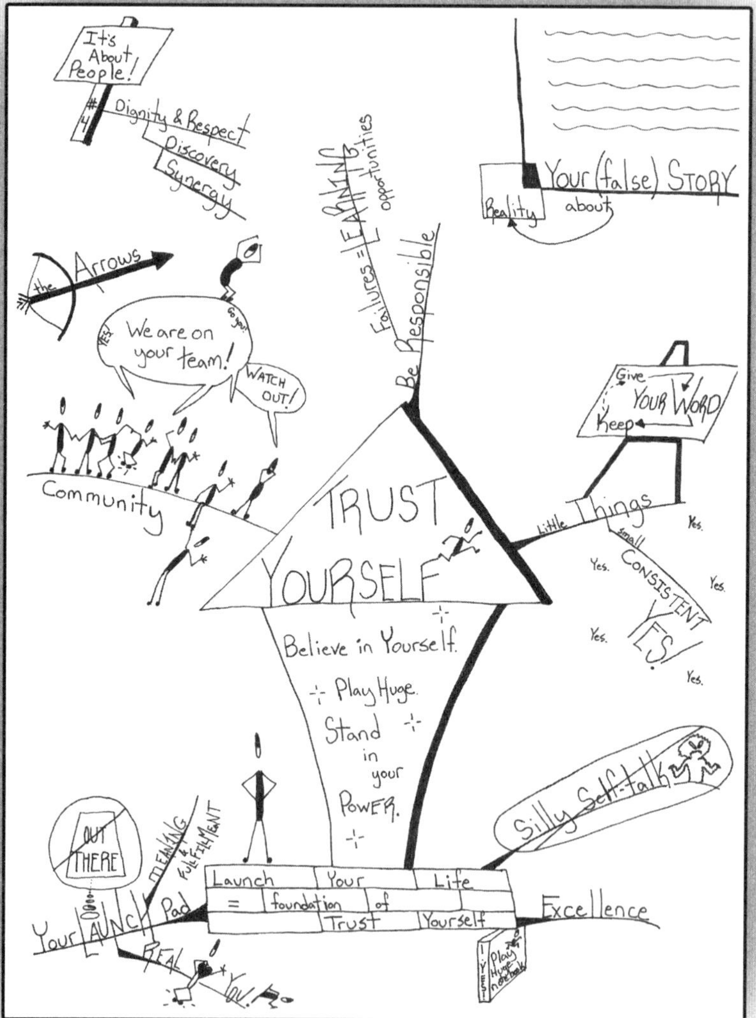

It's About People!
#4
Dignity & Respect
Discovery
Synergy
Failures = LEARNING opportunities
Be Responsible
Your (false) STORY
about
Reality
the Arrows
We are on your team!
Yes!
Go you!
WATCH OUT!
Community
TRUST YOURSELF
Give YOUR WORD Keep
Little Things
small
CONSISTENT
YES!
Yes.
Believe in Yourself.
Play Huge.
Stand in your POWER.
Silly Self-talk
OUT THERE
MEANING & FULFILLMENT
Your LAUNCH Pad
REAL YOU!
Launch Your Life = foundation of Trust Yourself
Excellence
YES! Play Huge notebook

YOUR SIMPLE TRUST YOURSELF

You know what you want. You have opinions. You have ideas of how you want to handle situations. You have reasons for doing the things you do. You go through your days making decisions and reacting to situations.

But often your actions don't reflect your knowing, and your life does not follow the script you want it to.

You end up in situations that the Real You doesn't want to be in.

The reason this is happening is you don't Trust Yourself.

To Trust Yourself is to know that, when you make an effort—an honest effort—you will be able to handle what you create.

Trust Yourself is all about action—Playing Huge. You are ready to Play Huge because you are confident about the Real You.

Your Know Yourself provides a conceptual foundation for who you are, how your brain works, and what you Stand for. When you Trust Yourself, you take this conceptual understanding and put it into action.

Trusting Yourself builds up your resistance to the messages of the Test Score Culture; you learn how to answer the questions ("What are you doing next year?"), you quiet your Silly Self-Talk (and stop making up false stories), and you create a community of people around you who love and support the Real You.

When you Trust Yourself, you Stand in powerful self-expression. You feel shakeproof. You love being on the Play Huge Stage, because all you can see up there is opportunity, opportunity, opportunity.

206

The whole idea of making a mistake gets flipped on its head, from avoiding it at all costs to welcoming—maybe even craving—the next one.

You'll have a whole new perspective on the world as you Trust Yourself. And that perspective will grow and grow as you learn and practice.

Imagine yourself on the Play Huge Stage in full, zestful expression, celebrating you and Standing in your power. And then someone from the audience throws a tomato at you. However, instead of getting nailed in the head by it, you know it is coming, so you catch it, slice it, add it to your salad, and say thank you while the people you invited to the performance stand and applaud (and enjoy your delicious salad).

That is Trust Yourself.

TRUST YOURSELF EXPLAINED

Your Know Yourself—the combination of your experiences and how you interpret your experiences—makes you who you are.

Knowing Yourself is essential, but not sufficient. To Launch Your Life, you must Know Yourself *and* Trust Yourself. Trust Yourself is where the difference is made; it is where you become one of the 3 out of 100, not one of the 97, and you honor the Real You. When you Trust Yourself, you have the opportunity—and the challenge—to believe in yourself enough to Stand in your full, zestful expression as you live your everyday life.

Trust Yourself shows up in all your actions and interactions. Trusting Yourself is about believing what you discovered about the Real You. You are able to share who you are and stand up to challenges or questions people have about you. You stop apologizing for who you are. This courage leads to your expressing yourself, feeling successful, and sharing your gifts and your challenges with the people in your life.

My First Eighteen Years

For the first eighteen years of my life, my perspective could have been summed up as, "Everyone else gets it, and I don't."

THE SITUATION	MY EXPERIENCE
Academics	I don't get it.
Social	I don't get it.
Artistic	I don't get it.
Athletics	I get it! But, it is not significant unless you are really, REALLY good. So, cute dream...good luck. How are your grades?

Then, eventually, finally, I began to understand my Know Yourself and develop my Trust Yourself. As I did, my self-confidence and self-image grew. As that happened, my perspective began to change.

THE SITUATION	MY EXPERIENCE
Academics	I can get it if it is presented in a certain way.
Social	I still don't get the girl part. Dang. But there are other ways I am really good at this—people seem to like and respect me.
Artistic	I have some potential, but I have got to get over the shyness.
Athletics	This is not going to be my career, but it is going to be a source of fun and enjoyment forever! Yahoo!

Trust Yourself also sets you up for the ability to Empathize—to get out of your own private world and out into the world of others. Trusting Yourself creates a sense of safety, and that opens up the opportunity to know others in new and deeper ways. And, when you connect to people in this way, you create Sustainable change for your life.

Trust Yourself is about confident self-expression and not living in shame. The three components of Trusting Yourself are:

1. a solid foundation in the ideas from *Launch Your Life* up to this point—that is, feeling connected to the Real You, knowing what you Stand for, being willing to Play Huge, believing in the Upward Spiral, being the OPERATER of your life, and Playing Above the Line;
2. Standing in your full, zestful expression in that moment on the Play Huge Stage when the lights are on and the audience is ready for you; and
3. Standing your ground. Not everyone will like your performance, but that doesn't mean it was a bad performance. To Trust Yourself will take being willing to be different and to defend yourself.

Your ideas and opinions and all the concepts identified in the Know Yourself exercises and surveys have value. They make up the Real You. Trusting Yourself is knowing this, believing it in your core, and making your actions match your passion.

Your Solid Foundation

YOUR LAUNCH PAD

When you Trust Yourself, you easily and consistently connect with the Real You. You are easily able to identify the Gnawing Feeling, and now have at least an idea of what you value and what you care about. This foundation—hopefully captured in your Play Huge Notebook—helps form your Trust Yourself.

QUIET YOUR SILLY SELF-TALK

23

Your Silly Self-Talk shows up here, too, just as it does in every part of Launching Your Life. The skills you have learned to quiet and control your Silly Self-Talk will be needed to Trust Yourself.

The farther you travel on the Upward Spiral and the more you Trust Yourself, the quieter your Silly Self-Talk becomes and the better you get at dealing only with what really exists. You handle situations with honesty and accountability. When you approach life with courage, confidence, and a clear head, you will find a tremendous amount of extra time, more energy, increased health, and greater opportunities.

YOUR STAND(S)

152

You may still be learning and exploring to find your real Stands, but, hopefully, you are *not* still lost in the place of "I don't know what I want to do with my life" or "What should I do this weekend?" or "I don't care what kind of job I get." At this point, you know the answers that honor the Real You. You believe in the gifts you can share with the world. And you know your learning style. The more solid you are in how you learn and what you Stand for, the farther you will be able to travel on the Upward Spiral.

When you Trust Yourself, you usually have a beautiful vision of what you want your life to be and who you want to become. You are clear on a way of being that you believe is powerful. You may not always make choices congruent with your knowing, but you are not unclear on what you want.

You are able to analyze, see the big picture of the situation, and not get drawn into the temptation to compromise the Real You through your choices. Or, if you do get drawn in, you are able to reflect about what happened and figure out how to avoid it happening again.

It is important to have the beautiful vision and the powerful Stand(s), but they are not enough.

EXCELLENCE

When you Play Huge, you push your Learning Edge and say Yes! at all the challenging moments you create. You have learned that everything you want in your life happens little by little as you get going on the Upward Spiral. You have learned that, when you deal with challenging moments from *inside* experiences, you can call *Time-out* and remember the Real You.

And you know that you want to play on a high level. There is no need to bottom-feed with low standards that create meaningless and insignificant "wins." You also know that talking about how great your performance is going to be, is very different from standing on the stage and performing. When your actions match your passion, you honor the Real You and play with a high level of excellence.

Your Full, Zestful Expression

POWERFUL SELF-EXPRESSION

As noted above, your ideas and opinions and all the concepts identified in the Know Yourself exercises and surveys, have value. They make up the Real You. The next step is to share these ideas and opinions so you can align your life with the Real You.

It can be tempting to back down from your full, zestful expression. It can be easy to begin to doubt yourself. It is challenging to Stand powerfully for yourself. But—no more living in shame.

When you Trust Yourself, you begin to share your secrets. You have the confidence and courage to share what you are experiencing.

IF YOU...	INSTEAD OF...	YOU WOULD...
Have a crush on someone	Being embarrassed	Tell him or her
Have a terminal illness	Hiding it or shutting others out	Share your experience and accept love and support
Want time for yourself	Worrying how it affects the other person	Ask for it
Are gay	Keeping it hidden	Share openly with a community that supports who you are
Want to travel after graduation	Being the good soldier and getting a job	Stand strong and make your arrangements

The choices you make don't have to be life-altering choices. Trust Yourself happens in all your choices. The key aspect is aligning your choices with the Real You.

PRESSURE AT THE OFFICE

The guys at the office may be going out tonight, and it may seem the cool thing to do, but hanging out in bars is not your thing and you want a quiet night to talk more intimately and intensely with some friends. But, when asked if you are meeting for Happy Hour, it may be easier to say, "Yeah, I guess so." It avoids conflict and seems nice.

However, it is not powerful. The Real You would say, "No. I'm going to meet some friends and hang out." And then you meet your friends and feel powerful about your decision.

The choices and decisions get bigger as you gain confidence in expressing yourself. For example, students about to graduate from high school often get asked *the question*: What are you doing next year?

Sometimes it feels like the correct response has to be "I am going to college" or "I have a job starting in July." Because society values education and working, those responses get approval. But, if your Real You wants to travel or pursue another direction, you might fear disapproval.

Regardless of the reaction, if your response is aligned with the Real You, you already have your own approval. When you Trust Yourself, your self-esteem is not determined by the approval of others.

ALLISON AND "THE QUESTION"

When asked the question (What will you do when you graduate?), Allison would answer, "Well, um, well, I'm not really sure. You see, well, this summer I'm, well, traveling and hanging out with some friends. Then, in the fall, well, I might, you see, my sister is in LA, so I figured, that, well, I'll hang out with her. And, I um, will look for some kind of work there."

Every time she was asked the question—which was constantly—it threw her into the place of self-doubt and feeling bad about herself. In her head, she began comparing herself to other friends she perceived as successful and having it all together. Her Silly Self-Talk was making all kinds of negative comments to her.

She began answering the question with what she thought she should answer. "I'm looking for, um, a real job, maybe consulting, maybe the stock market, maybe"—under her breath—"a nonprofit organization."

She began getting more positive responses from people she talked to, but she didn't feel very good about what she was saying or doing. She was not expressing herself, and she was not feeling powerful.

She really wanted to explore more, keep on traveling, and visiting friends.

She practiced how to respond to the question by expressing her Real You.

Here is what she began to say: "I created a cross-country trip with several friends to learn about myself, learn about the country I live in, and visit friends. Then, I am going to go live in LA with my sister, because we have always dreamed about living together. While I'm there, I'm going to look for a meaningful job that will have an impact in the world because that is what matters to me."

This was all true for her, and, when she said it, there was energy in her voice. Her body language was more positive. And she reported feeling powerful, excited, and hopeful, when she shared what her real plan was.

Allison faced *the question*. At first, it sent her into a tailspin, but, eventually, she began to trust herself. Then she was able to answer *the question* powerfully.

When she stopped trying to prove and validate herself, what emerged was the playful, creative, energetic, healthy, excellent, committed, spontaneous, passionate person she is. She realized she was not compromising her being, and her actions were consistent with what she wanted to be doing in her life. She was being true to her Real You.

NO MORE COMPROMISES

I had a client who shared this as she began to trust herself: "I got it. My work is exactly what other people think it is supposed to be. My phone message has said what I think it should say, not what I want it to say. I have been wearing clothes I think other people expect me to wear, not the ones that I love.

"I am going to reorganize my office to represent who I really am. I am going to change my language. And what is really going to change is my story about myself. I am going to be able to say, 'This is who I am. This is my authentic expression.' I will no longer live trapped in the place of feeling like I have to be a certain way, do certain things, and compromise what I know is true for me."

SETTING YOURSELF UP FOR SUCCESS

Another level of zestfully expressing yourself is setting up your life in such a way that it works for you. We all have things we like and things we don't like. We all have patterns that work for us and patterns that don't.

In the work to Trust Yourself, setting up your environment to work to your strengths is helpful. If you know you are not a morning person, scheduling morning classes is not a formula for success. If you know you feel much better, healthier, and more energized on days when you exercise, then set up your day to support your exercise. If making time during your week to volunteer for an organization you care about makes you feel you are contributing to the world in a way you value, then create a schedule in which that happens consistently.

By setting up your life in the ways that work for you, you are eliminating all the little barriers that can prevent you from zestfully expressing yourself and, ultimately, Trusting Yourself.

153

RIDING MY BIKE

I ride my bike around town. I live in Portland, Oregon, and it rains sometimes. When it is raining, it's very tempting to drive or simply not go places. In fact, when I began riding, I would avoid going because all the logistics would take too much energy. I had to remember my rain gear, my helmet, the right gloves, any necessary lights, the locks, keys for the locks, a change of clothes, water, food, a map, and whatever other miscellaneous items I might need—and this did not include any stuff for the kids.

But, whenever I did not ride, I was mad at myself, grumpy, and felt I had compromised my Stand.

I began to set myself up so that getting on the bike was easier. The first thing I did was make a checklist of things I needed to remember for most of my trips. That was mildly helpful, as I no longer had to remember all the items I needed for my ride.

But I was still not riding as much as I wanted to be, so I made some more changes. I decided to keep my lights and keys in the pocket of my biking coat—always. In the other pocket were my hat and cold weather items. I figured out a place on my bike to keep a lock. I put up a coat hook for my rain gear, my helmet, my gloves, and my bag. I put up another one for the kids' stuff as well. I put some energy bars in the bottom of my bag.

These changes have made it easier for me to get out of the house and onto my bike. It took several months of trying things out, and I am constantly refining, but I feel quite good about my system.

I now can quickly leave the house and trust that I have what I need to get where I'm going. When I began this whole process, I was spending a lot of energy and using brainpower to get myself going. Now, because I am in action honoring one of my Stands, my energy and mental energy are focused on different and bigger things.

Many times, the challenge of zestfully expressing yourself—whether it is what you want for dinner, what you are going to do when you graduate, or how to set up your life in a way that works for you—comes from your lack of organization. When you set yourself up for success by being the OPERATER of your life, by
116 getting your Play Huge Notebook working for you, by learning how to create consistently a resourceful state or focused attention, you allow yourself to live each moment in full, zestful expression.

BLURT

When you are set up for zestfully expressing yourself, you will notice you have a lot to say that is currently going unspoken. You will notice the "giant pink elephant" in the room. The giant pink elephant is the energy, the tension, the excitement, or other feeling that often exists in conversations or meetings—the thing everyone knows is there, but no one is saying anything about. In your full, zestful expression, not only will you begin to notice the giant pink elephant, but you will blurt out, "Hey, there is a giant pink elephant."

STAND FOR YOUR STAND

Trust Yourself is not about words; it is about actions. Knowing what you Stand for is essential, but not sufficient. The difference gets made when you take real-life action to do something about it.

WORK YOUR LEARNING EDGE

When you show up in your full, zestful expression, you will make mistakes. All you have to remember is that your Learning Edge is the place where you balance taking risks with taking care of yourself. Trust Yourself that, when you make a mistake, you will be able to do something about it, and make it a learning experience.

ACCEPT FEEDBACK

When you are in this place of full, zestful expression, you can take feedback in a powerful and positive way. If you're not in that place, feedback often feels like deeply biting criticism and you may become defensive.

Being in full, zestful expression allows you to hear feedback—even if it is meant as criticism—as support for your learning and growing. You can genuinely say, "WOW! Thank you." As a result, you can transform even the most difficult feedback into an opportunity to do things differently in new and more powerful ways.

PLAY AT THE LEVEL ABOVE SIMPLE

Finally, the last aspect of your full, zestful expression is a reminder that you want to play with excellence. Full, zestful expression is not living at the level of simple. It is living on your Learning Edge and Playing Above the Line. The importance of this is much greater than the outward expression of yourself. You know in your heart whether you are being honest with yourself. And, when you are working to Trust Yourself, any compromise in your heart undermines your effort.

Stand Your Ground

It takes courage to Trust Yourself. It takes courage to get in touch with what you believe is right about the world, and then it takes more courage to say it and Stand for it.

When you are new at Standing powerfully for yourself, you will generate many different kinds of reactions, and that generates a lot of opportunity for you to make up stories in your head about what people are thinking and saying. It will then feel safe to retreat to a place that is less risky, but this is where you must learn to Stand your ground. To do this, you will have to Trust Yourself.

BE WILLING TO BE DIFFERENT

It can be emotional when you express yourself and people don't agree with you. But think back to Know Yourself; Know Yourself is about realizing that you have your own perspective, your own learning brain, and your own Stands. Everyone is different. There is nothing wrong with you. You are not broken. Just like everyone else, you are different.

If you need to call *Time-out* and go back to your Organize and Plan, do it. Quiet your Silly Self-Talk, and get yourself back on track.

DEFEND YOURSELF

You have the tools to defend yourself. You can lean on any of the concepts you have learned in *Launch Your Life*, but your Know Yourself is a good place to start. You can say, "Thank you for your opinion. I know how my brain works and I know what is best for me, and my ideas reflect this." Or, you could ask for more information to understand what the person really means. Remember, in Know Yourself, there was a story about a friend of mine choosing a major (see page 181)? In that case, her own ego tripped her up.

A POWERFUL AND GROUNDING CHOICE

But, with another friend of mine, the situation was different. He spent a lot of time doing reflection on, and evaluation of, what he wanted to do with his life. After long deliberation, he made a decision he was excited (and relieved) about. But, when he began to express his choice, people—including his parents— had reactions that were less than supportive.

He almost bailed out and followed his parents' desires, but then he calmed himself down (he was really hurt and angry), and remembered that he had based his decision on what he is passionate about and what he thinks he is best at. When he got connected to this, he was able to have a conversation with his parents. In the conversation, he asked lots of questions to clarify their perspective, and then he defended himself and explained the basis for his decision.

DEAL WITH COMPLEXITY

These kinds of conversations can be uncomfortable and complex. There might not be easy answers, and there might not be agreement about the right course of action. But, when you are willing to engage in these kinds of conversations, it sends a message to the Real You that you are ready to Trust Yourself, just as avoiding any complexity and not Standing your ground send the opposite message to the Real You. By being willing to be honest in adverse situations, you build a foundational level of Trusting Yourself. 324

TAKE RESPONSIBILITY

It is not possible to defend yourself if you don't take responsibility. Remember to Play Above the Line. When my friend made his case to his parents, he was making a commitment that he was going to be responsible for his actions. It is the difference 200 between talking the talk and walking the walk. Talk means nothing; it's just words, unless you back them up with action.

Wrap-Up of Trust Yourself Explained

When you Trust Yourself enough that you are not unconsciously engaged in conversations in which you spend the whole time trying to prove yourself and validate that you are okay, the whole world slows down. You are able to understand the structure of the conversation you are in...you have a feel for the context of the discussion...you grasp the big picture.

When this happens, you can watch other people figure out their Know Yourselfs and Trust Yourselfs.

You can see when people are not in control of their emotions and are saying and doing mean things. You are able to see the insults coming and sidestep them. As your consciousness of the communication's situation gets engaged, you go into slow motion.

Great athletes talk about the game moving slowly. They can anticipate how the play is going to happen, where the players will be, and what they can do to take advantage of the situation. That is what made the greatest hockey player ever, Wayne Gretzky, so good. He was able to see the game in a different way. He was not reacting to what was happening; he was reacting to what was going to happen next. The game slowed down for him! When you Stand powerfully, the "games" slow down for you, and you begin to be able to see the dynamics of the conversation.

What starts to happen is that people seem to be changing their behaviors and actions, but it is really not the people around you who are changing; it is that your Trust Yourself is allowing you to change your perspective.

HUSBAND AND WIFE GOING DIFFERENT DIRECTIONS?

Emily's husband began to talk about leaving their family. He felt like things were not working and that they needed to separate. She was sad, hopeful, disappointed, frustrated, and a whole lot of other things. Despite all these emotions, she was able to understand the situation as if she were looking down on a maze from a bird's-eye view. In the midst of the highly emotional breakup of the family, with the possible ending of her marriage at stake, she trusted herself. She understood that her husband was not confident about who he was and what he was about.

Instead of getting wrapped up in all her emotions, Emily was able to see that he was really struggling. She did not take their struggles to be about her (and they were not about her). Even when he was yelling at her, and blaming her, she could see the structure of his hurtful and angry communication because she was in her Trust Yourself.

In the slow motion, she was able to reach out to him and extend a piece of their relatedness to him despite his anger and criticism. She was able to avoid getting personally hooked by his verbal attacks, and, when she did, she was able quickly to let it go and move on.

Emily was able to stay out of the emotion when she needed to, and express it when she needed to, or when she felt it was appropriate. By being able to see the big picture, she could evaluate the questions of what was going to support him and what was going to support them working through this.

Her Trust Yourself supported her not making up stories about what she thought was going on. She was able to rely on herself and deal with reality.

Emily was able to see the big picture, understand her husband's feelings while not agreeing with them, and then search for solutions. She did not get sucked into the emotion of the situation, and she was able to protect herself.

- Trust Yourself is the courage to Stand powerfully in your Know Yourself.
- Trust Yourself is the faith and belief that you can make happen what you want to make happen.
- Trust Yourself is the confidence to perform on the Play Huge Stage.
- Trust Yourself is the zestful expression of the Real You.
- Trust Yourself is not reacting to how other people react to you, or what they think of you.
- Trusting Yourself is knowing that life is complicated, but that you can step right into the challenges and figure out solutions. In fact, when you Trust Yourself, you want to create the learning opportunities that exist in the difficulties of life. You welcome the frustration of life's challenges. You want to get into the complex situations that don't have easy solutions. You want to solve the most difficult problems, because you know they are the ones that matter most—as was true for Emily and her husband. The solution for them was not in avoidance; it was in getting to the real issues.

You want to be in those moments because that is living. You feel confident with the Real You, so you enter into the challenges, complexities, and difficulties because, otherwise, there is a compromise in your being.

If you constantly avoid the challenges, complexities, and difficulties, you miss out on life. When you live in your Trust Yourself, your living creates Meaning and Fulfillment.

THE PATH TO TRUST YOURSELF

On the journey to Trust Yourself and to Launching Your Life, you are constantly faced with choices and decisions. How you respond to these has a significant impact on your Trust Yourself. The impacts your actions have on your perception of yourself are as significant as the external impacts of your actions. The path to Trust Yourself is based on how you feel about yourself. The more deeply you believe in yourself, the more profound your expression will become. Every moment presents an opportunity to be courageous, build confidence, zestfully express yourself, quiet your Silly Self-Talk, honor the Real You, and create community.

Execute the Little Things— Create Consistent Successes

The first step on the path to Trust Yourself is to execute on the little things. The goal is to build your Powerful Portfolio so you can Stand powerfully and Play Huge. The idea is to get to the place where you trust that, when you give your word to do something, you will do it. Further, executing on the little things is trusting that, when you make decisions, they honor the Real You.

Through this process, you build your Trust Yourself by committing to actions that align with the Real You, and then by following through on your commitment to execute what you give your word to.

Your journey to Launch Your Life is one during which you will be creating new patterns in your life. Standing powerfully for your Real You, no matter how small your expression, is part of the creation of these new patterns.

THE RED SOX—PITCH BY PITCH

In 2004, the Boston Red Sox were trying to win their first World Series in eighty-six years. In a series in which the first team with four wins advances to play in the next round—and the loser's season is over—the Red Sox were down three games to none, and to their biggest rival, the New York Yankees.

The story goes that the players had a meeting. In the meeting, the players created a strategy for the rest of the series. The strategy went something like this: "We can't win four games at a time. We can't even win one game at a time. What we can do is work to win each pitch. If every one of us works on winning each pitch, whether we are in the field or hitting, we can start to win each at bat. Once we begin winning pitches and at bats, then we start to win each inning. Then we start to win the first three innings, the first six innings, and, eventually, today's game. When we win today's game, then we go on to tomorrow's game and work to win the first pitch, then win the second pitch, then win the first at bat, then win the second at bat, then the third, and so on."

During the meeting, the players made a commitment as a team to begin executing the little things.

As they began executing the little things, they gained confidence, and the little victories came more and more easily. They shifted the momentum of the series. The pressure had been on them because they were three games down, but now the pressure began to be on the Yankees because the Red Sox were winning and getting closer.

The momentum in a series like this is an example of a Cusp moment. Cusp moments are challenging and take supreme focus and attention, as illustrated in this example. But once the shift happens, winning the little moments and executing the little things becomes much easier. Just as happens on the Upward Spiral, when things begin to go well, keeping them going well is easier and easier.

The Red Sox came back and won the series, four games to three. They won four games in a row, and then, riding their momentum, they won another series to capture their first World Series in eighty-six years. They did it by executing the little things.

You learn and grow to Trust Yourself by executing the little things. You cannot go from no trusting to, all of sudden, being immensely successful and confident, just as you cannot go from wanting to go to college to, all of a sudden, graduating.

What are the little things? What are the little things you've got to do each day?

When you give your word to someone or something, keep it. Be on time. Be conscious of eating the way you want to be eating. Be more positive. Be more kind in your interactions with people. If you want to drink eight glasses of water, then drink eight glasses of water a day, one at a time. Get up at the time you want to get up. What other things do you care about?

Start to execute the little things because, if you are not executing the little things you are committed to, then you are compromising your integrity. And, when you're constantly compromising your integrity, it's very, very difficult to Trust Yourself.

Stop ripping yourself off. You know you want more than you have in your life. Start to build your confidence by keeping your commitments to yourself. Keep your word. Guard your word. Build your integrity. As you execute the little things—just like winning each pitch, winning each at bat, winning each inning—what you're doing is adding to your Powerful Portfolio. Start the positive momentum and believe in the Upward Spiral.

Quiet Silly Self-Talk

It takes courage to Trust Yourself. It takes courage to get in touch with the Real You. It takes courage to Stand for what you believe is right about the world. Then it takes more courage to express it and even more yet to defend yourself.

When you begin to think about standing in your full, zestful expression, you might notice that you begin to run stories/scenarios in your head. You will recognize the false stories as those of your Silly Self-Talk. Here is another chance to practice jamming it.

Organize and Plan

116 You want to honor your Real You.

In the Your Launch Pad section, you created a Play Huge Notebook; this notebook can assist you in setting up a structure and infrastructure that work for you, and support you being Organized and Planned. It will help you keep your actions consistent with how you Know Yourself and the Real You.

For some people, being Organized and Planned is making sure you have time every single week to look ahead to anticipate your next week. Whether it's Sunday night, Monday morning, or some other time, what is important is the structure and consistency. Knowing you have that time set aside helps you Trust Yourself. It is keeping an appointment you have with yourself. If you don't keep the appointment, you know that your Silly Self-Talk will grab that lack of execution and unlock the keys to a downward spiral.

There are limitless ways to Organize yourself, but, whether you Plan every month or you sit with a friend and talk through the week, what's important is that you set up the time with your Play Huge Notebook, remember that you Know Yourself, connect with your stand, and Organize and Plan yourself. This allows you to be the OPERATER of your life and sets you up for success.

YOU KNOW

You know what you want to accomplish this week and/or this month. And, if you don't, Trust Yourself and act as if you do. You know who you want to connect with. You know how you want to take care of yourself. You know what challenges you will face. And you know how you are going to get yourself out of a funk. The challenge is not in knowing these things; the challenge is remembering them and remaining connected to them, and that is where being Organized and Planned comes in.

What you create for yourself will be personal. Your structure will be based on what works for you, and it may take time to develop and refine it. You Know Yourself, so you know what works for you, so set up the structure that sets yourself up for success.

PLAY HUGE NOTEBOOK

What you have already collected in your Play Huge Notebook are the ways to get inspired. You have your collection of movies, songs, podcasts, quotes, recommendations, and kind words people have shared with you. You also have a list of activities that help you get into a resourceful and powerful state.

Since you first began your Play Huge Notebook, you have collected information about your learning brain, including your learning style, intelligences, and brain dominance, as well as all the information that led up to what you Stand for.

And, of course, you have been adding to your Powerful Portfolio whenever you feel good, make an effort, or create something excellent.

If you have not already, it is time to put your Play Huge Notebook to work. And add to it.

Your Play Huge Notebook is a perfect place to get yourself Organized and keep your Plans.

By collecting these resources you set yourself up for success.

MY PLAY HUGE NOTEBOOK

While writing *Launch Your Life*, I have used my notebook and the materials in it every day for two years. It has been a constant challenge to get and stay engaged as I write. I use my music, my quotes, and favorite inspirational talks to keep myself forwarding my action.

I have a set of music I can listen to—some with words, some without words; some uplifting, some calming—but all of it allows me to generate and maintain my concentration.

When I am really lost, or trying to capture the idea of a concept that is, for some reason, being elusive, I listen to one of the talks from people who inspire me, or I watch a movie I know will reconnect me with the ideas that matter. Once I do this, the idea I was trying to capture always becomes clear.

My Play Huge Notebook is where I Organize and Plan myself and where I keep all my resources; this way, I know exactly where all my stuff is, so that, when I need it, I can find it easily. I don't want to have to search for it; I don't want to have to go collect resources; I don't want to have to think. I know that when I'm in a funk and am not trusting myself, I need to be able to go right to the place where I keep my Play Huge Notebook, open it up, read the quotes, watch the movie, look at my Plan—get myself going.

It is critical to realize that, when you are in a funk or having trouble getting in action, you don't have the capacity to figure out how to get out of it. You will be in an emotional place in which you are not able to think clearly. You might remember the idea of being in the right thinking and feeling mode from the secret of being the OPERATER of your life (see page 116). When you are in a funk or having trouble getting inspired, you will not be in big-picture mode; you will be inside the experience, dealing with the challenge. The Play Huge Notebook blasts you back to when you were in a powerful space in which you felt inspired to act. This gives you perspective on your current challenge.

A LETTER TO HERSELF

A friend of mine added an element to collecting and organizing her notebook. She dealt with bouts of depression, so she set up a place in her drawer that she called the Depressed Resources Space. This held a collection of her favorite clothes, a food treat, the friends' phone numbers, and a photo album of people she loves and who love her.

And she wrote herself two letters. One she wrote when she was feeling good, and one she wrote when she was feeling down. She knew she had trouble remembering what it was like to be down when she was feeling good, and what is was like to feel good when she was down.

She used the letters to remind herself what it was like in the other place, and to remind herself to appreciate the good times, or kick herself out of the down times.

LETTER WHEN FEELING GOOD	LETTER WHEN FEELING BAD
Dear Me, I have a great, great ability to be creative and playful and loved in the world. I am a brilliant writer and will someday write movie scripts. I am a loving and patient mom, and I love spending time reading and going to the park with my daughter. Take her to the park and listen to her laughter and her joy. Push her on the swings. Look at her smile. I have a network of friends who care about me, listed at the end of this letter (with their phone numbers). When I am not feeling well, call a friend and say, "I am not feeling well." They have agreed to talk with me, go to dinner with me, and to hang out with me. Love and Hugs, Me	Dear Me, I want to feel loved. What I need is support getting up in the morning. What I need and what I want is to connect to some of my friends. I want to feel like I have a future to look forward to. What I want is to wear the clothes that make me feel powerful and loved. Most of all, I want to connect with my daughter because I feel far away from her right now. Love and Hugs, Me

She called her friends and said, "I'm writing this letter and, when I'm in this place, I would love to be able to call you and say, 'Hey, I'm not feeling well, and I would like you to take me out to dinner, come and hang out with me, or whatever you think will be helpful.' But, when I call from that space, I am not going to be able to ask for help, and I will probably resist it when you offer. So I am asking you now, because I feel good and I know that I need help when I am in that place." Most of her friends were thrilled to help, and some were not, but she then knew who to put on her list and who to keep off her list.

She set herself up for success. She put the letters in her notebook and put that in a place where she would know she could find it. She collected and organized her resources so she would take care of herself when she was feeling depressed and when she was feeling great.

My friend's situation illustrates the challenges of wanting to get something done or feel a certain way, but struggling with accessing the motivation to make it happen. The Play Huge Notebook is intended to provide support to break through this challenge. It will help, and there are other ways to make it happen as well.

Take Responsibility

DEAL WITH REALITY

Like all people, you are a meaning-making machine. You take all your experiences and you try to make meaning out of them, because you want to have an understanding of what's happening and what's going on. Very often, what you're doing is making up stories that aren't true. When you do this, you compromise your foundation.

Dealing with reality happens in very small ways, and it happens in really big ways. But one element of Trusting Yourself is to begin to deal with reality and not with the false stories. When you deal with the false stories, you waste a tremendous amount of time and energy and good moods, dealing with things that aren't really there.

Usually what happens is, the false stories push you onto a downward spiral. Sometimes they affect your whole day, and, before you know it, your whole day goes down the tubes because of something that is not real—something you made up. This is not a strategy for building trust in yourself.

But, by dealing with what really exists, by engaging in the conversation, by having the courage to clarify the situation, you start to take steps on the Upward Spiral and begin to build that fundamental belief in yourself. Imagine this scenario:

WALKING DOWN THE HALLWAY

You're walking down the hallway when you see a boy you have a crush on, and you say to him, "Hi, Scott." And Scott walks right past you without saying anything. Then you think, "Crap. He doesn't like me. He just ignored me. I can't believe it."

And, in that moment, you start to make up false stories about what happened: "He doesn't like me. He thinks I'm ugly. He thinks I'm dumb. He doesn't want to have anything to do with me. He's never going to talk to me again. There's no way I'm ever going to go out with him." Often, once you have made up these kinds of stories, you're in a bad mood the rest of the day.

It's possible something happened that you don't know about. Whatever the circumstances, you want to be certain you are dealing with reality. Don't try to deal with what you *think* is reality.

TAKE ACTION

The opportunity and challenge here are for you to approach Scott and say, "Scott, this morning I was walking down the hall, and I said hello to you, and you didn't say anything back."

This gives Scott a chance to say, "You know what, I was totally preoccupied. I'd just gotten out of a class. I did really poorly on a test, and I was just totally focused and didn't hear anything anyone was saying. I didn't even hear you say anything."

Or, Scott might say, "Oh, you know what, somebody had just asked me a question and I was turning to respond and I just didn't even hear your question."

Or, Scott might say, "You know what? I'm not interested in talking to you."

Whatever his answer, by getting the information from Scott about what happened, you are now able to deal with reality and not waste energy on something that didn't happen. Without engaging him, you don't know what really occurred. What you probably did was make up stories about him not liking you, thinking you were dumb or unattractive or whatever.

Until you ask someone, and hear what they have to say, you are not dealing with what really happened. You are making an assumption. Once you have the real information, you are able to say, "Oh, he just had gotten out of a bad test. Right on." So now you can deal with that reality, and say, "Okay, great. Scott, you know what, I'd really like to go to lunch with you. Can you have lunch today?"

FROM CRITICISM TO LEARNING OPPORTUNITY

In one of my adventures on the Play Huge Stage, I was learning to facilitate groups of fifty to one hundred and fifty teenagers for SuperCamp. My job was to be on the stage, present all the material, and lead all the activities for ten days—and the idea was to be a fun, engaging, friendly, and inspiring teacher.

The learning process to become a facilitator was intense. The two most important elements of doing it were courage and confidence. The training included practicing delivering the content and activities in a fun, engaging, friendly, and inspiring way.

It was a nerve-racking experience because all the practice happened in front of the other facilitators—who were already excellent at being fun, engaging, friendly, and inspiring. They were experts at doing what I was learning to do.

When I began, my Silly Self-Talk was loud. I was making up lots and lots of different stories about getting up on the stage. But, the one story that was the loudest, came directly from my memory of when I did my ninth-grade lip sync to John Cougar Mellancamp's song, "Pink Houses," by air guitaring for four minutes and forty-four seconds (see page 87).

The voice sounded like this: "Phew, everyone's going to think I'm totally lame at doing this. They are going to laugh while I am presenting. They are going to wonder how in the world I got hired. They will think I don't deserve to be a facilitator. And then, after telling me how bad I am at this, they will fire me."

There were days I would get up on stage and not remember what I was supposed to say. I couldn't remember how to be engaging and inspiring in my delivery of the information. I felt I wasn't really doing anything well. At the end of the session or at the end of the day, I would just feel totally crappy about myself. That false story in my Silly Self-Talk would go on and on and on, and cause me to be in a really bad mood.

Then, when my next opportunity to get on the stage happened, I was still in the bad mood, and so my performance was poor. I was on a downward spiral.

Finally, I talked with one of my friends and fellow facilitators about my challenges. His response really surprised me. He said, "Well, I really admire your effort and your willingness to be up there, to go for it and to learn like that. You've been more courageous than anyone else, and it has inspired me to get up there also. Thank you for your effort."

Around the same time, I started to get some acknowledgment and positive feedback around my presentations. Then I realized, "You know what? I'm making up all the negative stuff going on. The other facilitators are not saying all that stuff I thought they were saying. No, I'm not doing as well as I could be, but I am learning and I am trying and I am going for it, and here is the reality. This is a learning environment, and they don't think that I'm really bad. If they did, they are honest enough that they would tell me. They think I do have talent, and they want me to keep on learning and getting better and better and better."

I became the OPERATER of my life.

I started to anticipate that, when it was my turn to practice, my Silly Self-Talk would get louder and I would start to feel bad. So, I decided to figure out how to quiet my Silly Self-Talk and believe in the reality that I did belong there and they did want me there. And, as I began to feel the positive energy, my perception changed. I realized that what people were feeling when I was on the stage practicing, was the same thing I was feeling when somebody else was on the stage—namely, support, encouragement, and admiration. And—wow!—support, encouragement, and admiration feel very different from lame, discouraged, and not capable.

LEARN TO TAKE RESPONSIBILITY

200 Taking responsibility is all about personal accountability. It is beyond the place where excuses live. You are responsible for your actions. You are responsible for your life. It is where you Play Above the Line.

This may be a familiar scenario for you:

You have a paper due in a class today, but you are not finished.

"Mr. Johnson, you see, I have not been getting much sleep because my brother has been sick. I meant to turn in the paper in on time, but I have been really busy lately."

Maybe you use a different excuse, like my computer crashed, my dog ate it, I also had a paper due in another class, or I have been out of town.

In these examples, let's look and see who is being blamed:

	BROTHER SICK/ LITTLE SLEEP	COMPUTER CRASH	BUSY	OUT OF TOWN
WHO IS RESPONSIBLE?	You	You	You	You
WHO/WHAT IS BEING BLAMED?	Brother's illness and sleep gods	Computer	Busyness	Travel Schedule

If you want to really Trust Yourself, then stop making excuses and blaming circumstances. It's been said before, but, when you make excuses, you are compromising your own integrity. And, when you do this, you will not have a foundational confidence on which to build your Trust Yourself. Instead of making excuses, you could have the following conversation with your teacher:

Talking with Mr. Johnson

"Mr. Johnson, I am disappointed with my effort on this paper.

"I apologize that I turned the paper in late. My commitment is to have it in early next time.

"I knew, weeks ago, that this was going to be a busy time for me. Next time, I will anticipate my schedule, and, as soon as I can, I will ask you if we can work something out."

By taking responsibility for your actions, you are sending a message to yourself and the other person that you can handle the consequences, you are interested in learning from your experience, and you realize it has an impact on everyone involved.

It is so easy and so common to justify our actions, blame external circumstances, deny the activity is that important, or just blow it off. As soon as you are aware of how common it is to shirk responsibility, you will see it all over the place. Then you can see for yourself what it looks like when you are playing small.

The amazing thing is, this happens when you do good things, too. It is very easy to give the credit for an excellent effort to some external circumstance:

Giving away your credit

"My paper was good, but the teacher was grading really easy."

"Yes, I did well on the test, but it was a really easy test and everyone did well."

Or, "I got lucky."

The measure that matters here is your own effort. What grade do you give yourself? If you know you did not make an effort but give yourself a good grade, what message does that send? What about if you did make a big effort, and still don't give yourself credit?

What would the Huge You do? What do you know is the choice that will honor the Real You? What is the decision that, when you look back on it, will feel awesome, not crappy?

You know the answer. Make it happen.

Create Community

Secret #4 is It's About People. The bottom line of the secret is this:

You cannot get where you are going, alone. You must create a community of people who love, encourage, and challenge you, and who don't let you get complacent.

Creating community is the best place to begin your focus on relationships with people. Early on in *Launch Your Life*, I made the point that Meaning and Fulfillment come from relationships with other people.

So far in the path to Trust Yourself, you have learned to execute the little things, quiet your Silly Self-Talk, Organize and Plan, and take responsibility. These are foundational components for you to start to create community.

MAGIC

In Palo Alto, California, near Stanford University, there is a community called Magic. It's a group of people living together in what they call "intentional community." They're all immensely respectful of one another, of each other's abilities, of who they all are, and of what they want to learn and to create. They support each other to make their lives awesome.

They also hold each other to a really high standard, because that is what each one of them wants. They know that the reminders and accountability are what will get them what they want. If someone is not being the citizen they want to be, or is not being honest with herself, or is not executing his life plan, their friends and their community are there to say, "Come on. Come on. Not enough effort here. You're a better person than this. You can do better than this. What do you need?"

They don't do it in a mean, harsh way; they do it in a loving, caring way that helps stimulate action. They consistently help each other get into action.

They handle the little things every day, they are experts at dealing with complexity and discomfort, and so they continue advancing on the Upward Spiral. The little things that once were challenging have become routine, which allows them to take on more powerful and challenging things that, in turn, also become routine, and the Upward Spiral continues.

They have been at this for many years, and they are a powerful group of people. When you look for the 3 out of 100...well they make it 9 out of 9.

Building your community doesn't have to be people living together in the same house. It happens when you start to build that kind of network and the kind of relationships that they have at Magic. When you have these kind of connections with people you start to have that network in which people don't let you get away with not being incredibly powerful.

Creating community is tremendously, tremendously important in Trusting Yourself. It begins to create synergy on your Upward Spiral. The impact happens on a whole number of levels because, once you begin to know that people are with you, you start to be able to be more honest and more courageous. When you are more honest and courageous, you get and share more acknowledgments, and you begin to create a higher level of accountability. When you live with a higher level of accountability, you Stand in your power, you stop apologizing for who you are, and you take on bigger and bigger risks. On this journey, you begin to Trust Yourself because your confidence and courage are growing up the Upward Spiral.

There are four steps to creating community:

1. Prepare to share your Know Yourself.
2. Create support networks, surrounding yourself with people who demand that you step up and Play Huge.
3. Let go of, or create distance from, the people who don't support your journey. (This is challenging initially, but, with time, becomes liberating.)
4. Reach out and join the community of people you know and care for.

1. SHARE YOUR KNOW YOURSELF

You Know Yourself. You have gotten in touch with the Real You. It is now time to practice Trusting Yourself. When you communicate with people, Stand powerfully for who you are. Tell them the things you Stand for, and learn how to talk about your life in powerful ways.

Be prepared for the questions: "What are you doing after school?" "Where do you work?" "How do you spend your time?" "What are things you love to do?" "What do you Stand for?"

When you are in a learning situation, notice how your learning brain can be helpful to you, and then share that. Talk with your teachers, boss, friends, and community, so they know you are taking care of yourself and you want to be engaged and thoughtful.

These are all great opportunities to Stand powerfully and zestfully express yourself. Take advantage of them.

2. CREATE SUPPORT NETWORKS

Creating community is beginning to surround yourself with the people who are going to support the Real You. They are the people who are going to Sustain you while you create what you want in the world.

You want to gather resources in your friendships, your family, your professional community, your school community, and with mentors and coaches. They are going to love and acknowledge you, and are going to be there even when you fail...even when you fall down...even when you try something and it doesn't go well. When this community is with you, you trust that, when you take risks and are courageous, you will always have people behind you clapping, cheering, hugging, encouraging, giving feedback.

One of the easiest ways to execute on the little things is to enroll your community. When my clients successfully enroll a friend as a workout buddy, they always begin to work out. When they don't enroll a workout buddy, they sometimes begin to work out but it usually takes them a lot longer to make it happen. Every time a client or a friend has expressed the desire to run a marathon, and subsequently joined a marathon club, they have achieved their goal. The added accountability of meeting someone at the gym gets you enrolled in a different way than if you only make the commitment to yourself.

Ask your friends to execute the little things with you. It takes courage, but it is one of the little steps to get you where you are headed.

When you ask your community to support you, you want them to support the Real You. You want them to provide honest feedback. There are times when being nice is important, but, if you are making choices in your life that are not in your interest, you don't want nice—you want strong, assertive, and loving. As in the story about Magic, you want people who don't let you get complacent. You want people in your community who continue to challenge you to keep learning and keep growing.

3. CREATE DISTANCE

There is another piece of building community to be aware of, and that is the challenge of letting go of some of the people in your life and in your world who aren't supporting the Real You. When you assert yourself, you want to be building a team of people who support who you are and say, "Right on. Go You!"

When my mom was a kid, her dad made this comment to her: "You will never amount to anything!" I have clients consistently come and share about friends and family who don't support them, just as my mom's dad did not support her. Someone who says to you, "You will never amount to anything," has no place in your support community.

So, what do you do about it? Here's an example of what you can say to people when you are uncertain if you want them as part of your community. Say, "Hey, here's who I am, and here's what I want to create with my life. And I want you to be on board and support me in getting there, but I am not going to put up with negativity, laziness, teasing, and apathy. If you want to support my success, right on. And, if not, well, good luck to you, because, if your path is headed that way, I want you to know that my path is headed this way. Please know you are invited to join me, but that way is not the journey I am on."

But there may be a situation where you cannot distance yourself from the person being negative; perhaps it is a parent you are living with (as with my mom), a kid on the school bus or in your class, a co-worker, etc. How do you handle that? First, realize that they are sharing their opinion, and you don't have to agree with them—Trust Yourself. Second, manage your Silly Self-Talk. It is easy for your Silly Self-Talk to take a comment like, "You will never amount to anything," and repeat it again and again and again. Then the statement someone said to you becomes a statement you are saying to yourself. Jam that dialogue! Third, use the path to Trust Yourself to establish a belief in yourself so you are able not to get hooked by this negative comment. Be powerful and Stand for who you know you are!

And be prepared for a reaction by being the OPERATER of the situation. Know it is coming, so that, when it comes, you are able to sit back and see what is happening.

Again, whether you find this challenging or easy, you will eventually learn that, when you have your supportive community that is free from negativity, it is massively liberating.

4. HELP OTHERS TO BUILD COMMUNITY

Creating a safe place for people to express themselves is an essential element of creating community, whether you are doing so as an individual or as someone working with other people. As an individual, you will be dealing with parents, kids, teachers, or friends, and joining other people's communities will enhance your commitment to live a life full of Meaning and Fulfillment. Similarly, when dealing with a group of people, creating a safe place for people to share will allow them to trust themselves and take steps on the Upward Spiral.

Empathize is the next section of *Launch Your Life*. Empathy is the ability to enter into another person's world and understand that world from their perspective. It is a beautiful extension of an open hand in support of another person and their effort to discover Meaning and Fulfillment.

Just as you are looking to find people to be part of your support community, others are looking for the exact same thing. Your willingness to be part of a friend's life opens the doors. You will learn what it feels like to be a part of a support community, while realizing that everybody else is also looking to create community so they can trust themselves.

MY SHY FRIEND

In a recent gathering in which we were discussing Sustainability issues, there was one shy and quiet woman. We were all answering a question and making an opening comment, but she did not speak up and got skipped as we went around the circle.

Thankfully, one of the group members asked her, "Do you have something you want to share?" In response, she jumped right in and began sharing. She had ideas, opinions, reflections, and reactions, but she did not have strong skills in how to enter into a conversation. Once invited, she absolutely had things to say. She just needed someone to notice her, and open the space for her.

The simple gesture of noticing and extending an invitation gave her the confidence that it was a safe space for her. When explicitly extended the invitation to share her ideas, she spoke the first time, and then she continued to enter the conversation for the rest of the evening and in future meetings.

Remember that I already disclosed the biggest part of Secret #4—It's About People: you cannot get where you are going, alone. And part of creating community is the awareness that the secret is *not* "It's All About Me." Being part of other people's journeys is an important component of creating community.

CREATING A SAFE PLACE

As youth workers, parents, teachers, and colleagues, and also as a friend, the more you can get stories flowing, the more connections you will create among people. Remember, stories are powerful to us as humans. They resound with who we are and fill us with learning and understanding. When you share your stories with other people, you create connections and liberate yourself from the space between your ears.

Creating safe enough places for people to step out is a beautiful contribution to the building of community. Create the safe places, extend the invitations, and then enjoy the beauty and wonder of people.

When you are creating a safe place in which to share, there are four simple rules to follow:

- Be assertive. You have to eliminate the awkwardness and difficulty by being in charge. By doing this, you will alleviate the fear that someone is going to get skewered if they say something.
- Create consistency and stay consistent. When you set up the structure for sharing, keep it consistent, so that everyone knows what to expect, how to engage, and how to respond. Then, keeping that structure consistent creates the safe space.
- Acknowledge the nervousness and offer an invitation: "You might be feeling those butterflies in your stomach, and that is a great indication that you have something to share, so, when you are ready, we want to hear from you."
- Acknowledge every effort. Thank people when they start to share, and make everyone present pay attention. Then listen intently, using your Real Listening (see page 332). When they are done, be certain everyone supports the effort.

SUPERCAMP LARGE GROUP SHARE

I worked at a summer camp called SuperCamp. It was ten days of action-packed learning and challenge. The campers were pushed to their Learning Edge all day, every day. We ended each day with what we called Large Group Sharing, an opportunity for the campers to come up on stage and share what they learned that day. As you may have heard, public speaking is among the scariest things for most people, so, to come up onto the stage and share about your experience in front of more than fifty of your peers took courage.

We structured Large Group Sharing so that it was the same every time we did it. As the leader, I set the ground rules, assertively maintained them, and kept the structure consistent. The kids always shared from the same place; they were always asked to speak loudly; listeners were always expected to practice Real Listening. Then, whenever someone came up to share, we acknowledged the effort and the courage it took by snapping respectfully.

By the last day of camp, almost every camper would come up, sit in front of the group, and share.

In contrast to this experience, I watched a youth worker attempt to get his students to share at a school assembly some ideas on a project about Oceans they had just completed. At least one hundred older kids were in the audience.

He began by asking his students to speak loudly and stand up strong. However, they were scared and nervous, so the first kid didn't stand and only whispered. The second kid stood up far behind his classmates and mumbled, so he could not be understood. The youth worker meekly tried to get order and have the student speak up, but quickly realized it wasn't working, so he began to doubt the structure of sharing in this way. When the third student stood up, he said nothing. And that was the last student who stood up, despite the leader's effort to encourage them. Eventually, he stood up and shared about the project on behalf of his students.

Now, both these examples are about groups, but the same idea applies to interactions with friends, parents, kids, and anyone else. Creating a safe space for people to be honest and vulnerable will greatly enhance their desire to share their stories and ideas.

WRAP-UP OF CREATE COMMUNITY

You now have some tools and ideas for creating community. Remember that creating community is tremendously, tremendously important in building your Trust Yourself. It begins to create synergy on your Upward Spiral. Once you begin to know that people are there, you start to be able to be more honest and more courageous, and you're able to get and share more acknowledgments, and bigger and bigger things in your life. You begin to create a higher level of accountability, there is less apologizing for who you are, and you take on bigger and bigger risks because your confidence and courage are growing on the Upward Spiral. And you learn how to avoid the arrows that people fling at you (see page 266).

Learn to Apologize

Learning to apologize is an important step in Trust Yourself. First, it's important to do it because it conveys that you are taking responsibility for your actions and the results of your actions on other people. Second, it shows you are courageous enough to zestfully express yourself, and confident enough to deal with whatever reaction you get.

I call the tool I use to apologize, the Huge Apology. It has four steps:

STEP ONE	Acknowledge	"I was late."
STEP TWO	Apologize	"I apologize for being late."
STEP THREE	Empathize/Acknowledge Impact	"My being late caused you to worry and waste time waiting for me."
STEP FOUR	Learn and Commit	"I will start wearing my watch, so I know what time it is and can show up when I am supposed to."

In the case of my friend (see page 237) who was defending himself against his parents when they disapproved of his decision, his Huge Apology went like this:

STEP ONE	Acknowledge	"I made a decision you are not happy with."
STEP TWO	Apologize	"I do not apologize for taking care of myself, but I do apologize if I have done something to disappoint you."
STEP THREE	Empathize/Acknowledge Impact	"I know you have other ideas about what you want me to do, and it might be hard for you that I am choosing to do something different."
STEP FOUR	Learn and Commit	"I realize you think this is risky, but my commitment is to make my path work for me. I am hopeful that you will be proud of me if I create a life for myself that I am excited about and makes me happy. I want you to know that I am 100% committed to making it happen.

Notice that there is no step for explaining yourself or making excuses.

You have certainly been in the situation in which you were expecting something from someone. You know how it feels when they didn't follow through on their commitment and, instead, gave you an excuse. Taking responsibility and being willing to apologize make it so you don't create that feeling in others because of your actions, or lack of actions. And, if you do create it, you are willing to take responsibility for it, apologize, and do what it takes to clean up your mess.

POSSIBLE BARRIERS

Internal Challenges

175

You will face challenges when you make an effort to Trust Yourself. In a similar way to the challenges you faced in Know Yourself, these will put you in a vulnerable position and make it tempting and easy to compromise the Real You. By anticipating the challenges, Knowing Yourself, and having the tools to connect to the Real You, you can make a conscious effort to avoid slipping onto a downward spiral.

External Challenges

184

It's worth going back to look at the possible barriers to Play Huge and Know Yourself, because elements of those challenges will certainly be present as you learn to Trust Yourself.

Remember: you live in the Test Score Culture, in which what you do is more important than who you are. It is very tempting and very easy to get trapped in the messages from society, your peers, parents, and schools that say, *You should...You are supposed to... If you had this product, then you would be...*You are inundated by these external messages, usually accompanied by flashing neon lights. This constant barrage compromises and eats away at Trusting Yourself and can make it supremely challenging to Stand up on the Play Huge Stage and assert: Here is who I am; here is how I learn; here is what I Stand for.

And all these voices convey the same message:

- Who you are is not okay.
- You should do things differently.
- You should be different.
- If you did ________________, you would be okay; in fact, you would be much happier, cooler, and smarter.

What goes in the blank? Choose one of the following: buy these jeans, use this shampoo, do well on this test, get into this college, smoke this, drink this, say this, pay attention to this, etc.

Society, peers, parents, and schools are all challenges to Know Yourself and Trust Yourself. The biggest challenge with Trust Yourself, however, does not come in standing in the full, zestful expression you are working on, but, more insidiously, in avoiding the eating away of your internal belief in yourself.

The incessant messages, teasing, and test scores create small seeds of doubt in you. They may seem insignificant, but seeds can grow. These powerful forces can cause a slow slip away from your natural way of being and into a way you come to believe you are supposed or ought to be. They provide water for the seeds, which do grow—unless you have the skills to keep them down.

All these possible barriers can be held in check by using the path to Trust Yourself. You learn to quiet the stories about who you should be, and you begin to trust and express who you are.

In addition to the standard internal and external challenges faced in Play Huge and Know Yourself, you may run into two additional Trust Yourself barriers: getting nailed by the arrow, and your traps and your Silly Self-Talk.

Getting Nailed by the Arrow

People fling arrows all the time. Arrows are things people say or do that provide you a choice. An arrow can be a general and neutral comment in a conversation, or it can be a direct criticism in an argument, or anything in between.

You can react to the comment, or you can sidestep the comment, because when an arrow gets flung, it creates a choice for you. You get to decide how to react.

Learning to avoid the arrow is another step in Trusting Yourself. When an arrow nails you, it kicks you toward a downward spiral. It usually triggers your Silly Self-Talk, activates your self-doubt, makes you feel alone, and undermines your creation of community.

Events happen all the time and people say things all the time that you can take personally and make mean something. When you "make something mean something," you take an everyday, normal, and neutral experience or comment, and turn it into something negative about you. The arrow nails you.

Some typical arrows happen when you make a comment in class...when your parents ask how your grades are...when you get your SAT scores back...when you decide not to apply to college...when your best friend gets into college...when you get into, or don't get into, college...when someone doesn't like something you believe in...when you are applying for a job...when you're looking for work...when you're interviewing for a job...when you ask someone out...when you're learning how to be in a relationship with a friend or significant other.

In all these cases, information creates a choice about how to react. You may feel these are easy or challenging to deal with, but they are, for the most part, meant as neutral comments.

Sometimes, however, the arrow is a very direct and purposeful comment intended to stick you, perhaps in the form of teasing and taunting, criticism, or judgment. It may sound something like this:

- Oh, that shirt really looks bad on you.
- You aren't any good at that.
- You don't care about me.

- You will never amount to anything.
- That was the most stupid comment I have ever heard.

Getting nailed by that arrow can really hurt. Because these kinds of arrows are directed at you, they can be more challenging to avoid, but, like the more neutral events, you have a choice about how to react.

When you can sidestep the comment, and let the arrow fly past you and land on the ground, you stay out of the ugliness that has been presented, and you stay in your power. From your power, you can say something like:

- I'm sorry you don't like my shirt. It's one of my favorites.
- You seem to have strong feelings about my shirt.
- Thank you for expressing your opinion, but I disagree.
- Wow, where did that come from?

You get to express yourself and defend yourself.

You met my friend Allison (see page 230), the one who recently graduated from college and is looking for meaningful work. When people asked Allison *the question*, they were (usually) not trying to be difficult or nail her with an arrow. They were usually simply making conversation, but she had trouble avoiding getting nailed by the arrow. As soon as someone asked, she got nailed, and it sent her into a tailspin of self-doubt. Her Silly Self-Talk got going, and, pretty soon, she was feeling crappy about herself.

As soon as she learned to sidestep the arrow, she was able to stay in her power and answer the question in a way that validated herself.

As you are more able to sidestep the neutral arrows flying around, you will get better at sidestepping the arrows that get flung directly at you.

And a powerful thing happens when you are in an argument and you are able to avoid being nailed by the arrows the other person is flinging at you. First, it dissipates the tension and energy of the situation. Second, it creates relatedness, because, instead of reacting to the other person's anger, you are able to see beyond their anger to what is really going on. Usually they are feeling alone, wanting to be included, wanting to be listened to, and in a situation where they don't trust themselves.

Learning to avoid the arrow allows you to Trust Yourself. When you avoid getting nailed by an arrow, it allows you to continue on the Upward Spiral, because you are able to see your traps and quiet your Silly Self-Talk before it gets started.

Your Traps and Your Silly Self-Talk

When you know your traps and what your Silly Self-Talk sounds like, you can anticipate times when you will face challenges and learn how to set yourself up to handle those times effectively. In other words, you can learn how to be the OPERATER.

When do you get grumpy? When do you get your buttons pushed? When don't you feel so powerful? Where are the places that make you want to learn and grow? Who are the people who make you feel good, or make you feel bad? What is your Silly Self-Talk? When does your Silly Self-Talk happen? Is it critical? Does it make up stories not based in reality? Do you compare yourself with others? What are the things about who you are that keep showing up, that you can't explain? When are you vulnerable to getting nailed by the arrow?

My friend knew she suffered bouts of depression, so she set herself up to deal with feeling down by writing letters to herself (see page 246).

Your traps and your Silly Self-Talk are not in control of your actions or your decisions. The Real You is in control of your actions and decisions, so, by knowing the danger zones, you are able to be the OPERATER of your life in a way that supports the Real You being in charge.

ALLISON'S NEW RESPONSE

This summer, I created a cross-country trip with my best friends, because I have always wanted to learn about myself and the country I live in. Then, I have always wanted to live with my sister, and she is in LA, so, after my road trip, I am going to LA! Once I am there, I will look for meaningful work. I have always wanted meaningful work; I want to have an impact in the world, so I am going to find this kind of job. Then, who knows? I trust myself enough that I will figure it out when I get there.

Here is Allison again, but, this time, she has sidestepped the arrow and is being the OPERATER of her life and Playing Above the Line when someone asks her *the question*: what will you do after you graduate?

Remember Allison's first response? How did she begin to trust herself enough to be able respond to the question like this? Her first step was to realize where her traps and Silly Self-Talk were. Her second step was to figure out what to do about *the question* before it was asked. She knew that, whenever someone asked her what she was doing after college, it threw her into a space of self-doubt and kicked her onto a downward spiral.

The power of knowing your traps and triggers is that it allows you to create a plan to be able to deal with them when they come up.

Beyond the Barriers

Hopefully, you continue to Stand in your power. When you Trust Yourself, you build on your foundation to the place where you fully and zestfully express yourself. You step onto the Play Huge Stage and perform. It is your time to share yourself.

TRUST YOURSELF

Now that you have the idea and path to Trust Yourself, you can again imagine yourself on the Play Huge Stage in full, zestful expression, celebrating you and being powerful.

When someone from the audience throws a tomato at you, you are ready to defend yourself. You have taken the small and significant steps of building your internal and external expression of yourself, to the point where you are really feeling trustworthy.

You know the importance of Standing for yourself. So, remember, instead of getting nailed in the head by the tomato, anticipate it, catch it, slice it, and add it to your salad. Then say thank you for the feedback and enjoy the applause from your support network.

As you master being able to create a resourceful state and Stand powerfully in full, zestful expression, you will find it easier and easier to move beyond your focus on yourself and begin to understand other people. Not only will you begin to be more powerful and effective, you will be able to enjoy each moment of your life more, because you will be connecting to other people.

HUGE OUTCOMES—TRUST YOURSELF

DEREK

I used to think it was easy to **IGNORE** all my **FEELINGS** about not being honest with myself, but now I realize how much foundational **ENERGY** it takes.

My connection to **FRIENDS** is much **STRONGER** now that I trust myself. I have begun to create a strong **COMMUNITY** of people who support me and **CHALLENGE** me to be my best.

I **LOVE** the feeling of being challenged, by others or by my own **FAILURES**. Feedback helps me be more **EXCELLENT**!

It is so much **EASIER** to meet people. The confidence I feel with **MYSELF** helps me talk to and connect with new **PEOPLE**!

I feel a sense of **INTEGRITY** and **CONFIDENCE** in the core of my being that has been **MISSING** a long, long time.

Not only am I more and more **CLEAR** on what I Stand for and who I am, I also have a much better **ABILITY** to act on the things I care **MOST** about. I have taken a Stand, and now I **ACT** on it consistently!

It is **AMAZING** how different my relationships are, now that I don't always have to **PROVE** myself. I can now see how much **COMMUNICATION** is dedicated to people justifying and trying to validate themselves.

I feel **FREEDOM** in my head and in my Real You when I quiet my **SILLY SELF-TALK**. I am excited about the possibilities I can create in the **FREEDOM**. It is amazing how tiring it is when you don't **BELIEVE** in yourself.

Huge Outcomes—Text Version

And what does it feel like when you have an honest belief in yourself? How does it impact the way you live your life?

CONSIDER THE UPWARD SPIRAL

The outcomes offered here are ones I have seen and experienced myself, and could be categorized as the low-hanging fruit. They are the most obvious possible outcomes, so, what follows are the powerful outcomes you will very likely experience, but, by no means do these make up a comprehensive list of the possible outcomes when you Trust Yourself.

Consider the Upward Spiral as you consider possible outcomes because, once you Trust Yourself, the huge outcomes begin to open more and more possibilities for you.

BELIEF IN YOURSELF

The most obvious outcome is that you will feel more confident. By consistently following through on your commitments and honoring your word, you are creating a deep integrity that feels really good. Believing in yourself has a cascade effect on how you show up in the world.

This feeling allows you to become more courageous and willing to take risks. Increased confidence and deep integrity create more and more focus and clarity in identifying what you Stand for and what the Real You wants.

It also helps you quiet your Silly Self-Talk. At this point, the potential impact of quieting your Silly Self-Talk is profoundly more than the absence of things holding you back. In the absence of these things, there is freedom, and with this freedom enters an immense opportunity to become extraordinary.

EXCITED. INSPIRED. ENERGETIC.

Trusting yourself feels good. It will turn on your sense of passion and purpose.

Because you are honoring the Real You and beginning to deepen your sense of self and what you Stand for, your inner sense of integrity and confidence grows. And, as it does, your acceptance of lame justifications goes way down. Playing small becomes massively unpalatable, both in yourself and in others. You realize that it takes a lot of energy to be apathetic, bored, and lazy, and that you have lots of possibilities for what you can do to get your energy and excitement onto the Upward Spiral.

EXCELLENCE

You will awaken your spirit of learning. You will realize that Playing Above the Line helps you achieve high levels of excellence.

You will watch people who are doing inspiring things and making a difference in other people's lives in order to learn from them and open up possibilities for yourself. The perception that a failure is an indication of your ability or your talent—or anything about you—disappears.

It is an absolutely magical place to crave failures and honest feedback. When you get past the fear that a failure will crash your sense of self or cannot be fixed, you enter into the place where feedback turns into learning, because who you are is not at stake. You only compare yourself to others to learn, and to provide yourself with motivation to step up your level of excellence.

Once that happens, then the whole failure and feedback idea turns on its head, and you realize that the only way to become the person you want to be is to make excellent mistakes and use them as information and motivation.

You will get that feeling of stepping up to the challenge posed by a teacher, friend, coach, or even a failure. Instead of getting intimidated, uncertain, or small in the face of a challenge or failure, you are invigorated to dig in and work harder, and that feels good.

CONNECTED WITH PEOPLE

When you Trust Yourself, you will find a freedom in your expression. You will be able to say courageous and honest things to others. But, equally as important, you will not worry what people think about your ideas or your suggestions. When you Trust Yourself, you speak your truth, and you carry the perspective that, when people don't agree, they have the freedom to respond (or not respond), and you will be able to handle their response.

You used to perseverate on what people thought about your ideas or how they reacted to what you said or did, but now you let that stuff go very quickly and enjoy life. You will do much more listening. You are able to understand situations as if you are looking at them from above, so you are able to interact with people in thoughtful and meaningful ways.

And it works in the other direction also. When you Trust Yourself, your life slows way down and you are able to anticipate how people will react, what people will say, and what will happen next. When somebody says or does something you don't like, you are able to understand it from a new and different perspective, and, if necessary, bring it up to them in a way that honors their perspective as well as your feelings.

You will experience healthy and meaningful relationships based on honesty and the true expression of people, and you will have a community of people around you who support the Real You and keep you in your power.

MEET NEW PEOPLE

There are so many people who want to meet other interesting people, but it can be challenging. When you Trust Yourself, meeting new people becomes easy. You are bold enough to begin conversations with people; you are curious enough to ask people questions; you are powerful enough that people are drawn to you. Trust Yourself, and you will find yourself with lots of new possible friends.

GET OFF IT QUICKLY

It is unrealistic to think that you will never compare yourself unfavorably to others, get caught in your Silly Self-Talk, make up stories that are not real, and be critical of yourself.

A Huge Outcome of every section of *Launch Your Life* is that you learn to get off it quickly. You catch yourself before you send yourself onto a downward spiral. You begin to replay a conversation you had with a friend, making up stories about why they didn't react in the way you expected, but then you stop. You get off it. You let it go, and move on to more powerful ways of being.

Foundational Terms

Trust Yourself added yet again to the list of foundational terms from Your Launch Pad, Play Huge, and Know Yourself, and, again, some of the terms come from a secret. In this case it is Secret #3—Play Above the Line. It is exciting to begin to Trust Yourself, because it means you have a *solid foundation*; you are Standing in *full, zestful expression* of the Real You; and you are able to *stand your ground*. Because of your *Response-ability* and ownership, you are easily able to *execute the little things* and begin to *build your community*, which protects you from getting nailed by *arrows* flung at you.

WRAP-UP

It is action time on the Play Huge Stage. Trust Yourself is taking the conceptual understanding you developed in your Know Yourself, and putting it into action.

On the stage, there is another blob of clay to sculpt your Trust Yourself. You want to do something with it for your upcoming performance.

But you decide that, instead of sculpting a whole new image to go with the work you did on your Know Yourself, you will use your clay to bring your Know Yourself to life. You are going to animate it!

The play is about the expression of the Real You. While you are preparing, an audience member in a disguise jumps onto the stage where you are busy animating your sculpture, and asks if you want to cancel the performance.

This audience member shares that she has been in the auditorium while people have been coming in, and these people are aggravated about taking the time to come when they hear you aren't ready and are going to present something they don't like. She actually overheard your parents, and they are disappointed already. Several of your teachers are annoyed, and several of your friends feel like you are being uncool. So she suggests she can help tell everyone that the performance has been cancelled.

This all feels familiar, but, before you take any action, you realize that the "audience member" is your Silly Self-Talk in a disguise. You remove the disguise, remind your Silly Self-Talk it is not invited onto the Play Huge Stage, and escort your "guest" out the backstage door.

You hear applause, and turn around to realize that the curtain is open and the play has begun. You had been focused on taking care of small details of your Know Yourself and the Real You before you were interrupted. But, once the door closed behind your Silly Self-Talk, you got an infusion of energy and excitement. While your first temptation is to close the curtain, you feel inspired to continue. You get your sculpture and pull it to the front of the stage.

As you begin to show the capabilities of your sculpture, how it learns, what it values, and how it is smart, you take out your Play Huge Notebook, throw it to a friend in the front row, and ask him to take some notes about what is happening and any feedback that comes forth.

After a short while, you begin feeling like you are missing something important. You are not feeling settled. There is something not quite right, so you turn to the audience and say, "I am going to call a *Time-out.*" And you walk off stage.

There is confusion, some grumbling, and a couple of people get up and jump on the stage to do a Know Yourself improvisation about themselves. Someone asks what they are doing, and they say you have inspired them to share who they are and what they care about.

In the meantime, you are looking at your Organize and Plan for your Trust Yourself event, and remember you were planning to sing.

As you come back onto the Play Huge Stage, someone sees your banner (see page 196)—what you Stand for: creating meaningful friendships and relationships.

As you read it, you realize that, since you began fully and zestfully expressing yourself, you have gained more clarity on it, so it has shifted and is now closer to what the Real You wants to express.

I stand for treating people with dignity and respect! Always.

Then a crazy thing happens. A flaming arrow comes flying from the back of the auditorium, and then another and another. Then several people start chanting, "You will never amount to anything," "You are not a good sculptor," "You must not love us," "Who do you think you are?", and more. But you see the arrows coming and easily sidestep them. They land harmlessly on the stage and lamely burn out.

Your powerful stance over the petered-out arrows provides a perfect transition to asking for feedback, so you address your audience and ask them for honest feedback about your performance. As people share, you are amazed that you are feeling energized and excited about people's honesty. You realize they have good ideas which will make your future performances much more excellent. And you realize there are a lot of people in the audience who are part of your community and committed to your creating what you want to create.

Finally, you wrap up the evening by saying, "I am hopeful that you enjoyed yourself tonight, and I am appreciative of your time, effort, and honesty. If you are leaving and not feeling good about your investment of an evening, I apologize. I am committed to filling my life with excellence through continued learning. I will Stand more and more powerfully, and hope you will give me another chance to create a connection."

SECRET #4
It's About People

You know the importance of Playing Huge. You Know Yourself and Trust Yourself. You have arrived at a Cusp moment, and, when you navigate it effectively, this Cusp moment will have a profound impact on your life and on the world, greater than the impact of anything else you have learned thus far.

The significance exists because it is the Cusp of shifting your focus away from you and into the world of other people. The secret that sits in this Cusp moment is, It's About People.

When it comes down to it, you will judge your life by two measures. The first is the strength of your relationships and the connections to people in your life. The second is the degree to which you treated people with dignity and respect.

In Your Launch Pad, you learned that Meaning and Fulfillment come from your relationships with people. Now you are ready to learn that the way to have powerful relationships with people is to embrace It's About People. Further, the way to make a difference and leave the planet a better place than you found it, is to act on It's About People.

Three principles make It's About People happen:

- treating people with dignity and respect
- being discovered and discovering
- creating synergy

When you effectively implement these three principles into your life, you will have the answers to the following questions (among others):

- How do you create lasting friendships and partnerships?
- How do you build and Sustain a successful business, organization, movement, initiative, or partnership?
- What does it take to be comfortable dealing with complexity, discomfort, conflict, and challenging situations?
- How do you get people to help you?
- How do you get really good at doing something?
- What does it take to be an extraordinary learner?

When I think back to the days after my dad died, I am amazed at how much time I was spending on things that really did not matter. And I am amazed at how many things in my life I was taking for granted and not appreciating.

I wanted my dad back. I wanted to know him as an adult and be known as one by him. I wanted to have another pillow fight. I wanted more hockey and baseball games. I wanted to share my ideas with him and learn from his insights. I wanted a hug. And I wanted more chances to deal with the challenges that we had, my frustrations with him, and his frustrations with me. From my new perspective, this all seemed so small and easy to do, yet it had been underappreciated and ignored when there was something we could have done about it.

There was no *thing* I could have or get that would replace him. And, as I walked along the train tracks from the movie theatre to my dorm room, or as I sat overlooking Seneca Lake in Geneva, New York, remembering the good times and the challenging times, and wondering what my life was going to be like without him, I did not want to be alone. But I was.

And, while I walked and sat, a phrase came to me, and I remember speaking it out loudly again and again (often through tears): "It's About People."

While I have spent the last twenty years exploring and discovering It's About People, the basic ideas have not strayed far from the raw feelings I had back then:

- Friendship is massively valuable. Feeling loved and loving makes us whole.
- Where is everyone?
- Treating people well makes a difference.
- Existing institutions are not preparing people with the skills and values necessary to make the connections with other living things that will make their lives meaningful and fulfilling.

Nothing can replace a relationship you have with another person. When you connect with the Real You and realize you want to make a difference, you will also realize that the most profound way to make that happen is to remember that It's About People. That is what matters most.

TREAT PEOPLE WITH DIGNITY AND RESPECT

When you Launch Your Life, there is no room for a lack of dignity and respect. Taking advantage of people, exploiting people for your personal gain, lying, being deceitful, or any of the other ways there are of harming people, will never lead to a life of Meaning and Fulfillment.

217

Instead, these behaviors will lead to a life of regret, sadness, disappointment, emptiness, and being lonely. When you do not treat people well, you know it. At that foundational level, you cannot deceive yourself. Even if you say you do not care, or justify it by saying that it's the way other people do things, or have convinced yourself that you "have" to do it that way—in your heart, you know. Deep down, you know, and you cannot escape that knowledge.

The way to Launch Your Life is to be honest, hold people to high standards, Play Above the Line, coach people to learn, listen deeply to people, and be willing to work through uncomfortable situations.

Whether in formal situations (school, work, family time, etc.) or informal situations (at the gym, a restaurant, grocery store, etc.), you have the opportunity to practice treating people with dignity and respect. The opportunity exists in your life every single day. The basics include returning a phone call, responding to an email, saying hello to a friend or person walking down the street, working to remember someone's name or something about them, or not answering your phone while talking face-to-face with someone.

Eventually, you hold people big enough to be able to be completely honest, apologize for mistakes, take responsibility for your actions, consider their circumstances before interacting with them, and Stand for their excellence by not letting them get away with weak efforts. These are just a sampling of the possibilities, because there are endless ways to act with dignity and respect.

It is a gift to humanity and all living things when you live in this way.

Regardless of the venue—whether it be at school, in an intimate relationship or a friendship, as a parent, as an employee, or as a leader of an organization—the bottom line is that people are most creative, energetic, positive, and inspired when they feel good about who they are and what they do.

You will do better in school and at work and be a more effective person when you feel good about who you are, and you will be more likely to make good on your commitments to the Real You. Because of these things, your life will be filled with Meaning and Fulfillment.

BEING DISCOVERED AND DISCOVERING

You learned in Know Yourself that everyone desperately wants to be liked. You want to have friends, you want to be included, you want people to be thinking about you, you want people to do special things for you, you want to be part of groups—everyone does.

Being discovered builds on the desire to be liked. You know you have unused potential and you wonder what your life would be like if you realized your potential. You want to be amazing, make a difference, and share your gifts with yourself and with the world, but it's not happening on its own. You really want to Play Huge, and you wonder what it will take to get yourself unlocked.

FEELING ALL ALONE

I sat overlooking Seneca Lake wondering what everybody else was doing and how it could be that I was the only one wanting to talk, wanting to laugh, feeling lonely, knowing I am talented but not fulfilling my potential, and wanting to do something amazing.

You have an idea of what your life could be like if only…if only …something! The something is, if only you were discovered. If you were discovered, you would be connected to people in a way that could help you realize your potential.

You know that, when you get discovered, it will unlock your belief in yourself and give you the opportunity to move towards your powerful and zestful expression. And so you wait…

And wait…And wait…

Or…you use what you have learned in *Launch Your Life*, and you Play Huge, because you know that the way to get discovered is to put yourself in situations where people can begin to understand you and learn who you are and what you Stand for.

But there is also another part of being discovered, and it took me a long time to realize it. You have to be willing to discover others.

If everyone is just waiting to be discovered, there is no one out there to do the discovering. So everyone waits around for that lucky moment when they get the BIG break. But that is not the way the Meaning rEvolution works. Change and meaning do not happen to us someday; you make it happen. And this is the Cusp you are on—the Cusp of Empathize. In Empathize, you get out of your own world and into the world of others.

This element of It's About People breaks apart the focus on you and puts focus on someone (or something) else that wants to be discovered. When you unlock someone's potential and give them the gift of being discovered, not only does it break the pattern of waiting around for someone to Play Huge and navigate the Cusp, it creates a crack in the dam. And as soon as the water starts to flow, watch out.

When you are willing to discover others, there are others willing to discover you. The discovery happens by using Real Listening, slowing down, and appreciating life. Then you stop asking, "Where is everybody?" and begin saying, "Thank you for being here."

CREATING SYNERGY

ALVIN'S CLASSROOM

254

My friend Alvin is an amazing teacher. He has the beautiful combination of discovering students and challenging them to Play Above the Line, Play Huge, and use all their potential. His class is massively challenging. His demands are significant. His expectations are high. And the students love it!

Everyone craves being a part of a learning community. Amazing things can happen when a group of people gets together with a focus on a common goal, the passion to make the goal happen, the creativity to do what it takes to make it happen, and the ability to listen and acknowledge people. If you have ever been part of a situation like this, you know exactly what it feels like, and I am certain you want more of it. If you have not ever had this kind of learning experience, find one and get involved. It will transform your life.

Synergy happens when a group becomes more powerful than each of the individuals in the group. Possibilities open up. Creativity thrives. Each person becomes more and more powerfully and zestfully expressed.

When you have a community of people around you that supports the Real You, it helps you feel confident. It provides the foundation for the courage to be who you are. You feel discovered. And, because discovering happens, your community knows what you like and what you do not like; they know what you are good at and what your challenges are; they support your efforts to Play Huge; and they hold you to high standards.

Fulfilling your potential and honoring the Real You and your pursuit of excellence is not possible to do all by yourself in a Sustainable way. Everyone has moments when they get inspired and on-target; these are the moments that provide the tastes and dreams of what is possible for our lives. The only way to create and Sustain this is through creating synergy with a community of people.

BACK TO ALVIN'S CLASSROOM

Alvin and his students created synergy in their classrooms. They became a group of people driven to excellence, learning, and making a difference. They had a ton of fun and they worked hard. The mentality of students getting by, doing the minimum amount of work, not caring, and not being engaged—all that disappeared. It was a classroom where discovery was happening and everyone was being challenged to unlock their potential, because people were being treated with dignity and respect, discovering and being discovered, and everyone in the class was passionate, creative, and connected to each other.

The success of any initiative you want to take on is dependent on the people in your life. You. Cannot. Do. It. Alone. Remember: It's About People! And being part of other people's communities and discovering them is a key part of life, because they cannot do it alone either.

IT'S ABOUT PEOPLE IN ACTION—REAL WORLD EXAMPLES

This secret is simple and has profound implications.

MULTIPLICATION BY LIZZY

Lizzy is a first-grader. She sat for twenty-five minutes with a counter containing one hundred beads; she was working different strategies to multiply eighteen by five. She did not get frustrated, and she eventually got the answer, prompted only by an occasional "Is there another strategy you can use?" from the teacher. When she felt she had come to a solution, she immediately asked two friends how they got the answer. After listening to their strategies, she reset the counter and got the answer a new way.

On the Yes! side of the Cusp, in the upcoming chapter on Empathize, there will be more stories like this, in which Lizzy was treated with dignity and respect in being trusted to find the answer. Her way of thinking was being discovered, which opened her up to discover her friends and create synergy. The teacher was completely connected to Lizzy and her friends, and she did not force any learning, but, instead, she let the discovery happen and allowed the students' sense of self—not just their math skills—to expand.

Everything looks/sounds/feels different in the world of It's About People. Here is the distinction in perspectives:

- **It's About Me**: I have to tell that person the right way to get the right answer.
- **It's About People**: How can I coach this person to get the answer in a way that will make complete sense to him, will honor how she thinks, and enhance his belief in his Real You?

If you force someone to do something, the outcome will be ineffective. But, when someone learns through the way their learning brain works, then the outcome is effective and Sustainable.

The following example is unfortunately more common than you might think. I use it as an illustration of systemic failures to treat people with dignity and respect, which I fear models for us an unacceptable way of being.

THE LONELY TEACHERS

Imagine teaching in a school in which all the teachers are alone all day long. They are so busy that they don't have a chance to go to the bathroom, eat lunch, or talk with an adult all day. Then, at the end of the day, they have a meeting in which they are told that their students are not doing well enough and they have to work harder. The next day their supervisor comes in and sits in the back of the rooms taking notes. After an hour, the supervisor gets up and leaves without acknowledging the teacher.

How effective do you think you would be as a teacher in this school? Would you like to be a student in one of these classrooms?

IT'S ABOUT PEOPLE TEACHERS

Now imagine teaching in a school in which the teachers work in groups. Each group gets to create its own structure for making certain that everyone is taken care of. Everyone gets breaks during the day and eats with at least one other person. Some of the other groups create workout teams before or after school, and others schedule times to go learn about new ideas they can use in their classrooms.

The school believes that when teachers (and staff) are healthy, rested, and taken care of, they will then be more effective with their students. The school has a belief that, when people are treated well, they will treat other people well. They know their students watch how the adults around them interact, and they learn how to interact with each other based on those interactions.

The groups of teachers meet regularly to set up ways always to be on their Learning Edge, because they realize the importance of modeling learning for their students, and how important it is for them to consistently challenge themselves to improve their craft.

How effective do you think you would be as a teacher in this school? Would you like to be a student in one of these classrooms?

You could create a similar scenario for workers in a factory, a bookstore, or any office; for families and friendships; for a group of people with different values; or just about every situation you find yourself in every day.

This seems so obvious. Would you rather have people in your organization feeling powerful and passionate, or lame and unempowered? Who would be a more effective student, employee, teacher, leader, or friend? People feel powerful and passionate when they are understood, when they are listened to, when they feel like a part of a team, and when they are given the opportunity to contribute their gifts to the world.

People also feel powerful and passionate when they are on the path to creating new habits, dealing with challenges effectively, and confronting difficult situations.

JULIE AND THE PROFESSOR

I went to school with a woman, Julie, who was having a difficult time with her health. She was committed to staying in school, but her health was making it challenging. She was also shy, so very few people knew what she was dealing with.

One of our professors was disappointed with her performance and was quite aggressive about it. She would call her out in class, would be harsh in her comments on assignments, and curt in all their interactions.

It was obvious the professor was frustrated and I knew that my friend didn't feel good about the situation either. They kept trying to force each other to change, by giving a failing grade, making an insulting response to a question, leaving angry messages, ignoring requests, or showing indifference. They tried all kinds of tactics, and it was clear that neither of them was being powerful. Something had to change.

One day after class, our professor said hello to Julie as she was leaving class. Then one of those awkward comic moments occurred, during which they both began to talk simultaneously, trying to explain and apologize for what had been happening. That day they talked for an hour, and they scheduled an hour each week for the rest of the school year to talk some more. They realized they were both going through challenges in their lives. By talking, they stopped making assumptions about what the other person was doing and, instead, made a real connection.

Julie ended up doing very well in the class, and our professor became a trusted advisor and mentor for her.

There is It's About People in action. In many situations, people are not willing to treat each other with dignity and respect; instead they make assumptions about who people are and the reasons for their actions. It is when you are willing to discover another person and allow yourself to be discovered that a connection is made.

This happens all the time with parents and teenagers. There's
374 no listening, but there is lots of force, wrong assumptions, and a lack of dignity, respect, discovery, and synergy. The relationship becomes like holding jello—the more you force it by squeezing, the more it squirts out of your hands.

It's About People is not about forcing people to be a certain way, to think a certain way, or to do what you think is right. It's About People is about being with people and discovering ways of solving challenges in ways that match their learning brains and their Real Yous. When you practice It's About People, people feel validated, challenged, and understood. When people feel validated, challenged, and understood, they share their gifts with the world.

It's About People is the idea that you are far more effective and powerful when the Real You is acknowledged.

You simply cannot be as productive in your life without connections to other people. When you are treated well, you in turn treat others well. We all are our most creative, energetic, positive, and inspired when we feel good about who we are and what we do. Whether in a family, a school, a friendship, or a place where you work, treating people with dignity and respect makes a difference.

ONWARD TO EMPATHIZE AND PART III

This is the critical moment of transition. The Cusp between inward focus and external focus happens in the space between Trust Yourself and Empathize. When you begin to get out of your own world and into the world of others, you will begin to feel your world shift.

It's About People challenges you to acknowledge the truth that Meaning and Fulfillment come from connections with people, not from material possessions and self-interest. The awareness of this is critical, but many of you may realize that all your existing skills, abilities, and maybe even interests are currently focused on acquiring more stuff and taking care of yourselves.

If this is the case, there is nothing wrong with you; you are simply ready for a learning experience. You now get to enter into the complexity of dealing with the unknown. You get to enter into the world of other people. And this is the work of Empathize.

Congratulations for making it to this point. Now you have the opportunity to explore and learn what it feels like to live in the world of Empathize—where It's About People.

AROUND THE DINNER TABLE
SO ELLY, I WAS ABLE TO GET A NATURE DOCUMENTARY FROM THE LIBRARY.
I DON'T FEEL WELL. I'M GOING TO BED.
OK HONEY, GET SOME REST. WE'LL SEE YOU IN THE MORNING.
REALLY I JUST NEED SOME REST, I'LL BE FINE IN THE MORNING.
I'M ON MY WAY. CAN YOU PREHEAT THE OVEN FOR ME?
I'M GLAD YOU'RE HERE FOR MOVIE NIGHT.

WHAT WILL IT TAKE?

SINCE YOU GOT HERE YOU'VE MET AND HELPED OUT A LOT OF PEOPLE.
PEOPLE FEEL LISTENED TO AND UNDERSTOOD WHEN THEY TALK WITH YOU.
THOSE ARE VALUABLE SKILLS YOU HAVE.
REALLY? HUH. I LOVE THAT STUFF. A JOB LIKE THAT SOUNDS APPEALING.
SOUP'S ON EVERY-BODY.
I HOPE YOU ALL LIKE LASAGNA.
MMM... SPEAK OF APPEALING!

WHAT WILL IT TAKE?

I SHOULD STILL BE ABLE TO MAKE IT OVER TO AAP.
PAT GILBERT
PPLIN
10:30

WHAT WILL IT TAKE?

IT'S LATE. WHAT'S THAT RACKET?
JENNY CALLED AND SAID THE COM-MUNITY CENTER IS ON FIRE.
WELL, I DON'T LIKE THE PLACE BUT THAT'S TOO BAD. WE SHOULD WAKE THE KIDS AND TELL THEM.
ELLY?
JAMIE?
THEY'RE BOTH GONE! THIS WAS NEXT TO ELLY'S BED.
EAT WITH
SPEEDING TO AAP
I SWEAR TO YOU MARK. OUR CHIL-DREN ARE GOING TO BE GROUNDED TIL WE'RE GRANDPARENTS.

WHAT WILL IT TAKE?

LET'S GO HOME. I'VE DONE ENOUGH DAMAGE TONIGHT.
I'M SO SORRY LESLIE I'LL TRY TO... I'M SORRY.
HOW DID IT GO SO WRONG?
COME ON. I'VE GOT THE NICEST COUCH IN THE TRI-STATE AREA.

PART THREE

INTO the WORLD

EMPATHIZE

I have come in contact with many individuals who have achieved an incredible degree of outward success, but have found themselves struggling with an inner hunger, a deep need for personal congruency and effectiveness, and for healthy, growing relationships with other people.

Stephen Covey

There is a revolution happening in the medical world. It is the stunning realization that patients get healthier faster when doctors listen.

Patch Adams

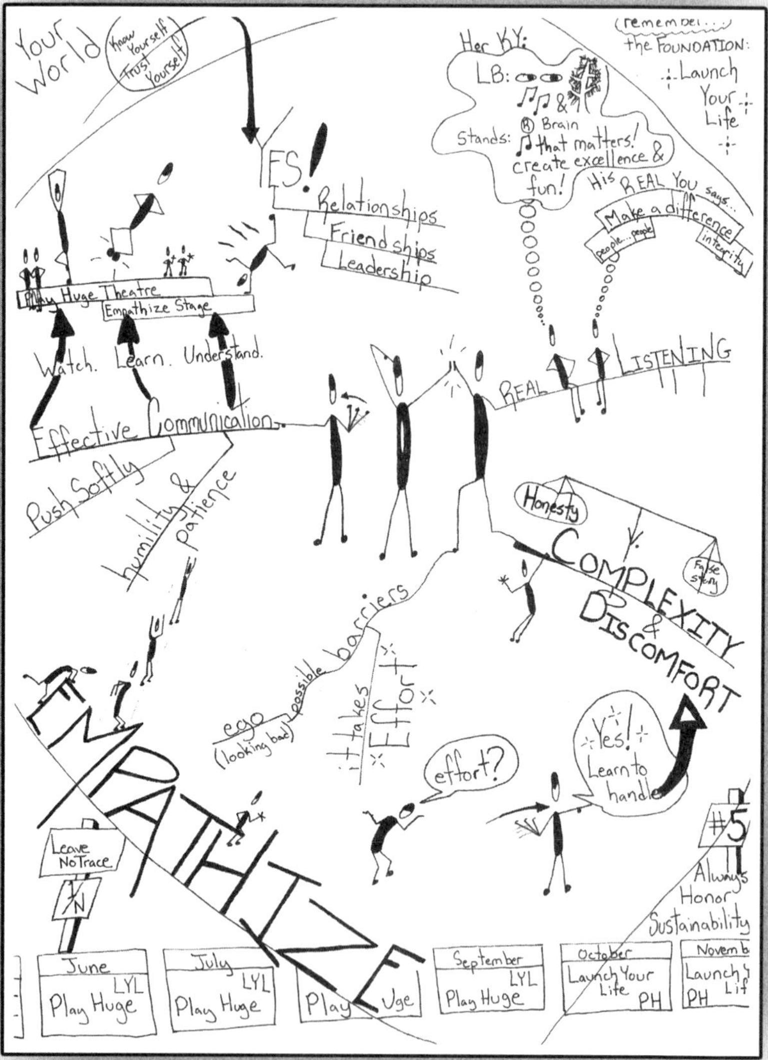
Your World
Know Yourself
Trust Yourself
YES!
Relationships
Friendships
Leadership
Her KY:
LB:
Brain
Stands:
that matters!
create excellence &
fun!
the FOUNDATION:
Launch Your Life
His REAL You says...
Make a difference
people...people
integrity
Play Huge Theatre
Empathize Stage
Watch. Learn. Understand.
REAL LISTENING
Effective Communication
Push Softly
humility & patience
Honesty
False story
COMPLEXITY & DISCOMFORT
possible barriers
ego
(looking bad)
it takes Effort
effort?
Yes!
Learn to handle
EMPATHIZE
Leave No Trace
#5
Always Honor Sustainability
June
LYL
Play Huge
July
LYL
Play Huge
Play Uge
September
LYL
Play Huge
October
Launch Your Life
PH
PH

YOUR SIMPLE EMPATHIZE

Empathize is where you create Meaning and Fulfillment because Empathize is about people.

When you Empathize, you understand other people on their terms. You leave behind your need for self-validation, and you escape your own Silly Self-Talk. You enter into their understanding, into their experience, and into their interpretation of life events, and, when you do, you create a relationship with another person.

It is in the profound simplicity of relationships with other people you love that you will feel loved, and awaken to the possibilities of passionately fulfilling your potential. Ultimately, it is where you will find Meaning and Fulfillment.

EMPATHIZE EXPLAINED

Up to this point, *Launch Your Life* has focused on you. It has focused on you because the only way for you to create the kind of meaningful relationships the Real You wants is to *stop* focusing on you.

Empathize is where your foundation of Knowing Yourself and Trusting Yourself allows you to focus on other people. Empathize is the space in which arrogance turns into respect, aggression into compassion, and assumptions into understanding.

When you Empathize, you step into the world of other people:

- The teacher who teaches each student in the way that student learns
- The student who understands that each teacher is different, and adapts his learning to account for the differences
- The friend who listens, is able to see the world from your perspective, and accepts you for who you are
- The parent who puts aside his agenda and works to learn about you and what you want to make with your life

- The boss who, instead of telling you what to do, asks you what you think is the best course of action, and respects your thoughts and opinion

When you live your life with Empathy, you will find that people open up to you and live in their full, zestful expression around you. They share their stories, they convey their understanding of the world, and they take risks to live their lives fully and zestfully expressed.

You invite your friend (or child or parent or student or boss) onto the Play Huge Stage with you, and you allow them to tell their story. You encourage them, cry with them, support them, and make a difference in their life by being 100% in their world.

But, unfortunately, in our culture, it is not that easy. You are now familiar with the Test Score Culture you live in—in which what you do is more important than who you are, and self-interest drives your decisions. The messages that inundate you every day will make it challenging to move to the Empathize Stage in the Play Huge Theatre (see page 184).

But, because you Know Yourself and Trust Yourself, you are up for the challenge. It begins with further understanding the concept of Empathize, and then moves to the path to get there. This part is about the concept, so what follows are three sections to enhance your understanding. The first provides a frame for getting beyond yourself and into the world of others, and introduces the distinction of Know Yourself. The second explains the elements of empathetic communication. And, finally, the third section looks into the places where you will use Empathy.

Again, with your foundation, you are ready to use Empathy in a personal relationship, at school, at work, or as a teacher, parent, or leader. You are ready to use Empathy to make people feel understood and, therefore, powerful.

Into the World of Others

KNOW YOURSELF

Here I am going to add a distinction to Know Yourself for the purpose of Empathy. In Empathize, you are working to know another person. That means you want to be able to distinguish your interpretation of the world and their interpretation of the world. Another way to think about Know Yourself is that it's what you know about the world based on your interpretation of your own experiences. It is what you know and how you understand the world.

Know Yourself will be referred to throughout this chapter because it is the foundation of understanding other people. And, in order to understand other people, you have to be willing to put your own Know Yourself aside and listen for theirs.

To Empathize is to begin to understand another person's Know Yourself.

It is easy to assume that your interpretation of an experience is the same as someone else's interpretation of the same experience, but meaningful relationships only happen when you get beyond that assumption, when you deal with situations and feelings that really exist, and you take responsibility for how you respond.

Remember: everyone has a different catalog of experiences in life, and unique interpretations of those experiences; therefore, everyone has different interpretations of situations and events. This is your opportunity to learn about them.

GET BEYOND YOURSELF

When you put yourself aside, it does not mean you have to agree with the other person's actions or her perspective on things. The objective is not to agree or disagree. The objective is to understand.

When you believe you are right, it is easy to assume that other people see the world or an event in the same way you do. Getting out of your own head is shifting your awareness from seeing the world through your eyes, toward listening to the environment and other people, in order to see the world from a perspective other than yours.

I WOULD BE HER CELL PHONE

A friend recently was asked, "What would you want to be if you could be anything in the world?" He responded, "I want to be my girlfriend's cell phone."

His girlfriend is known for always picking up her phone every time it makes a noise, no matter what situation she is in. When asked about that, she always has an excuse for why she needed to answer the call, respond to the text message, or reply to the email.

Like many people she is self-absorbed; she is caught up in all the messages of the Test Score Culture.

Depending on how well you understand the concept of Trust Yourself, you may have just reflected that she does not trust herself, and, therefore, she is not able to be present with her boyfriend.

You might also realize that, like many people, she is not Playing Above the Line. She blames circumstances (the phone ringing) rather than being in control of her response and remaining present with her boyfriend.

The point of understanding is not to place judgment or be critical, but rather to use it as information. Later in the chapter, you will learn about knowing the type of communication that is happening and the impact it can have.

The most fundamental concept to understand when you begin to Empathize is based on being present and engaged with another person. In order to do this, you have got to put yourself aside.

You now Trust Yourself, so you know you don't need to prove yourself and you can Stand for who you are. You are beyond the need for the temporary validation.

Now, this may be easy to understand intellectually, but it is often challenging to put into practice.

MATH CLASS, PART ONE

When I was in my midtwenties, I taught math to sixth-, seventh-, and eighth-graders. I became a math teacher because I like math and am good at it. The fact that I wasn't trained as a math teacher did not enter my thinking.

Growing up, I learned math in a traditional way. The teacher gave me a problem, showed me the steps to get the answer, and had me practice until I could do it that way. When I became a math teacher, I did the exact same thing, but many of my students struggled.

When they did not understand and struggled, I assumed that they needed to work harder and care more, so I explained more, and pushed them and drilled them on the correct steps, over and over again.

Despite my efforts, the students were not more successful; actually, they became visibly defeated. I was trying to fit all of them into the same mold I had come out of, but that wasn't working.

In the end, I realized two things. The first was that I was offering only one way to learn—my way—and, for many of my students, my way was not going to work. There had to be other possibilities. The second thing I realized was that I was desperate to validate myself as a good teacher.

INTO THEIR WORLD

In the moment when people are struggling to understand and are not putting ideas into action, an opportunity arises. It is a Cusp moment.

MATH CLASS, PART TWO

In my classroom I believed there was a right way to do any problem. One way. My way. I mistakenly believed I had nothing to learn; after all, I knew how to do the problems.

But part of my responsibility was to open up to new possibilities ...to remember that I know myself and trust myself...to step past my triggers and my buttons and continue to listen. Eventually, when a student asked a question, rather than try to force my way, I side-stepped the arrow, and asked the student a question. I remembered to focus on understanding the Know Yourself of my student. In that moment, I began to learn how to listen and to start to understand.

In order to be Empathetic and build relationships, you need to be open to new possibilities and new perspectives. Too much time spent in your own head, trying to make sense of the world and your experiences, is dangerous. It becomes easy to blame others or circumstances for how things are going. While it is challenging to examine your actions and evaluate your part of the situation, that is how you Empathize. You begin to spend time working to be in the world of other people and other living things.

Here are a couple of scenarios of what it looks, sounds, and, perhaps, feels like to step into somebody else's understanding.

EVENT OR SITUATION	BLAME AND SELF-PRESERVATION	EMPATHIZE
My classroom	The students are not working hard enough. They are not smart enough. They never listen to me. I have to prove how smart I am. I have to prove what a good teacher I am.	How does each student learn? How are they thinking about this problem? How can I answer the question in a way they will understand and that will help them solve the problem in their own ways?
Argument with friend	He is stupid. How come he doesn't care about me? What is wrong with him? He never does what I ask him to do.	How did he understand the situation? I wonder if something else was going on. What effort did he make? What assumptions am I making about what I expect from him?
Doing community service	My effort will not make a difference. I have better things to do. It's uncomfortable to go into situations in which I don't know what I'm doing. It would be inconvenient for me to do that.	My effort makes a difference. My convenience is not the most important consideration here. There are people in the world who are less fortunate. I am grateful for what I have, and want to help in any way I can. What is important is bigger than my comfort and convenience.

DEALING WITH REALITY

You certainly remember that your Silly Self-Talk is great at making up false stories, creating scenarios that haven't happened, or interpretations of events that have happened. You may also remember that part of being the OPERATER of your life is to be Realistic. When you get wrapped up in this stuff, you are not dealing with reality.

You spend a huge amount of time and energy dealing with things that never happened or are never going to happen.

MATH CLASS, PART THREE

In my classroom, I was frustrated and angry at my students. I was convinced they were not working hard and they didn't care. Because of this evaluation, I spent a lot of time trying to figure out how to get them to work harder and care more. Then, when my efforts didn't work, I became convinced they thought I was a bad teacher and didn't care.

But never in this process did I validate my assumptions. Everything I was doing was based on the conversation going on in my own head. I was not dealing with reality; I was making up false stories.

Here are just a couple of examples of situations in which you may not deal with reality.

Not Dealing With Reality

- You may think your parents don't care, or don't want to talk with you.
- You may think your teacher doesn't like you.
- You may be convinced that the reason your girlfriend is not going out with you tonight is because she likes someone else.
- You may be freaking out about what happens if you don't get into college, or don't get that job you really want.

Earlier in the book (see page 249), there was an example in which you made an assumption about your friend Scott ignoring you. When you got upset because you thought he ignored you, you were not dealing with reality.

And here is an additional challenge with not dealing with reality. When you make up a false story, you will work hard to collect all the evidence that you can, to prove that your story is true.

It happens all the time, and you will save yourself time and energy, and create Meaning and Fulfillment, when you understand the real issue.

But there is yet another challenge. Sometimes when you learn what the real issue is, you don't like it. And then you have to deal with the difficulty and discomfort of handling it.

MATH CLASS, PART FOUR

I eventually asked my students how things were going. They said they were working hard and they did care. But, they felt like I was not giving them credit for their effort. And, though they were questioning whether I was a good teacher, they did think I cared.

Then I knew what was real and what was a false story. I could then let go of my anger and frustration, but I did have to face the reality that they didn't think I was a good teacher.

Thankfully, I was able to use that as motivation to improve my teaching. I was willing to take responsibility for my actions.

PLAY ABOVE THE LINE

Remember: when you Play Above the Line, you are responsible, you take ownership, and you take accountability. Regardless of the circumstances, you begin to see the world as in your control. You Stand in your power and you begin to take charge of what happens in your life. This is how the necessary perspective shift happens, and it is how it happened in my classroom. 200

If you constantly have the perspective that things are not fair, nothing is your fault, and you are a victim of circumstances, then your journey to Meaning and Fulfillment will be very, very long and unfulfilling. Until you shift your perspective, you will be stuck.

Your foundation of Knowing Yourself and Trusting Yourself makes it okay for you to make a mistake or be at fault, so you are confident enough to be open to understand other people.

Empathetic Communication

When you have something at stake—which is always, when you Launch Your Life—it is your responsibility to communicate effectively and act appropriately. The key to understanding people is to learn what "language" they speak. You want to communicate and act effectively, so you take it upon yourself to figure out a way for the listener to understand, and for your actions to be helpful.

LITTLE KICKERS SOCCER

My six-year-old son is playing soccer under two excellent coaches.

They have a lot of skill, a ton of knowledge, and they have a lot of interest in conveying their knowledge of soccer effectively. They know the game of soccer like experts, but, what makes them excellent coaches is that they are able to understand what level and amount of information each kid is capable of absorbing. Their language is age-appropriate, their body language is age-appropriate, and the concepts they're teaching are age-appropriate. They are able to convey soccer concepts in a way so the kids can hear it, like it, understand it, and are able to execute it.

And guess what? The kids absolutely love Coach Ryan and Coach Brian.

The steps to Empathetic communication will be explained in this section. It begins with Real Listening, continues with paying attention to meaning, chunking information, being able to identify the type of communication that is happening, and matching style and language. Then the section wraps up with pushing softly, entering into the complexity, and, finally, Playing Huge.

These are the concepts that help explain the brilliance of Coach Ryan and Coach Brian.

REAL LISTENING

Real Listening is working to hear what the other person is saying and how that explains the way they understand the world. Real Listening is putting aside your need to be right and relating to what the other person is saying. Real Listening leads to understanding another person's Know Yourself. You want to validate other people's Know Yourselfs.

Real Listening happens when you sit with someone and work to hear the words coming out of her mouth, to interpret her body language, and you are present and engaged with her. You are open and ready to be receptive to what she has to say.

If your Silly Self-Talk gets turned on, or if you are in an emotional space (e.g., angry, sad, excited), you will not be able to do Real Listening.

When you listen to validate *yourself*, you are listening for something someone says that you can relate to, something you can agree or disagree with, something you have ideas about, some experience you have thoughts about, or something you feel intelligent about. Then, once the other person says that something, you begin either to respond verbally, or you get into your own head and begin thinking about your own understanding.

There are times to validate yourself or test out theories, but, when you do Real Listening, you listen to learn about another person or another living thing.

Real Listening is the difference between saying, "I know exactly what you mean," and asking, "What do you mean by that?" When you ask a thoughtful question, you validate another person's Know Yourself.

THE MEANING OF THE COMMUNICATION

The meaning of any communication is the message received by the listener. As the listener, the idea in Empathize is to understand the meaning the speaker intends to convey, not how what the speaker says applies to your Know Yourself.

As the speaker, it is essential to remember that the meaning of your communication is the message that is received by the person you are communicating with. If you have a brilliant idea, but convey it in a way that doesn't make sense, you can't assume that the person you're speaking to understands what you are saying.

This happens in classrooms all the time, including my math classroom. I wanted to help my students learn math, and I was able to do it, but the way I was communicating didn't work for them. The meaning of my teaching was not what I intended it to be; the meaning of my teaching was what they were receiving—which meant there was no meaning in my communication.

You certainly have had a teacher who was brilliant but boring. No matter how brilliant the idea he wanted to convey, if it was not able to be understood, it had no meaning at all.

CHUNKING INFORMATION

I remember visiting a preschool classroom filled with three- and four-year-old kids. A parent who was an accomplished musician was visiting the classroom that day to talk about music. I found it fascinating, but not a single one of the kids understood anything he said. He was talking about music as if he were talking to adults with some musical intelligence. He did not chunk his information at all, so his fascinating knowledge was rendered irrelevant because he did not Empathize.

UNIVERSITY PROFESSORS

Many professors are brilliant thinkers. But many have room to improve their communication skills. The reason (often) is Empathy and their inability or unwillingness to communicate their brilliant ideas in a way that is accessible to the students. Contrast this with Coach Ryan and Coach Brian, who are brilliant and excellent at empathetic communication.

In responding to someone, you want to chunk the information so you provide them the appropriate amount of information and at an appropriate level for them to understand. The professor with a huge amount of content knowledge about his subject has to decide what part is relevant and realistic for the day's class. I often ask myself, would I rather have my client take away any insight, or, would I rather have them take away nothing, but think I am really smart (and, perhaps, intimidating)?

THE GUITAR TEACHER

Fred teaches guitar. Fred also plays guitar and has recently been learning about guitar theory, new playing techniques, how to write songs, and other advanced guitar skills. He has been working hard to improve his music making and is superexcited about his progress.

Fred had a new student who wanted to learn to play the guitar. Because Fred was excited about his own new learning, in their first couple of lessons, he shared all his new insights with his student. He tried to jam all the stuff he'd been learning into the lessons with his beginning student. He forgot that he knows how to play the guitar, has been studying for a decade, and has spent tens of hours recently improving his skills.

As could be expected, the first lessons didn't go well. There was a complete mismatch of purpose, since Fred did not chunk his information. Because the student didn't feel understood, he didn't return after a couple of lessons.

Fred later reflected that he was not a very effective teacher, as several of his students did not return. He was always grateful when people came back after he had taken the time to reflect on his process and evaluate the level of the student. He then would slow down the process, and not jam stuff down their throats.

When you Empathize, you are able to realize that you don't need to share all the information you have with the student/learner. You are able to plug into the level of the learner, and the information the learner needs and wants. You are able to chunk the information to an appropriate level of challenge to keep the learner growing and learning. Then, you are able to extract from your knowledge base the tiny bit of information that you know will be relevant for the learner (its relevancy determined through your Real Listening). Then you can provide that information in a really meaningful way.

When you don't need to validate yourself by sharing the whole scope of everything you know, you can be profoundly powerful and effective. The ability to convey information in a meaningful way at the appropriate level of challenge is what makes you a great teacher, a great coach, a great leader, and a great friend.

IDENTIFYING THE TYPES OF COMMUNICATION

116 Through your work to Know Yourself, Trust Yourself, and be the OPERATER of your life, you have gained a lot of knowledge about how to reflect upon and evaluate your actions. When you Empathize, you use the same set of skills to understand another person.

By Empathizing, you bring understanding to the type(s) of communication someone is using. You can evaluate whether she is justifying herself in an attempt to trust herself; you can evaluate if he is an auditory person; you can identify how much the person knows about a certain subject. You can use any idea in *Launch Your Life* to reflect upon and evaluate what type of communication is being used by the person with whom you are interacting.

DANIELLE AND THE COMPUTER STORE

Danielle works at a computer store. When someone comes into the store to buy a computer, she has been trained to evaluate quickly that person's level of understanding.

Some customers know a tremendous amount about computers and can talk the language (processor speed, memory, resolution, etc.), and some know that they simply want to be able to turn it on and use it.

Danielle is evaluated by her company on how quickly she identifies the type of customer she is working with; she is also evaluated on how well she uses a kind of communication that helps the customer feel understood and able to make a smart choice. If she starts talking bits, bytes, RAM, 400 GB hard-drive to someone who just wants to know how to turn on the computer, a sale is unlikely. Similarly, if she talks about the on/off button to someone who is deciding between the new Intel processor and the seasoned Pentium processor, a sale is equally unlikely.

MATCHING STYLE AND LANGUAGE

When you Empathize with someone, you want to match their language. When you do so, you gain credibility and build rapport because it makes that person feel like you are listening and paying attention to him or her—because you are.

The more effective Danielle is at matching the style and language of the customer, the more likely she will be to have an effective interaction. If she talks about things that are too complicated for the customer, the customer does not feel knowledgeable. If she talks about the computer in terms that are too simple, the customer questions her credibility and capability of helping. The same idea can be applied to any interaction you have with friends, family, teachers, or anyone else.

PUSHING SOFTLY

I learned to push softly when I taught middle school math.

MATH CLASS, PART 5

In my classroom, I wanted my students to learn and understand math. I wanted them to retain the information they learned in order to be successful in future math classes. When they were having a bad day and were struggling to understand (or, more likely, I was struggling to communicate with Empathy), I pushed harder. I increased the pressure on them, I challenged them to work harder, and I gave them more work to do. As soon as I pushed harder, it became obvious that my students felt more threatened, blamed, dumb, ineffective, and overpowered.

It was like I was talking to someone who doesn't speak English, and, when they didn't understand, I spoke louder and more slowly, as if there was something wrong with them. Instead, I could have realized that the problem was that we were talking different languages, and I needed to figure out a better way to communicate.

Whenever I reached a Cusp moment—where something was at stake—I either fell back into my need to know myself or trust myself, or I pushed harder and tried to cram information into my students by force. I got louder and more stubborn.

Remember the Cusp moments from Play Huge (see page 80)? The time when you either say Yes! or no? The Cusp moment in Empathize is the moment you decide to understand somebody, and the challenge is, it always comes when you have something at stake. It might be in an argument with a friend, teacher, or parent. It might be when you have to make an important decision. It might be during an emotional experience. Whenever it comes, it will be tempting to push harder. But, when you Empathize, you push softer.

Water is fluid, soft, and yielding. But water will wear away rock, which is rigid and cannot yield. As a rule, whatever is fluid, soft, and yielding will overcome whatever is rigid and hard. This is another paradox: what is soft is strong.

Lao-Tzu (600 B.C.)

Pushing softer means honoring Secret #5—Always Honor Sustainability, because it means opening up to understanding another person or other people. It means reading the other person's body language, using your Real Listening skills, asking questions, and matching their style. It does not mean getting louder, insisting you are right or know what is best, or making demands. It is realizing that the way to get to your goal—Meaning and Fulfillment—is taking the path of understanding people.

List A	List B
FEELING...	**FEELING...**
Supported	Threatened
Cared for	Blamed
Understood	Attacked
Challenged	Dumb
Capable	Ineffective
Resourceful	Overpowered
Empowered	

- Choose which list would help you accomplish a goal.
- Choose which list helps people learn most effectively.
- Choose which list will create Sustainable results.
- Choose which list makes people feel loved.
- Choose how the Real You wants to make people feel.

In my classroom, this meant listening to students' questions and providing information in a way that made sense to them.

When you push softly, you help people feel powerful, capable, and ready to Play Huge. You also engage in the kind of relationships that will make a difference in the world.

ENTERING INTO THE COMPLEXITY

Remember the part of the story about my math classroom when I had to deal with the reality that my students did not think I was a good teacher?

When that happened, it was a Cusp moment for me. I was faced with the choice either to ignore the issue, or to sit with it and figure out a solution.

You are faced with issues like this whenever you have an argument with someone or you disagree with something someone says or does. When there is a difference of opinion, an emotional response, an action that causes a reaction, a difference in values, or a difference in how to get to an outcome, it can be an uncomfortable and challenging space.

The ultimate measure of a person is not where one stands in moments of comfort and convenience, but where one stands at times of challenge and controversy.

DR. MARTIN LUTHER KING JR.

This uncomfortable and challenging space is one we too often avoid because of the potential complexity. But this is the space in which Meaning and Fulfillment grow and develop. A life well-lived is a life that goes toward complexity and discomfort, not away from it. Play Huge and enjoy this space, because it is where you connect to people and where you learn. Getting good at navigating this space will lead to lots of good things, including the life the Real You desperately wants.

When you reach real ability,
you will be able to become one with the enemy.
Entering his heart, you will see that
he is not your enemy after all.

—TSUJI

PLAYING HUGE

79 In this entire section about Empathetic communication, you have the chance to say, "Hey, this is not my responsibility," or ask, "How come I have to do the work and compromise?"

You might want to argue that it's the student's responsibility to adapt to a boring teacher. You might want to argue that tough love is better than coddling people, so pushing softly sets people up for failure. You might want to advocate for avoiding complexity, but, if you do, check how huge you are playing.

You get to choose how you want to play. Are you going to play small or step up and Play Huge? Remember that when you 200 Play Above the Line, you don't make excuses. And also remember that, whether or not other people perceive you playing small, it doesn't matter—you know. It is in your heart.

The more huge you play, the more profound your impact in the world. There are constant opportunities to Play Above the Line. The question is simple. How Huge are you going to Play?

Situations in Which You Will Use Empathy

The ability to Empathize can be used in many different situations. The most basic distinction is whether you are a listener or an information provider. In a friendship or family situation, Empathy is used mostly to understand other people and to build a relationship with them. But, in a professional or leadership situation, Empathy can be used to provide information in the most meaningful way possible.

PERSONAL AND COLLEGIAL RELATIONSHIPS

Being Empathetic will greatly improve your relationships with your parents, your friends, your teachers, your kids, your boss, your colleagues, and any person with whom you communicate.

At the essence of Empathize is the ability to respond to other people in a way that is congruent with their Know Yourselfs. By using their language, matching their body language, by doing something they would want you to do, by asking for further explanation, and/or by perceiving accurately their understanding of the world, you will gain credibility and rapport. People will feel at ease around you. Whether with a friend, a significant other, a parent, or a teacher, when you indicate you are making an effort to listen and to understand, they will feel validated and their self-esteem will increase. They will be more trusting. They will feel cared for. And they may begin to take more risks to connect to their Real Yous.

SYLVIE AND THE BIKE

My daughter and I ride our bikes to school every day. When I take my bike out of the garage, I have to balance it before going to shut the garage door. It's an unpleasant moment in my day because my bike often falls. One day, Sylvie walked over, put her hand on my bike seat, and held the bike up. I had not asked her to do it, but she realized she could be helpful, and she made an effort to help me.

It made me feel incredibly loved and understood by my four-year-old. That day, and whenever she did it, we had a fun and playful bike ride to school because we both felt happy and connected.

When you respond in the world of others, you will find that conversations are much easier because people open up when you enter into their worlds. While you may not agree with their ways of thinking and their actions, at least you will be showing that you are willing to consider their perspectives. They will be more willing to engage in a solution conversation, and will certainly be more open to your perspective when you are open to theirs.

TEACHING OR LEADERSHIP RELATIONSHIPS

In this scenario, it is likely you will be using many of the concepts in Empathize. But, when you are in the position of providing information to other people, whether in a classroom or professional presentation, as a teacher or a leader, you will want to pay close attention to skills like Real Listening, the meaning of the communication, chunking information, pushing softly, and entering into the complexity.

When you bring consciousness to how to convey your knowledge, and you practice humility and patience, you are able to engage people's own natural curiosity and motivation. People then start to grow and to expand how they know themselves and how much they trust themselves.

LEADERSHIP

As a teacher or as a leader, you want people feeling like they understand, they're creative, and they're smart. When you have a group of people feeling positive about themselves and knowing they're able to create outcomes you want, then you start to have powerful results in a classroom, business, or on a sports team.

Great teachers and great leaders are able to understand how their peers, students, or employees understand information. Then they are able to convey information in a way that will motivate and inspire. By using Empathy, you are supporting people feeling great about themselves, and you are providing information in ways that are congruent for how people know themselves.

A Teacher with Four Students

Imagine a teacher who has to convey the same information to four students. When the goals are for each of the students to understand, to feel like an important part of the team, and to be motivated and inspired, great teachers know they're going to need to convey that information four different ways to reach each of the students.

Great teachers know that the meaning of the communication is the message received. They realize they must provide the information in the way that is most meaningful for each person.

They want to build relationships, create synergy, get people to feel great about themselves, start to be motivated, and feel a sense of urgency and agency.

"THROW IT TO SECOND"

I coach my son's little league team of six-, seven-, and eight-year-olds just learning to play baseball.

One player on the team is always very hesitant to throw the ball when he picks it up. My assistant coach, Britany, and I were trying to figure out what was going on.

Whenever he picked the ball up, we would say, "Throw it to second. Throw it to second. Throw it to second." And he would stand there, hesitant and confused.

Our assumption was that he wasn't paying attention, didn't understand the game of baseball, and just didn't care very much.

Finally, one day Britany was talking with him, and began to do Real Listening. He said, "When you tell me to throw it to second, I don't understand why I would throw it to a base. You've told me to throw the ball to my teammates, and make it easy for them to catch. I don't understand why I would throw the ball to the base and not to my teammate standing on the base."

When my assistant reported this, we were fascinated. It would have been easy to blame the player for not understanding what we meant, but instead we were fascinated. He didn't understand the baseball term "throw it to second," which means throw it to the player on second, and so he was confused. And he didn't understand why we were saying, "Throw it to second," and not saying, "Throw it to Ezra" (who was covering second).

Once we understood how he was interpreting our words, we were able to explain to him what to do in a way that was helpful for him, both so he could learn baseball terms and so he could understand what to do with the ball when he picked it up.

Being able to Empathize will have a tremendous impact on every one of your relationships. It will enhance the work you do and your ability to create the life you want to create. I believe that the ability to Empathize is what truly creates positive change in life. It's About People.

THE PATH TO EMPATHIZE

Up to this point, *Launch Your Life* has been about you. This is where it transitions to be about the other people (and living things) in your life and in the world. Now, Playing Huge, Knowing Yourself and Trusting Yourself, Playing Above the Line, and your ability to be the OPERATER of your life are your foundation to embark on the path to Empathize. Here is where you move beyond yourself. Your foundation will open the doors to Real Listening, effective communication, and entering into the complexity of relationships.

You will have to Play Huge on the Empathize Stage to create Meaning and Fulfillment. It's the place to practice, practice, practice, and then practice some more, and what follows is the playbook for how to practice your Empathize.

The Chapters

PLAY HUGE

Remember (see page 79) that there are three steps in Play Huge: (1) make an effort, (2) failures and challenges, and (3) fun and feeling good. The first step on the path to Empathize is being willing to engage in the process. As you learn this skill, you will have to bring awareness and consciousness to your interactions with people. Having Empathy will not happen by accident; initially, it is a conscious effort.

By now you have learned to navigate many kinds of Cusp moments, and there are more opportunities ahead. Yes!

KNOW YOURSELF AND TRUST YOURSELF

The reason Know Yourself and Trust Yourself are all about you is so you can get to a place where you can Stand powerfully and feel confident with the Real You. When you doubt the Real You, then your ability to be available to other people is significantly compromised.

The degree to which you Know Yourself and Trust Yourself is the degree to which you can Empathize. These foundational steps provide the building blocks to connect with other people and live a life full of Meaning and Fulfillment.

The Secrets

PLAY ABOVE THE LINE

You are in control of your life. You are powerful. There is every reason to Stand in your power and your abilities.

When you compromise this by making excuses and blaming circumstances, you enter into a compromised place in which connecting with people is much more difficult. This step is all about making the process of creating relationships easy for you.

Live with ownership. Take responsibility. Keep challenging yourself to higher levels of the Upward Spiral.

BE THE OPERATER

The ability to call *Time-out* and get connected with the big picture is a great skill for yourself. But the power and possibility of it are greatly amplified when you Empathize.

This step—using your ability to see the big picture so you can understand where other people are in their process—is crucial to Empathy.

There are two levels on which this ability comes into play. You have to be able to manage yourself and to keep yourself from getting sucked into a confrontation or unproductive emotional situation. And, you want to use your skill to understand what is happening with the person/people you are interacting with.

That is your foundation. It's what has led you to this point at which you are ready to learn the components of the path to Empathize. Get ready to learn Real Listening, effective communication, and the opportunity to enter into complexity in dealing—with Empathy—with the challenges you will face.

Learn Real Listening

317

The way to learn how to listen is to practice, practice, practice.

REAL LISTENING–THE BASICS

There are some basic, and, perhaps, obvious, things to pay attention to when you are listening to someone. This applies to everyday listening, but has added importance when you want to use Real Listening to connect with someone.

GOOD PRACTICE		UM...NOT GOOD
Eye Contact	**EYES**	Wandering, looking around, focused on anything other than the person you are with Staring intently
Open, positive position–at your side or folded in your lap	**ARMS**	Crossed (any kind of "closed" position) Hands dug into your pockets
Open and available	**EARS**	Headphones, earmuffs, anything covering, or in, your ears
Calm and receptive Facing them	**BODY LANGUAGE**	Turning your back, looking at a book (or anything), engaged in something else, distracted
Remember to breathe!	**EXTERNAL INFLUENCES**	Phone ring, email messages, text messages, headphones, etc.

All the things on the *Um...Not Good* list are things that send a message that you are not ready to listen to, or be engaged with, the other person. How you hold your body impacts how the other person feels. Studies estimate that upwards of 90% of communication is nonverbal. This means your words communicate less than 10% of what you are saying. The impact of this, while listening, is to be certain to hold your body in a position that communicates you are ready to listen to the person/people in front of you. You want to make them feel they are important, you care about them, and you are ready to Empathize.

ASK CLARIFYING QUESTIONS

When you ask questions, be guided by your curiosity. But, be careful not to steer what the other person has to say, simply because you are curious.

When you do Real Listening, you can ask questions, but the kind of questions you ask is important. When asking questions, your intention should be to deepen your understanding of the other person, while allowing him to maintain or deepen his thought process. The intention of your questions should not be to validate yourself, to agree or disagree, or to stump the person. Empathy is not about proving you know something about the situation being spoken about. You want to use questions to deepen your understanding of the situation and the person.

One way to do this is to use open-ended questions, rather than yes-no questions. The easiest way to do this is to begin your question with "how" or "what." When you ask this kind of question, there is an endless number of answers, and you encourage a response of many words.

YES OR NO RESPONSE		OPEN-ENDED QUESTIONS
Are you thinking about what I said?	**Becomes...**	What do you think about what I said?
Do you like the movie?	**Becomes...**	What did you like about the movie?
Do you have anything to prove your point?	**Becomes...**	How can you prove your point?
Did you think about what majoring in that subject will mean?	**Becomes...**	What considerations did you take into account before choosing that major?
Did you consider any other schools?	**Becomes...**	What were the criteria you used in choosing schools?

Asking people really to be clear about what they mean helps you understand their Know Yourselfs. If they use a term, rather than assuming that you're using the term in the same way, ask them to explain it. One of my clients recently said she's often "white-knuckling it." I had some idea of what she meant but was curious about what exactly she was saying, and, in the spirit of Empathize, I asked, "What do you mean by white-knuckling it?"

REPEAT BACK

A great technique I use with my clients in every coaching session is repeating back what I hear. I remember, when I learned the technique, that I felt goofy repeating back what I had just heard, but this has at least two functions. It tells the speaker you are listening, and it gives her a chance to change what she said or meant.

In order to begin to repeat back effectively, practice the following techniques. The first is mirroring back what they say to you. If they are telling a story and there is a pause, you can say, "What I hear you saying is...," and you say what you remember them just saying. When I do this, my clients often pause and reflect. Hearing their own words repeated back to them creates a moment of reflection. If nothing else, they feel listened to.

USE THEIR LANGUAGE

Another technique to use while you are repeating back and asking questions is to use their language. If they are talking about their hopes and dreams and they keep using the phrase "when I *get what I want*," then you can repeat, "What will happen when *you get what you want*?" By using their language, you step into their worlds. If you accidentally change their phrase from "get what I want" to "living your dreams," that sends a message that you are interpreting what they are saying, in your own understanding.

Remember: when you Empathize with someone, you want to match their language. Making them feel like you are listening and paying attention to them—because you *are*—sends an unconscious message that you understand them. Feeling understood in that way opens doors for them to feel at ease, to learn, and to trust themselves.

LISTEN FOR THE DEEPER MEANING

The powerful teacher, the powerful parent, the powerful leader, is able to see the meaning behind the communication. He or she is able to hear and understand what is really going on, by 119
identifying the structure of conversations. It is like calling the *Time-out* when you are the OPERATER of your life.

When you are talking to someone, there is often a difference between what they are saying and what they are conveying. As you get better at Real Listening, you can challenge yourself to listen for the deeper meanings of what people are saying. It is like listening between the words and getting down to the meaning of what they are saying and how they are saying it.

You can use *Launch Your Life* as the context of your understanding:

Oh, look. There is someone who is really trying to express his Real You. There's someone who is trying to validate herself and compare herself to another person. That's a Trust Yourself challenge. He just explained how stuck in an experience he is, and I can tell he can't see the big picture. He could call a Time-out. Her motivation is to be really good at something, but she is not willing to do the little things that will get her there. She just wants the results. He thinks he can just jump onto the Upward Spiral wherever he wants, but that is not a path to Honor Sustainability.

What is his learning style? What does she value? What does he Stand for? How does she trust herself? Is he trying to prove himself? What excuses is she making? Is he confident about who he is and how he is living his life? How does she handle Cusp moments?

You have begun to notice your Know Yourself and your Trust Yourself when you Play Huge, Play Above the Line, or use any other secrets. You do this as OPERATER of your life, and when you reflect and evaluate. But Empathize is not about you. This is when you take your knowledge and apply it to someone else's life.

In my coaching sessions, I have some questions with which I begin each session, and, while I'm listening, I am evaluating the place where my client is on that day. I am listening to what they're saying, and I'm also listening and observing the structure of their communication. I do this to get a feel for where they are so I know best how to coach them. I want to know if someone is entrenched in an emotional experience, or if they are in a reflective big-picture space.

They may be in a Trust Yourself moment. They may be doubting whether they know themselves. They may be trapped in an experience and are not connected to their Organize and Plan. Or, they may not answer the question that was asked, because they just keep on talking, or, perhaps, because they are thinking about something else.

118

Your ability to connect to the deeper meaning will enhance your understanding of people.

STUDY BODY LANGUAGE

As you just learned, body language is incredibly powerful and conveys significant information. But it is not just body language that is significant; you must pay attention to posture, energy level, and voice intonation.

THE SLOUCH

A seventeen-year-old client was talking about her hopes and dreams. When she began, she was sitting up in her chair, but, as she shared what she wanted in her life, she began sinking down in the chair. It looked like she was melting. Her words were saying how excited she was about her future. Her body language was communicating something very different.

Here are some other examples of differences in what people say with their words and with their body language:

- A person talking about how excited she is about her new job, in a completely lazy, unenthusiastic monotone.
- A person saying he is happy, while slouching, moving slowly, and dragging his feet as he walks.
- A person saying she really wants to talk to you while looking at a book, not making eye contact, not responding right away, and unable to remember what you just said or even what she herself just said.

When you look at someone's posture, notice if they are slouching, standing up straight, or somewhere in between. You can sense a person's energy level by noticing if they are energetic or tired, moving slowly or moving quickly, walking with a "hop" in their step or dragging their feet. You can pay attention to voice intonation, too; listen to whether a person is enthusiastic in what he is saying or if she is not very excited about what she is saying.

AVOID INTERRUPTIONS

The most common interruptions in today's world are provided by phones, emails, and text messages, but there are other ways to interrupt the person you are supposed to be listening to. Beware of relating their experience to your experience, finishing their sentences, and assuming you know what they are saying or going to say.

> **INTERRUPTED BY A PHONE CALL**
>
> I used to have a colleague who would answer his phone whenever it rang. We would be in a meeting, talking about something important, and the phone would ring. He would sometimes spend fifteen minutes on the phone while I waited.

Remember back to the story, "I Would Be Her Cell Phone" (see page 310)? The unconscious message when you are sitting with someone and they respond to someone or something not right in front of them is, "You are not as important as the call/email/text I am getting." In the same way, when you interrupt or finish someone's sentences, it sends the message that you are not interested in what they have to say, and you are absorbed in your own world and your own interpretation.

When you Empathize, you want to send the message that you care about the person you are with. You want them to feel cared for and safe. And you want to understand *their* world from *their* perspective.

ESCAPE ASSUMPTIONS

132

It is easy to assume that your interpretation of an experience is the same as someone else's interpretation of the same experience, but meaningful relationships only happen when you get beyond that assumption, when you deal with situations and feelings that really exist, and you take responsibility for how you respond.

Remember: everyone has a different catalog of experiences in life and unique interpretations of those experiences, and, therefore, everyone has different interpretations of situations and events. This is your opportunity to learn about them.

Remember my friend who was learning to Play Huge (see page 91)? He was making an effort to stop saying, "Like, ya know." And the first step he took was to become conscious of saying it, because he knew there was no way he was going to be able to stop saying it until he noticed when he was saying it. Then, once he got good at noticing when he was saying it, he began to shift what he was saying.

In the same way as my friend, you can begin to notice when you are making an assumption, and then learn how to ask a question that clarifies the assumption you are making. Then you get to decide which part of the assumption you want to pay attention to—the definition of terms, the impacts it has, whether the other person likes or doesn't like it, the intensity they feel for it, or how much they know about it.

MATH CLASS, THE END

My listening was getting softer and I was beginning to Empathize, but I was still pushing hard. I focused again on listening to the questions and explanations from my students. I worked to begin to understand their thought processes. I somehow realized that I had to be responsible for the communication of the material. I had to stop playing below the line and begin Playing Above the Line. And the challenge for myself that I came up with was to ask questions or answer their questions in ways that would keep them in their understanding of the problems. I wanted to make my responses congruent with the ways they were understanding and the ways they were working to solve the problems. Doing that dramatically increased their ability to do the problems and consistently get the right answers.

When I was listening to their questions and their explanations, I was able to get out of my world of understanding and into their world of understanding. I was able to provide answers congruent with their ways of understanding.

And, remarkably, once they felt acknowledged for their ways of thinking, and I shifted my criticism to understanding, they reported (and displayed) increased self-esteem. As their confidence grew, they shifted to another level of understanding, of feeling challenged, of feeling capable, and of being empowered to discover solutions.

They were able to evaluate whether their ways of doing the problems were the most effective way, and they were interested in doing so. They began to listen to the other students in a different way. They were no longer fighting for their own survival, so they could learn from their peers. Through this listening, they began to understand that there were many different ways to do the problems, and that learning many ways would allow them to be able to choose the easiest way for them to get the solutions. They were more open to the methods of other students.

When I Empathized with my students, a dramatic shift happened. When my objective as a teacher became to support the students learning on their own terms, their confidence increased, and, with it, their openness to solutions and possibilities. My challenges had been to be open to learning with my students, and to be the teacher without always being the expert (and having to be right).

Effective Communication

Two aspects of building relationships are key aspects of the path to Empathize. The first is to understand people. The second is to communicate effectively and respond to people. The following ideas all correspond to these two key aspects.

COMMUNICATE EFFECTIVELY

When you Empathize, the world starts to shift, your community starts to shift, and your relationships start to shift. Knowing people and having people know you has profound implications for Meaning and Fulfillment, as well as for change.

These things shift because you are understanding information and providing information on the level the other person is capable of understanding. You begin to be able to communicate information so that it's appropriate for the level of the person you're providing the information to. Your actions also begin to communicate your openness and willingness to connect with people and other living things. The profound shift is based on the amount of energy that is redirected from feeling bad about yourself and dealing with things that don't exist, to a place where all of us Play Above the Line and understand that It's About People. That is Empathy.

USE YOUR REAL LISTENING

When you have a solid understanding of someone and are ready to respond to him, you again focus on your Real Listening techniques. Asking clarifying questions, repeating back, using his language, escaping assumptions, and listening for the deeper meaning are all important for responding with Empathy. Continue to enhance your ability to use the Real Listening techniques and bring awareness to how people are responding to you.

Real Listening Cheat Sheet

Here are some questions you can use to prompt your listening and your efforts to understand people:

- What are elements you notice about his Know Yourself?
- Where does she Stand in her Trust Yourself?
- What is his perspective on the situation?
- What experiences inform her perspective?
- How would he explain what is happening?
- What are the things you notice that are different about your interpretation and her interpretation?
- What is his body language saying?
- How congruent is her body language with what she is saying?
- What are the real issues here?

When you understand people, it sets you up to respond to people, and, through your ability to understand them, you learn how to vary your communication to match what they're capable of understanding.

PUSH SOFTLY

Remember that, when you push softly, you use your Real Listening skills to gather information about the Know Yourselfs of other people. You read the other person's body language, ask questions, repeat back, and match their language when you provide information to them. You realize that the way to get to your goal of Meaning and Fulfillment is to take the path of understanding people and make them feel everything on List A.

List A
FEELING...
Supported
Cared for
Understood
Challenged
Capable
Resourceful
Empowered

Be Humble and Patient

Two key elements of pushing softly are humility and patience. When you are patient, you allow your Trust Yourself to emerge, which allows you to be present and engaged with another person. And, in that place, your humility helps you Trust Yourself and not have to be right. You are then ready to understand another person's Know Yourself.

In my teaching, I was eventually able to be patient when my students were asking questions and explaining their processes. Rather than interrupting or curtailing my listening, I stayed in my Real Listening. This patience allowed my humility to engage and for me to remember to trust myself, so I was able to let go of being right and be open to extracting information from my Real Listening. All that helped me Empathize.

In the Classroom

Everyone has experiences with teachers, speakers, or friends who are very smart people who don't convey information well. Failure or success when communicating is based on the ability to Empathize, because, when you do, you provide information congruent with the level of the person listening.

When you bring humility and patience to how you convey information, people can have fabulous learning experiences. People engage their own natural curiosity, and they thrive. They start to feel they know themselves and trust themselves, they expand their comfort zones, and they begin to create Sustainable knowledge bases.

CHUNK INFORMATION

Because you have an understanding of a person's Know Yourself, you can chunk the information you provide them. When you do that, you match an appropriate amount of information, and at an appropriate level, for them to understand. You are able to decide what part of your information is relevant and realistic for the person you are communicating with. Again, I often ask myself, would I rather have my client take away a small insight, or would I rather have her take away nothing but think I am really smart (and, perhaps, intimidating)?

UNDERSTAND PEOPLE

You want people feeling like they understand, like they're creative and playful and smart, and like they're good communicators. When you have a group of people feeling positive about themselves and knowing they're able to create outcomes they want, then they start to have powerful results, whether it be in a business, a classroom, or on a sports team.

LEADERSHIP

Great leaders are able to understand how people understand information, and how to convey information in a way that will motivate and inspire them.

If they have four people to whom they want to convey information, they know they're going to need to convey that information four different ways. The goal is for each person to understand, to feel like an important part of the team, and to be motivated and inspired.

A leader knows that the meaning of the communication is the message received. A leader, like a teacher, realizes he must provide the concepts he wants to get out into the world in a way that is meaningful for each person. She wants to build relationships, create synergy, get people to feel great about themselves, to start to be motivated, and to feel a sense of urgency and inspiration.

LEARN FROM PEOPLE

Finally, the path to effective communication, and therefore Empathize, includes the opportunity to learn. When you open yourself up to other people, you will begin to notice things about how other people live their lives, the ways people think and express their values, the Stands they take in the world, the impact they have with their colleagues, and the relationships they have with their families and friends. You may well find that some of those ways of being are of interest to you.

In many cases, this is how you learn. You notice other people doing something you think adds value to their lives and, then, you work to emulate it. Other people inspire you, and you make the effort to incorporate that into your life. This is an opportunity for you to expand your Know Yourself or challenge your Trust Yourself.

Enter into the Complexity

GET TO THE REAL ISSUE

At this stage of *Launch Your Life*, you are well aware of the importance of being able to step out of the moment to look at the context of the situation. The real issue is what is really happening in the world, not what is happening in your Silly Self-Talk. The way you get to the real issue is by calling *Time-out*, stepping back, and realizing you are getting sucked into a false story.

324

217

As you practice and get better at doing this, it becomes easier and easier. You are quickly able to realize if you are lost in a false story.

You are also able to recognize when the person with whom you are communicating is lost in a false story. You do this by using your Real Listening skills to understand how somebody else is interpreting events. If it is something that has happened, then you can ask direct questions, to clarify and learn how someone is feeling; if it's something that hasn't happened yet, you can be patient and wait for the event to occur. Whatever you do, the goal is to get beyond your assumption of what the issue is and identify the real issue so you can determine if it is something to let go of, or something you have to deal with.

DEAL WITH THE REAL ISSUE

There are many times when arguments can be avoided, and life energy can be saved, by simply uncovering upsets caused by misperceptions and assumptions. But, there are also times when a difference of opinion, an emotional response, an action that causes a reaction, a difference in values, or a difference in how to get to an outcome, is real. That can be an uncomfortable and challenging space.

It is a space you too often avoid because of the potential complexity and discomfort. But this is the space where Meaning and Fulfillment grow and develop. A life well-lived is a life that goes toward complexity and discomfort, not away from it. Enjoy this space. It is where you connect to people and where you learn. Getting good at navigating this space will lead to lots of good things, including the life the Real You desperately wants. Here is the Dr. Martin Luther King Jr. quote again, because it applies so well:

> **The ultimate measure of a person is not where one stands in moments of comfort and convenience, but where one stands at times of challenge and controversy.**
>
> *DR. MARTIN LUTHER KING JR.*

How do you navigate the real issues?

BE HONEST

375

You have a solid foundation in your Know Yourself and your Trust Yourself. You know how to Play Huge. And you are learning to Empathize. You don't have to pretend you are somebody you are not. There is no supposed to, or should, or anything. There is being honest and being the Real You. The opportunity when you are dealing with real issues is to be honest.

If you are angry, be angry. If you are disappointed at something that happened, then be disappointed. If you are at fault, Play Above the Line and take responsibility. If it is hard to take responsibility, say, "I am having a hard time taking responsibility for my actions." If talking honestly is challenging for you, then say, "Talking honestly like this is challenging for me." If you are making an effort to listen and understand, but the other person doesn't feel it, you can say, "I am meaning to learn to listen and understand you."

If someone did something you did not like, proceed as if you are helping them Play Huge by being honest about how you feel and what your thoughts are. When you hold each other to high standards, you honor the other person's Real You. When you get scared and are not honest, you let people off the hook. It may seem easier and feel more comfortable, but it does not create the Sustainable change the Real You craves.

USE SUPER REAL LISTENING

When dealing with difficult situations, being certain you understand the other person's perspective is crucial. Nothing diffuses a situation like an honest and sincere effort to understand. You should be ready for something unexpected to surface in the space of super Real Listening. It may be that someone is upset with you about something real that happened, but there may be more feelings behind the precipitating event. When you do Real Listening in the uncomfortable spaces, it creates a very safe space for people to share. Be ready for the unexpected.

STAY IN YOUR POWER

There is a big difference between saying, "You made me angry," and "I got angry when you said that." When you say, "You made me angry," you are giving up your power. You are saying that someone has the ability to impact your emotions and you are not in control of yourself. When you say, "What you did made me angry," then you are saying there was an action they took that you chose to react to. That is staying in your power.

You are in control of the Real You. You are in control of your emotions. You are in control of your actions. Take the responsibility for them. Take ownership of your actions and your reactions. And, if necessary, apologize.

PLAY ABOVE THE LINE

When you are responding to someone about a real issue, Play Above the Line. Be ready to take responsibility and ownership for your actions and your communication. Be ready to forgive other people for their actions and communication. Playing Above the Line in complex situations diffuses the energy in those difficult circumstances. And, even if you are hooked, you are able to let it go quickly.

NO FALSE GUARANTEES

Many times when you are in an uncomfortable situation, you want to try to make the uncomfortable feeling go away quickly. One way to do that is to say something to try quickly to diffuse the situation and make it "better." In Empathize, you learn how to respond in a way that is supportive, yet does not promise something you cannot deliver.

If you were late to a meeting with someone and she was hurt and upset, you may be tempted to say, "I promise I will never be late again," or "It will never happen again." But you cannot guarantee these results.

Instead, say something like, "I will recommit to being on time," or " I now have an better appreciation of how important my being on time is for you. I apologize."

I remember well the time right after my dad died. It was definitely an uncomfortable situation for most of my friends and other people who knew me. Many of them said to me, "I know exactly how you feel," and "It will be okay." I remember thinking, "You have no idea how I feel, and it is not okay, and it will not be okay."

Then a friend came up and said, "I am so sorry for your loss. I absolutely loved your dad and I am going to miss him tremendously," and gave me a hug. And I responded with an outburst of tears but managed to say what I truly felt, which was, "Thank you."

POSSIBLE BARRIERS

Ego

Your ego is a powerful thing. You learned this when dealing with the barriers in Know Yourself (see page 180). Your ego will want to compete, and you will want to compare your accomplishments with those of your peers and of others. When you go down the path of comparing your accomplishments with others, you fall back into focusing on yourself, and focusing on yourself is the work of Know Yourself and Trust Yourself, not of Empathize. So, comparing yourself with others is not part of understanding other people.

Inevitably, you will compromise your foundation; everyone does. But the question is how fast you will be able to get back to honoring the Real You so you can get out of your ego space and Play Huge.

It Takes Effort

Building your Empathy muscle is challenging. It takes a consistent and thoughtful effort.

This is not the place to get stopped in your effort to Launch Your Life. You have come this far, so keep on going. Hopefully, by this point, you will be feeling energetic and inspired to live with excellence and enjoy the process.

Disagree with People

When you enter into honest relationships with people, there will be disagreement. Sometimes you will realize that your values and the things that matter to you are different from those of the people you care about.

A disagreement with someone only becomes a barrier when you fail to navigate the Cusp effectively. A disagreement has the potential to be a barrier to Empathizing with people, but it can also be an opportunity to keep on learning.

Increasing Challenge

When you Empathize with people, you will be in a powerful place.

It is likely you have been in a pattern of communicating with someone (or several people) in which nobody is in their power. There are arrows flying everywhere, and no one is very good at avoiding them. So, when the pattern shifts, it will have an impact. (Note the opportunity for some Organize and Plan, so you can anticipate what is coming.)

266

That impact can raise a significant barrier to Empathize, because the arrows and energy the other person will throw at you may well be stronger, more mean, and more direct. They may try to recreate the pattern they have become accustomed to, by dragging you back down out of your Empathy.

STEPHANIE AND HER HUSBAND

Stephanie was a client of mine who worked with her husband, Phillip. Phillip was demanding, constantly asking for help from Stephanie. She would make an effort to help, but, usually when she did, Phillip would be critical. He had an image in his head of what he expected, and, if Stephanie's work did not exactly match his image (and sometimes even when it did), he let her have it by yelling at and criticizing her. This would often lead to a huge argument, with arrows being flung all over the place. She was really tired of it and began to change her pattern.

She worked to better understand Phillip before she did the work and also after she did the work. She Organized herself and worked her Plan. She stayed calm in the face of the yelling and criticism 118
which still came, despite her being more and more effective in her work. But she noticed that Phillip was getting more and more harsh in his criticism, and even more angry, as he tried to pull her back into their old pattern.

Eventually, Phillip began to respond, and was forced to change his way of communicating because he realized Stephanie was in a powerful place. He could no longer intimidate her and drag her down below the line.

The opportunity that exists here is to be strong, Stand on your foundation of Know Yourself and Trust Yourself, call *Time-out* as needed, and be open to keep on learning. You may find, as Stephanie did, that creating the change and relationships you want will take perseverance and a strong community supporting you, but you know how to make that happen. You can do it.

External Messages, Again

184 Will you be able to admit that you need to be more effective? Can you admit that something is your fault? Are you ready to take responsibility for what happens?

There has been a lot of energy given to the challenges you face because of our culture. There is advertising, there are schools, there are peers, and there are parents. And here comes more.

When we are faced with a complex situation, it is challenging to Stand up and take responsibility. It is so tempting to want to play below the line and revert back to justifying yourself. There are not enough people in our lives who Stand up and take responsibility. And without these role models actually Playing Above the Line and, worse, with the models of these people *not* taking responsibility and making excuses, it is easy to get lazy and play small.

Beyond the Barriers

You know better than to get trapped in these barriers by playing small and compromising the Real You. You know to get onto the Upward Spiral, begin with simple and easy steps, and, with perseverance and courage, enhance your skills. Once on the Upward Spiral, you can begin to build your community and remember the Real You, so that it is easier to Stand in your power.

You will feel deep satisfaction in your work to Empathize. It's About People, and your relationships with people are where you will find Meaning and Fulfillment in your life.

The beautiful thing is, that as you make the effort and learn all the skills it takes to Empathize, you will begin to create Sustainable change in your life. The solutions you create here are not short-term fixes and efforts. They are foundational aspects of finding Meaning and Fulfillment today, and for the rest of your life.

HUGE OUTCOMES—EMPATHIZE

I had **NO IDEA** how little I knew about my friends. It has been **WONDERFUL** getting to know people in a whole new and **DIFFERENT** way.

My **TEACHING** and leadership are so much better than they used to be. I love **LISTENING** to people and then working to create **NEW PATHWAYS** for them to deepen their learning and **PASSIONATELY** fulfill their potential.

I am able to see communication in a completely **DIFFERENT** way. I feel like my interactions with people have slowed down, so I can see the **MECHANICS** of the conversations and evaluate what is happening in my relationships. It makes me appreciate the **IMPORTANCE** of dealing with complex situations.

I feel like I am **PLAYING** at a much higher level. I don't make excuses anymore. I take **RESPONSIBILITY** for my **ACTIONS**. And I spend time considering possibilities I never even considered **BEFORE**.

I have more time and more **ENERGY**, and I feel much more alive. It is **AMAZING** how much time and energy I was wasting dealing with stuff that didn't exist. I feel **FREE**, **HEALTHY**, and ready to make a huge difference.

I have been exposed to many new **POSSIBILITIES** of ways to live my life. I am excited to keep on learning from **PEOPLE**, based on my listening to people.

My world has **OPENED UP**. When I treat people with **DIGNITY AND RESPECT**, they become more powerful, which makes me feel **POWERFUL** also. I am no longer the most important consideration in my **DECISION MAKING**.

I used to make all kinds of **ASSUMPTIONS** about people's motives. Then I would get really mad at them. Now I deal with **REALITY** and identify the reasons for their actions, and I can usually avoid my anger and **DEAL** with the issue.

Huge Outcomes: Text Version

And what happens when you get connected to people in a powerful way? What are the real-life ways learning to Empathize will help me make a difference?

THE WORLD SHIFTS

A world full of Empathy is a world that respects and thrives on difference and diversity. Instead of being ruled by self-interest and comfort, decisions get made through thoughtfulness and understanding. Decisions are made with future generations in mind. The field of consideration expands beyond what will be best for you right now and becomes one of consideration of others, awareness, and Sustainability. When this happens, challenges based on different perspectives are acknowledged and dealt with, not ignored or manipulated. When this happens, conflict is dealt with honestly and directly, not through deceit and power. The world shifts to a place where your field of focus includes what is best for the whole community. In the challenges we currently face, this is a crucial new paradigm of being.

FREEDOM

Your days become opportunities to transform your life and your community because you are able to deal effectively with complexity, and to be present with people. The freedom and energy you find in not being caught up in the private world in your own head, allows you tremendous freedom to have a positive impact on life. Your ability and willingness to Empathize will change your perspective on life into a world full of opportunities. This is the path to Meaning and Fulfillment.

Choices

Important choices in your life become clearer. You have the connection to the Real You and through Empathize you are able to deal with the implications, challenges, and communication of what you know is best for you.

RELATIONSHIPS WITH PEOPLE

Know Them

You will learn about people in new, different, and more profound ways. You will get beyond the surface and past all the superficial aspects of relationships, to enter into meaningful connections with people.

Increased Respect/Decreased Confrontation

You are able to understand the reasons for people's decisions, rather than acting on assumptions, or feeling there is a lack of respect. You are able to understand situations and react thoughtfully.

OPEN TO IDEAS

Thoughtful Consideration of Ideas You Previously Didn't Consider

You certainly have had disagreements with people about differences in what you believe to be important in the world or about how to do something. With the ability to Empathize and the knowledge that people have different ways they know themselves, you can use Real Listening to get inside their ideas. And, because you Trust Yourself, getting into their ideas will not threaten your belief in yourself, but, rather, will open up new avenues for your thinking and make you thoughtful about alternative perspectives.

Able to Agree and Disagree Thoughtfully

When you consider ideas you previously did not consider, you gain greater and greater understanding of what people are saying and their reasons for believing what they do. Being Empathetic allows you to understand their perspectives, and you can then make an informed and thoughtful decision about your own perspective and whether you agree or disagree with theirs. Because you listen to the alternative perspective, your disagreements are often respectful differences of opinion and, therefore, learning opportunities. You put aside judgment about people, which means everyone you meet is a possible member of your community, someone to learn from, and a potential friend.

LIVE IN REALITY

Profound Impact on the Quality of Your Work, Health, and Life

The freedom from the stress and anxiety created when you make up false stories will itself make you feel healthier and give you a positive perspective. But, further, when your Silly Self-Talk is quiet and you begin to deal powerfully with complexity, your confidence soars along with your courage. You are willing to live with discomfort and even desire the learning experience discomfort offers, because you Trust Yourself to know you can handle the situation.

When you enter this powerful place, you will enjoy an increase of creative thinking and problem solving, both of which are based on your level of Trust Yourself. In these ways and others, you will be more productive. Making the difficult phone call will become easy; things that used to seem like monumental challenges will just get done. You will feel free.

You will find you have a tremendous amount of time available to you. You will be able to be present in all aspects of life, enjoy life more, and, because of your courage and confidence, the quality of your work, health, and relationships will improve. You will become a powerful difference-maker in your own life, and in the world.

Ability to Impact Other Peoples' Production and the Quality of Their Lives

Beyond the impact you will have on your own life, through your willingness and ability to Empathize, that quality increase in your life will extend to the other people you interact with.

Your ability as a leader, a teacher, a parent, a child, a partner, and a friend, is enhanced tremendously. You have profound impact on people's lives. You honor the Real You and live in full, zestful expression, but, more importantly, you honor another person's Real You, and you make it safe for him to live his life in full, zestful expression.

When people are acknowledged for who they are, and they feel known and understood, they are more effective. The positive feeling of being known has a biological basis. When you feel safe, your brain functions in a way that allows you to be creative and playful, do critical thinking, and focus on what you want to focus on. It is called being able to do higher-order thinking.

When you feel threatened, scared, or vulnerable, you cannot do any higher-order thinking. Focusing only on your own survival, and not trusting anyone else, is not a very effective or pleasant way to live—and it is very lonely.

Your Empathy provides a gift to other people. It gives them the feeling of being known, which makes them feel safe in the world, which adds to the synergy around making a difference. This gift you give to people is the basis for *Launch Your Life*; it's the gift of Meaning and Fulfillment.

Foundational Terms

Despite *Empathize* being near the end of *Launch Your Life*, there are still foundational terms. And, in this case, there will be ideas included from two secrets, so you will get a review and a preview. They are Secret #4—*It's About People* and Secret #5—*Always Honor Sustainability*.

Amazing things will happen in your life when you *treat people with dignity and respect* and you *enter into their worlds*; you will begin to passionately fulfill your potential by using *Real Listening* and *pushing softly*. Your ability and willingness to *deal with complexity* will make it easier for you to *Leave No Trace* and *create community*, and you make a difference by including awareness of other people in your consideration of how you want to create your life.

WRAP-UP

The ability and willingness to Empathize is what *Launch Your Life* is all about. Because of its significance, it has its own stage in the Play Huge Theatre.

The moment you complete your Trust Yourself performance, a magical door you have never seen before opens up; a banner hangs above, saying, "Come, explore the Empathize Stage."

As you begin to climb the stairs toward the Empathize Stage, you get a strange sense that the number of stairs is dependent on the strength of your Know Yourself and Trust Yourself, but, around the next corner, you find a door.

What plays on the Empathize Stage is a story called "Resolution Corner."

"Resolution Corner" is about all the people in your life wondering about this Launch Your Life stuff you've been talking about. Some are curious about learning to launch their own lives. Others are highly skeptical about what you are up to. You are excited to tell people all about it, and you are getting ready to write a script to explain all your experiences and adventures, when you are interrupted by a loud THUD!

You look around, and see a notebook has dropped down in the middle of the stage. The cover says, "Read me before you proceed."

THE HISTORY OF RESOLUTION CORNER

Stephanie and Phillip were having trouble communicating (see page 351). They had very different learning brains and Know Yourselfs. Phillip liked direct verbal communication; Stephanie had difficulty with that kind of communication because she needed to be in motion.

After years of their kitchen being the location of their arguments, for some strange reason, in the middle of an argument one day, Stephanie walked out the door and down the street. Fuming mad and flustered, Phillip followed. They walked in silence for several blocks. Stephanie stopped at the corner eventually, looked at Phillip and asked, "What were you saying?"

It was the first time in a long time that Stephanie initiated the conversation. They proceeded to have a conversation full of direct verbal communication while they were walking down the street. Stephanie was much more able to walk and talk. Phillip found that he could explain himself as they walked without being interrupted. From that day forward, whenever there was a conflict or something important to talk about, they would return to their corner.

Resolution Corner was born: the place where what you care about is communicated to people you care about, in ways they can understand.

Resolution Corner is a place where you respond to the needs of other people because you realize it will enhance your ability to communicate effectively.

Resolution Corner is the place where you work to help people understand (and, in some cases, get onto) the Play Huge Stage, so, someday, they can mold and animate their own clay.

On the stage is a chair for you—your Real Listening chair. You are not the main character of this production; that role is reserved for all the significant people in your life. They come because they want to be understood. (Everyone wants to be understood. Everyone.)

At first you are excited that they are coming to see you, and, when they come, you barrage them with all you have learned in *Launch Your Life*, how it has helped you, and how it will help them. You are pushing them hard. They are courteous, and even nod a lot, but they usually don't come back for a second visit. You sense something is not working because no one is coming back to talk with you, so you begin to reflect and evaluate.

It occurs to you eventually that you cannot tell just one story about your path through *Launch Your Life*, because that one story works only for you. And who really wants to hear your story? People want to know how this will impact *their* lives.

With time, you begin to use your skills of asking questions, repeating back what they share, using their language, listening for the deeper meaning, and paying attention to their body language. And, when you engage in this kind of listening, you begin to learn about other people. You notice that, when you care about understanding them, they are far more willing to share honestly with you, and you are able to understand what is real and what is story. You begin to see opportunities to push softly by offering ways for them to get involved in your story about Resolution Corner.

But, just as you begin to think Resolution Corner is all fun and games, you realize that people carry a lot of emotion into relationships. The challenges people share with you help you learn to deal with complexity, and this reminds you that the journey to Meaning and Fulfillment happens on the Upward Spiral. It is not a place where everyone is perfect; it is a place where you (and hopefully others) are learning. There are plenty of arguments and disagreements on the Empathize Stage. But it is a place where the complexity of relationships is invited and worked through.

Thankfully, with time, you realize it is easier on the Empathize Stage to understand what the real issues are and what the stories are. Not a lot of time is spent dealing with things that don't exist, that were made up in someone's Silly Self-Talk.

With experience, it becomes obvious that the Empathize Stage is where you enter into the world of other people. Because of the freedom and increased energy created by being on the Empathize Stage, you feel the profoundly powerful place it can be. Exploring the creativity and challenge it takes to convey true stories makes you realize the potential for huge change to happen.

While in your seat on the Empathize Stage, you have developed the most honest and fun relationships you have ever had; you have increased your level of excellence tremendously; and people have consistently thanked you for the gift you have given to them in the opportunity to connect with their Real Yous and to be understood. As you reflect on Resolution Corner, you feel that your life is Meaningful and Fulfilling.

And it feels great.

Making a difference always does.

SECRET #5

Always Honor Sustainability

Launch Your Life is not intended to be hip and groovy. It is not intended to be sexy or the "in" thing. It is not a trend. It is not intended to create immediate gratification. It is not plastic surgery for your life.

Launch Your Life is intended to impact your life now and into the future. It is intended to guide you to make the kind of deep change in your life that you truly crave. The Real You does not want to hop from trend to trend to trend. The relationships you want are ones based in dignity and respect and that have been built on a foundation of Empathize. You want to create a life for yourself that is Sustainable.

As you get ready to take all the lessons from *Launch Your Life* into the world, and make your way around and around the Upward Spiral, there is one more secret to consider: Secret #5—Always Honor Sustainability

The way to make the Sustainable change you want is to take the moments when you feel inspired and most alive – those moments when you hear a lecture, read a book, see a movie, have a creative breakthrough, or whatever creates those moments—and create a way to feel that aliveness every day of your life. You commit to yourself that you are going to figure out how to continue to reenergize that feeling so it defines each day. Excitement and aliveness are easy to create; Sustaining the excitement and aliveness, however, is challenging.

What follows are the basics of what it will take to take on this challenge and Sustain the full and zestful expression of the Real You.

Practice Launch Your Life

Sustainability comes when you express your aliveness and honor the Real You. Sustaining a lie uses a lot of negative energy; Sustaining your authentic expression is energizing and takes acting on all the ideas from *Launch Your Life*.

The good news is that the tools and ideas from *Launch Your Life* were created with this secret in mind. The Play Huge Notebook and Powerful Portfolio help capture the moments of inspiration and the feelings of summer-camp-type experiences, so you can remember them at any moment. What you Stand for and all the ideas in Know Yourself, help you feel powerful in the world. Your Stand will help you remember what you care most about so you can align your actions to it. The Upward Spiral is all about taking small consistent steps; then, when you come to a challenge, you call Time-out (from Secret #2—Being the OPERATER of Your Life) and remember the Real You. And, in Trust Yourself, you learned to build a community that supports who you are. You take the steps to eliminate the negative, unsupportive relationships you have and build a community of people that demands that you show up and honor the Real You, every day!

See the Big Picture

As you learned in Secret #2—Be the OPERATER of your life, calling a Time-out allows you to see the big picture. Calling Time-out pulls you out of your experience and allows you to see the context of your decision. You avoid getting sucked into mistakes that are tempting but obvious when you look at your big picture Organization and Plan. You make decisions based on each of the variables in a scenario, not just the ones that favor your immediate best interest.

It works exactly the same when you honor Sustainability. You create a way of being that lasts a long time and takes all of the variables into account. And the way that happens is by honoring the Real You and not compromising what you know is right.

IMMEDIATE GRATIFICATION

Immediate gratification is an obstacle to Sustainability. Here are several examples of how immediate gratification results in a loss of Sustainability.

Cheating

A married person has a one-night stand, jeopardizing her marriage, her children's security, and her spouse's trust—all for the immediate gratification of an orgasm.

Buy on Credit

It's January and you are feeling the post-holiday blues. You see a big screen TV on sale and you think that having it would make you feel much better.

You do not have the money, but you buy this expensive item on credit because it's on sale right now, and there are "no payments due until next year." Despite having no plan for how to pay for this item, you create debt that may be with you for a long time, because you think that having this thing will somehow make that blah feeling go away.

Late Night Baseball

My son, Ezra, loves baseball. He loves playing it, he loves talking about it, and he loves watching it. But, unfortunately, he cannot watch any of the playoff games because he is asleep. He is missing out on the best time of the year for baseball—watching teams and players compete to win the World Series.

All adult baseball fans remember watching the playoffs as kids. It's the time when memories are created, players become legends, and the love of baseball is cultivated. (And, in our case, as Cubs fans, we learn to deal with disappointment.)

In the past ten years (or more), because of television ratings, and therefore, revenue, playoff baseball has been played at times when kids are asleep. Ratings are best when the games start at 8:00 p.m. Eastern Time. That means games end between 10:00 p.m. and 1:00 a.m. (A recent game ended at 1:47 a.m.)

This is a classic short-term win at the cost of long-term Sustainability.

The games used to be played during the day, creating a generation of people who love baseball, but the future is now at risk. There are no kids up that late on a school night, watching the magic of October baseball. They are missing out on the emotional connection to a game many of their parents love. And when they become adults, there will be no memories and no connection to the game.

Business

Many businesses deal with the issue of creating undesirable waste as a by-product of their manufacturing process. Oftentimes, they do not want to deal with the waste in a sustainable way because doing so is expensive, so they decide to get rid of it the easiest, cheapest way they can. They also decide to get their materials from a cheaper source despite the inferior quality of the materials.

In these actions they compromise the treatment of employees, the treatment of the environment, and the quality of the product. These decisions are often made because the company has to
129 report earnings every quarter; it looks good when profits are strong, which makes investors happy; they know that incurring the expense of safely disposing of their waste would adversely affect their short-term earnings..

This is a classic case of immediate gratification. The company is creating a big problem in the long term, both by not thoughtfully disposing of their waste and having employees deal unsafely with the waste. The company is also producing an inferior product, both because of cutting material costs and because of a disenfranchised work force. The long-term ramifications of the immediate gratification are that the business will lose customers, have to deal with an unmotivated work force, or—worse—hire and train new people (a huge expense), and deal with the implications of ignoring their waste.

NEW MEASURE OF PROGRESS

There are an increasing number of businesses who are defining progress, not on the financials from this quarter, but on the quality of their product, the health and passion of their employees, their ecological impact, or their leadership/stewardship in communities. They are choosing to base their decisions on what will sustain their business over time. They give up the sexiness and newsworthiness of immediate profits and prestige, to create security and Sustainability.

It would be convenient for a business to ignore the implications of their short-term actions, but it is not responsible and it is not good for the sustainability of their business. In a similar way, Baseball is compromising the future of their sport/brand for what is best for them right now. They will lament the absence of playoff memories in the coming years as their fan base decreases.

It is time to shift the way we do life and business. And along with the rest of *Launch Your Life*, a key secret is Always Honor Sustainability

Awareness of the power of honoring Sustainability is increasing dramatically, but reversing these trends and honoring Sustainability is not a new concept. Here is one historical iteration of this concept.

From the Great Law of the Iroquois Nation:

Look and listen for the welfare of the whole people and have always in view not only the present but also the coming generations, even those whose faces are yet beneath the surface of the ground—the unborn of the future Nation.

Bring Awareness to your Actions

Next you will learn about two concepts that will help you bring awareness to your own actions. When you practice the ideas of Leave No Trace and 1/N Consciousness, you create Sustainable relationships because these ideas are based on treating people, property, and other living things, with dignity and respect, like you learned in It's About People. By creating these sustainable relationships you are shifting your consciousness; by expanding your awareness beyond what is immediately convenient and beneficial to you, you are learning to see the big picture and honor Sustainability.

LEAVE NO TRACE

When you Empathize, you enter into the world of other people. Entering that place opens up your ability and desire to consider other people.

Leave No Trace is an idea that comes from the world of being outdoors, from hiking, camping, backpacking, and more. The idea is that you leave a place in better condition than when you found it.

If you use a picnic table in the local park, or a tent site in the backcountry, or a conference room in an office, or someone else's classroom, when you Leave No Trace, you consider the impact of your use on the people who will be using the same space after you. By cleaning up after yourself and improving the space, you make an effort to make their experience easier and more enjoyable.

You can do this by taking care of your trash—including dealing with messes left by others. If there is firewood available at the campsite when you arrive, then you ought to leave the same for those who come after you. If the trail is hard to find, then you can build a cairn to help those who follow identify the trail more easily than you did. If you move all the tables, desks, and chairs in a room you use, move them back as you originally found them. The specifics of what you do to Leave No Trace are not what is significant. What is significant is that you extend your consciousness beyond your own convenience. You never count on someone else to clean up after your mess.

Leave No Trace is a mind-set of personal responsibility as a consideration of other people. It is Sustainable because it keeps you out of the place where your self-importance undermines your treatment of other people.

Obviously a Leave No Trace ethic can be practiced anywhere and anytime. Your actions have a positive impact on the people who follow, as well as having a positive effect on the space you are using. It creates Sustainability because it feels good when you are thoughtful about other people, it honors It's About People, and therefore it enhances your journey to Meaning and Fulfillment.

1/N CONSCIOUSNESS

Extending your consciousness is a necessary attribute when you are part of any community, whether it be a group of friends, colleagues at work, classmates, or those with whom you live. In situations where your needs and your comfort are not the only ones to consider, your Empathize skills will come in handy.

While intentional communities are quite rare, and something not everyone is interested in, the challenges that arise in them are the same in other kinds of communities, such as groups of friends, work colleagues, or classmates, but they tend to be more intense.

Magic

There is an intentional community in Palo Alto, California, called Magic (see page 255). When I was at Magic, there were nine people living together in the same house. A great principle of theirs is to have a 1/N Consciousness. This means that you are just one out of "N"—that is, how many people you are sharing space with (in their case, nine).

This demands that you expand your awareness to include how your presence and actions will impact others. If you leave a mess in the kitchen, then someone else will have to deal with it; if you eat all the best food every day, no one else will get to enjoy it. In other words, there are basic considerations important to being a thoughtful member of a community.

This concept does not apply just to Magic, but many situations in which you will find yourself.

Donuts

Imagine that when you get to school in the morning, your teacher has brought donuts. Because you love donuts, you eat one and say thank you. But one of your friends get to school later than you, so she doesn't get one. Your teacher likes bringing donuts, and you consistently arrive early, so the same thing happens the next day, and the next. You likely are happy because you continue to get donuts, but your friend consistently misses out.

Or here is another scenario:

Dishes

You don't like doing dishes, so, when you use a dish, instead of washing it right away, you put it in the sink with all the other dishes. You figure that whoever ends up doing the dishes will not notice the one more dish you put into the sink.

When practicing a 1/N Consciousness, you take into account that you are not the only one who wants a donut and doesn't like doing the dishes. And, just because you get there first, that does not entitle you to a donut every day, just as your not liking to do dishes does not disqualify you from doing the dishes. The 1/N Consciousness allows you to have and enjoy the donut, but not every day. If you have it today, then tomorrow let others have a chance. Wait until all have enjoyed the treat before your turn comes up again. In the same way, you don't have to do the dishes every time, but, if there are three people putting dishes in the sink, then you ought to do the dishes 33% of the time (or work out some other deal using honest communication).

Like when you Leave No Trace, when you practice the idea of 1/N Consciousness, you are creating Sustainable relationships because they are based on treating people with dignity and respect. You live in a place beyond self-indulgence and self-focus and you base your actions on awareness of other people.

In the effort to fill up your life with powerful feelings, full and zestful self-expression, and Playing Huge, the implications of bringing awareness to your actions and respecting yourself and other people will have a huge impact.

Create Synergy with a Community

Creating Sustainability is learning from those moments when you go to a weekend workshop, have an inspiring conversation, hear a performance, or have a creative breakthrough, and you get that fired-up feeling, and commit to yourself that you are going to do something about it. But what happens when the next day comes, and you don't feel quite the same? It is hard to recapture the feeling. When you honor Sustainability, you figure out how to continue to reenergize that feeling so it defines every moment of your life.

I have seen this happen during the years I worked at summer camp. The campers would have these wonderfully powerful experiences, but, as soon as they got back home and into their daily routines around all the people who were not part of that learning environment, all the passion and excitement drained out of them. In your own life, think of the times that you have heard, seen, or done something that totally knocks you alive and you commit to yourself that you will get involved tomorrow, but when tomorrow comes you do not follow through.

Remember my friend Alvin who is an excellent teacher (see page 286)? Being in his class was amazing. Again, if you have ever been part of this kind of learning environment it is incredibly energizing; the learning is profound; and the challenge is massively motivating because the learning comes in the form of supportive community (let's hope that creating this kind of learning environment is the goal of all our teachers and leaders).

We all crave this kind of environment. We want to be challenged. We want honest feedback. We all want to be held accountable for our gift to the world.

But we cannot do it alone. Having your support community in place to create synergy helps make possible all those magical things you want to create. Magical things do not happen out of nowhere; they happen and they last because you are operating with a high level of excellence. And you operate with a high level of excellence when you and your support community choose to create a synergistic learning environment.

When you are honoring the Real You by treating people (including yourself) with dignity and respect, you are challenging your Learning Edge. When you have a support community that challenges you, honoring Sustainability just happens. Like everything, you have to work to create and Sustain it, but when you learn to live in that way it ceases to be something you have to do because it becomes who you are – the Real You.

Onward to Conclusion

Don't be satisfied with the amazing weekend retreat. Don't be satisfied with a great summer experience. Don't be satisfied with a job or a major that looks really sexy, but compromises what you Stand for. Don't be satisfied with that boy/girl who looks really sexy and has all the cool stuff, but is a complete jerk. Don't be satisfied with self-indulgence at the expense of others.

Be certain that you extend your consciousness to include other people.

Always Honor Sustainability and figure out how to take those amazing experiences and get them into every day of your life. If you experienced it at camp or on the retreat, you know it is possible, so use your Play Huge Notebook, your Stand, and your community to create it every day.

Remember: immediate gratification, despite how attractive it might seem, is an illusion; it is flashy and too good to be true, and getting away with it will never last. They always catch up with you. Launch Your Life is not a quick fix. It is not the pill that makes your symptoms magically disappear.

What the Real You wants is lifelong gratification. Launch Your Life works just like going to the gym every day…eating healthy food…honest communication (not successful lies). It is a way of being in your life that will dramatically shift how you experience the world.

This final secret challenges you to create change and Sustain it forever, and across all parts of your life.

TWO WEEKS LATER
DO NOT DISTURB
GOODWILL
COOK TO LIVE
RECIPES
SAUTES
CHEF
SOUPS
NOODLES
EGGS
I KEEP TRYING BUT I CAN'T GET ELLY TO EAT.
SHE JUST SITS IN HER ROOM.
AT LEAST SHE'S HERE. WHERE IS JAMIE?
I FEEL LIKE WE'RE LOSING THEM.
AT THE LIBRARY
THAT CURIOUS-ITY OF YOURS.
IT'S INTEREST-ING TO ME NOW.
I'VE BEEN DOING A LOT OF THINKING...
WHAT HAVE YOU BEEN THINK-ING ABOUT?
THE MORE WE HOLD ON TO THE KIDS THE MORE THEY'LL TRY TO GET AWAY.

WHAT WILL IT TAKE?

I DON'T LOVE IT. BUT I UNDERSTAND THAT IT'S IMPOR-TANT.
I'M UP TO A B AVERAGE!
B+
I APPRECIATE YOUR EFFORT.
YOU OK ELLY?
WHAT'S WRONG HONEY?
IT'S STILL MOVIE NIGHT SO I THOUGHT I'D MAKE ELLY'S FAMOUS BUTTERY POPCORN!

WHAT WILL IT TAKE?

COMMUNITY NIGHT
THE SAILING TRIP IS ALL SET AND WE'VE GOT THIRTEEN STUDENT SAILORS SIGNED UP!
GREAT! THANKS FOR INVITING ME BUT I'VE GOT SO MUCH TO DO THIS SEMESTER. I LOVE COUNSELING AND THE WORK IS FUN.
TONIGHT JAMIE AND THE BASEMENT BOYS
THANKS TO MY FAMILY FOR HELPING SET THIS UP.
HOW'S IT GOING COREY?
GREAT! DAD'S LEARNING A THING OR TWO ABOUT DOING REAL WORK.
NEW CENTER IS COMING SOON
HEY!
I'VE GOTTA GET IN ON THIS ACTION!

Conclusion

OUR JOURNEY CONTINUES—LET'S GO!

If you think back, you'll recall that this is where *Launch Your Life* started:

I remember taking his hands. I held them gently but firmly. I spoke to him quietly, hoping beyond hope that he could hear me: "Take my energy. I am healthy. I have lots of energy; you are just hanging on. Use my energy to get healthy. Please, please, take what you need."

My dad's death was a gift to me. It woke me up. It made me pay attention. It got me in action. But the gift came at too high a price.

My goal with *Launch Your Life*—as it is with my coaching, my speaking, and all my creations—is to help you launch your own life. Because you picked up this book, odds are you have a Gnawing Feeling that something is out of whack. You are not settled. You come ready; you want to Launch Your Life.

I want to give you the same gift I got when my dad died, but would never wish upon you the sadness and loneliness I continue to feel because of the loss of my dad.

What will it take? How can I convey the message without the heartbreak?

I hope I have provided a spark that gets you onto your own Play Huge Stage.

Remember, *Launch Your Life* is intended to be a wake-up call. It's either, "Hey, you could be doing more with your life," or, if you need the message to be more direct, it's "Stop making excuses, get off your lazy/insecure/apathetic/uncertain ass, figure it out. We need your brilliance, creativity, and passion, and we cannot afford to be complacent one more moment. Get. In. Action. Now."

It is time to get in action. There is no excuse to be complacent or complicit. *Launch Your Life* is my effort to scream out: LET'S GO!

My intention with *Launch Your Life* is to return you to what you have forgotten, and challenge you to get back the knowledge

- that life itself is bigger than material possessions, grades, test scores, college admittance, being right, a good résumé, the right clothes or latest gadget, or earning a certain amount of money. No hearse has an attachment for a U-Haul trailer. And your casket does not come with a self-storage unit.
- that you know this. You want to make a difference and your life will be complete only when you work to live every day in zestful expression.
- that a moment of laughter, a walk in the country, a creative exchange of ideas, simple touching, eye contact, or shared tears can create aliveness in a way that material possessions never, ever, ever will. Your relationships with people are where life happens.
- that the only moment you are promised is right now! You are mortal, and death is always in the background. If you take yourself in passionate—but not graceless—significance, you can have more fun than you currently have now, and be at least as effective.
- that all of us are humans. You are part of a we. And, yet, we are each unique.
- that you must unlock your listening. You must work to listen to and savor the uniqueness of other people. Real Listening challenges you to be present and engaged and to enter into the worlds of others, to where the gifts

of meaningful friendship, love, peace, understanding, and shared laughter reside.

- that all of you, young people *and* parents, stand a better chance of making it through life's inspiring and challenging moments as intimate and respecting partners, friends, sons, daughters, moms, dads, husbands, wives, and community members. We are not meant to make it through life alone. It's About People. Humanity is essential. Your community of loved ones and supporters is critical for your success, your joy, your meaning, and your laughter.
- that humor, celebration, gratitude, courage, passion, compassion, humility, powerful assertiveness, love, and creativity are all crucial elements to a life of Meaning and Fulfillment.

That is where *Launch Your Life* began, and now continues.

If I have done what I set out to accomplish, you are far beyond the Gnawing Feeling of Your Launch Pad and connecting with the Real You. If I have accomplished what I set out to, you are feeling inspired and energized; you are already in action and have logged some experience on the Upward Spiral. You know it is about the little things and the Upward Spiral Cycle—give your word...follow through on your word...give your word...follow through on your word. Create your foundation, make an effort, create mistakes and failures, and don't forget the key step of remembering the Real You.

You have gotten in touch with the Real You. By dealing with all the cultural messages, internal barriers, external barriers, and quieting your Silly Self-Talk, you have connected with that you, way down deep. By matching your actions with your deep desires, you have begun living the Real You, and it feels good. But more than just feeling good, it has begun to increase your core belief in yourself. This is Trust Yourself and has allowed you to enter into the world of others and help them reach toward their potential and their Real Yous.

Perhaps at some moments, you were struggling to get onto the Play Huge Stage, but that core belief in yourself made it easier. So now you are on the Play Huge Stage, and Playing Huge.

When you create failures, you Trust Yourself to be able to deal with the complexity and learn from what you create by (again) believing in the Upward Spiral and using the Upward Spiral Cycle. And your desire to challenge yourself toward excellence keeps on increasing as you honor the Real You by playing with high standards and Playing Above the Line.

Even as your energy level increases and you feel the freedom that honoring the Real You brings, you remember that, to create a life of Meaning and Fulfillment, It's About People. You reach out to your community to build a structure around yourself that supports you and enhances even more the level on which you Trust Yourself and Empathize.

The process of discovery and learning becomes delicious as you Play Huge and use your Know Yourself.

But life is challenging. Events happen and things you do can create significant difficulty and complexity. People get sick; people die; you make bigger and bigger mistakes; the stakes get higher.

Launch Your Life coaches you to enjoy today because tomorrow is not promised, and everything you want is available right here. You remember that you used to live in the place where change happened out there somewhere, where the life you wanted was out there only after you went to school, got married, changed jobs, or something else happened. But then you learned to Play Huge, and to take advantage of and enjoy all the opportunities and possibilities you have today, right here and right now, in your life.

But, still, you will face challenges, and you have learned that when you are in an experience, you have the capability to step back by calling *Time-out*; then you can look at the big picture, get grounded, and reengage as the OPERATER of your life.

And, in the challenging moments, because you treat people with dignity and respect and honor that It's About People and realize the importance of Playing Above the Line, people in your community (and outside it, too) will be there for you, and you will be there for them. People respond and respect when you are honest, responsible, and Empathetic. Because you are conscious of understanding other people on their terms and you remember the challenge to create Resolution Corner on the Empathize Stage of the Play Huge Theatre, you will be better equipped to handle the challenges that life inevitably will throw at you.

And all this leads to a life full of Meaning and Fulfillment.

Conclusion of the Conclusion

You have reached the "conclusion" but must be far from that. *Launch Your Life* must be the beginning of your journey. My intention was to provide a structure of activities and actions that will make it easier to maintain a Sustained effort throughout your life.

If *Launch Your Life* is a book that you read and then put down and never open again, I will have failed in my mission (a learning experience for me!)—even if you feel inspired and energized. Feeling inspired and energized is an essential first step, but it is not sufficient. It must be followed up by action. In order to make the difference you want to make, and honor the Real You, you must Always Honor Sustainability.

It will happen. I Stand powerfully for it.

We face unprecedented challenges in our lives today. We face ecological, economic, educational, moral, and human issues that threaten our future. Young people face a future that is increasingly uncertain. The dream of having each generation be better off that the previous one is in jeopardy.

You can make a difference.

I imagine a place in which everyone's life is launched and there is a huge event happening on the Upward Spiral. It is what I call the Meaning rEvolution.

In the Meaning rEvolution, everybody has a copy of their Play Huge Notebook, including their Stand and their Organize and

Plan. In the same way that people exercise in the morning or drink coffee to get themselves going, in the Meaning rEvolution people connect every day with what they Stand for, and reconnect with what they want to accomplish, and everyone shares their commitments for the day with each other. They talk about challenges, and they give hugs and high fives as they get ready to Play Huge and Play Above the Line.

In the Meaning rEvolution, we are inundated with positive messages that remind us how powerful we are. There are Play Huge Stages all over the place where we can be creative, take risks, make mistakes, and play, and where we get feedback about where we are on-target, as well as where we can improve. The feedback inspires us to Play Above the Line, and to remember that we are passionate about making the biggest difference we are capable of.

The most significant thing that happens in the Meaning rEvolution is that we are so profoundly connected to our Real You with a core confidence we can only imagine now, that we are always thoughtful about other people and we treat all living things with the respect and dignity they deserve. By creating relationships with people based on who we really are and who they really are, we spend our days in the freedom of feeling that our Real You is fully and zestfully expressed, Playing Huge, and loved.

You can make it happen for you. It is absolutely within your capability. As in Your Launch Pad, all you have to do is choose it. And, when you get past that Gnawing Feeling and connect with the Real You, visit *www.themeaningrevolution.com/launchyourlife*, where there are other people launching their lives. Please join us!

We will be waiting for your contribution to a future book called *Launched Lives: Real Stories of Playing Huge and Making a Difference on the Upward Spiral of Life (Your Experience Required!)*. The creation of that book starts today, so go—create your life in a way that will inspire others and will make the Meaning rEvolution happen.

Here we go. Ready? 1—2—3...LET'S GO!

Resources

Here are a few resources that you can utilize in your journey to Launch Your Life. The ones listed here are but a few; these and many more can be found by going to *www.themeaningrevolution.com/launchyourlife*. Good luck on your journey! Play Huge!

Learning Style Inventories

VAK Tests: This website contains a short test to determine your most dominant learning style: *https://olt.qut.edu.au/it/ITB116/gen/static/VAK/Tests.htm*

Personal Learning Styles Inventory: This is another website with a test that determines your most dominant learning style (this site requires that you fill out personal information before completing the test): *www.howtolearn.com/freelearningstylesinventory.html*

Visual Auditory Kinesthetic Learning Styles: A third website where you can take a test to see what your dominant learning style is: *www.vaknlp.com/*

Multiple Intelligences Tests: Based on the theories of Howard Gardner, these tests will help you determine your most dominant intelligence: *www.businessballs.com/howardgardnermultipleintelligences.htm#multiple%20intelligences%20tests*

Hemispheric Dominance Inventory Test: This website consists of a test to determine which side of your brain you use most, as well as exercises that will help to reduce hemispheric dominance in your brain, allowing you to more effectively utilize both sides of your brain: *http://pkab.wordpress.com/2008/01/23/test-dominan-otak/*

Community Organizations

Quantum Learning Network: Developer of SuperCamp, an academic summer camp that focuses on raising confidence and motivation. There are programs for youth in middle school, high school, and even college! *www.quantumlearningnetwork.com/*

inviteCHANGE: This coach training program is, in my humble opinion, one of the best. It is where I received my coach training. If you are interested in pursuing a career in coaching, visit their website at *www.invitechange.com/*.

Little Kickers Soccer in Portland, OR: One of the stories in *Launch Your Life* is about Coach Ryan and Coach Brian and their ability to connect to children about soccer in a way that the child can understand. If you live in the Portland area and would like to learn more about Little Kickers, go to their website at: *www.pdxlilkickers.com*

Resonance: I was fortunate enough to be exposed to the work that people are doing at Resonance, and their work influenced the model of the Upward Spiral Cycle. For more information on Resonance, visit their website at *www.ericwhitedesigns.com/websites/resonance/index.html*.

Magic: Magic is the intentional community located in Palo Alto, California, that is mentioned throughout *Launch Your Life*. They are up to incredible things—to check it out and become involved, visit their website at *www.ecomagic.org*.

Partners in the Creation of Launch Your Life

Melee Comics: Benjamin Dewey and Nathan Staples are the founders of Melee Comics. To see more of their work, go to *www.meleecomics.com*. They are great!

DoWriteEditing: If you are thinking of publishing your own book, and need an editor, contact Kathy Grow at *www.DoWrite Editing.com*. She did a fabulous job with my book, and I'm sure she'll do a great job with yours, too.

Dunn+Associates Design: For front cover design, contact Hobie and Kathi at *www.dunn-design.com*.

TLC Graphics: For interior design of your book, ask Tami, Erin, and Monica for help. Visit their website at *www.TLCGraphics.com*.

Write to Your Market: For your marketing copywriting needs, visit Susan Kendrick's website at *www.writetoyourmarket.com*.

UnTechnical Press: Michael Bremer is a great resource when publishing your own book. Visit his website at *www.untechnicalpress.com*.

Remember, we are waiting for your contribution to a future book called ***Launched Lives: Real Stories of Playing Huge and Making a Difference on the Upward Spiral of Life (Your Experience Required!)***. The creation of that book starts today, so go—create your life in a way that will inspire others and will make the Meaning rEvolution happen. When you are ready to share your story, go to *www.themeaningrevolution.com* and submit your story.

Visit *www.playhuge.com* to learn about products and services available to coach you in your process toward meaning and fulfillment.

SPECIAL THANK YOU

BENJAMIN DEWEY AND NATHAN STAPLES

I would like to acknowledge Benjamin Dewey and Nathan Staples for all of their work on the *Launch Your Life* graphic story. Ben spent countless hours creating and recreating scenes for each character, and Nathan worked to get the wording just right for each bit of dialogue. I deeply appreciate their work, and acknowledge that this book would not be what it is today without their contributions.

A question I get all the time is "Did you draw that?" And my response is, "Sadly, no. I wish I could draw like my friend Ben." Thank you for sharing your talent with us.

To learn more about Benjamin Dewey and Nathan Staples, please visit the resources section of *www.themeaningrevolution.com/launchyourlife*.

Index

- R -

- S -

- T -

ENVIRONMENTAL STATEMENT

I am conscious of the use of natural resources in my own life, and I am also conscious of the fact that publishing a book utilizes a lot of natural resources, i.e. paper. Throughout the writing and publishing process of *Launch Your Life*, I have made decisions to support the use of fewer of our natural resources, (digital copies, double sided printing, low ink settings, and more). I looked into alternative solutions to printing, including finding the mastermind behind the book *Cradle to Cradle* by John McDonough and Michael Braungart, which is a recyclable book but to produce is both cost prohibitive and in a big picture view of Always Honor Sustainability, is not yet an ecological benefit. With reservation, I ultimately decided to publish this book in print. I hired a printer who is a signed member of the Treatise on Responsible Paper Use, which is a part of the Green Press Initiative. To read more about my printer and their dedication to environmentally friendly printing, you can visit their website at *www.bangprinting.com.*

As an individual and as owner of Play Huge Coaching, LLC., I continue to be committed to sustainability and ecological awareness. I consistently make choices that are expensive, but ecological. My commitment is that all our products be created with minimal impact. If you care to support the effort by Play Huge Coaching, LLC to run a business in a sustainable way, whenever you purchase a product you will have a chance to share the cost of the ecological choices I make.

WHAT OTHERS are SAYING about MORGAN RICH and *LAUNCH YOUR LIFE*

"I have known Morgan for four years and have only good things to say about his character and abilities. I first met him as the director of the preschool family co-op which my daughter attended. He was a natural leader and facilitator, striving to find common ground between all members of the group. Later, I did some coaching sessions with him, and I found his insights and support were very useful.

"He is an exceptionally motivated individual who truly believes in the ability of all humans to live up to their potential. With his forthcoming book, he pursues his exciting quest to assist and inspire young people—nay, all of us—on life's path. I have no doubt that the enthusiasm, integrity, and insight which he brings to his work will pervade his new book…I can't wait to get my hands on a copy!"

AMY JACK, BSC, BARCH, MLA
Landscape Designer

"This book can be an owner's manual for your life. It's complete, concrete, challenging, validating, and inspiring. It can be read cover-to-cover, be used in sections as a resource, or be read in segments for support for what's up in the moment. It can be the theoretical foundation for making decisions or the practical guide to 'get 'er done.' Whether you're launching your life or looking for a course correction, this book has it all!"

JAN BERG, PCC
Partner, inviteCHANGE

"One of the greatest gifts that I have ever received is the friendship that has been shared with me by Morgan Rich. He is an amazing man who I can always count on to make me laugh, make me think deep thoughts, and, most of all, INSPIRE me. Morgan has a true gift—he not only plants the seeds of change but he stands close and cultivates them. Morgan has set the wheels turning in my heart and inspired me to make the changes in my life that I have been long afraid to set in motion. He is the kind of man I pray my son will grow to be—one who believes in himself, believes in humankind, and believes that, TOGETHER, we can be the change that we hope to see in this often scary world. It is with great anticipation that I look forward to his forthcoming book as I know it will only serve as a reminder that, if I stand strong for what I believe in, the beautiful results will follow!"

MICHELLE ELLIOTT
Mother of Three; Friend

"I have known Morgan as a coach for less than a year, but have already launched my life...well, a relaunch of sorts. And, when I achieve the goals we worked together on creating, I'll owe much of that success to my simple relationship with Morgan as someone on my side. The value of his perception resides in part in the purity of the relationship; his input is consulting, not corrective or placating to one's ego. I feel the work he is doing, by targeting youth, is even more important, because I believe that Morgan can transpose the quality of apathy into stewardship, being awake to the world, and playing huge, in even the smallest endeavor, as life's calling. And this should always be to the betterment of one's self, his environment, and to society's achievement as a whole. But, for me now, that simply means successfully launching a small business, learning new and advanced skills, while striving toward financial liquidity, as a respected and productive citizen.

MICHAEL EMERY
Coaching client; Founder, EmActiv

"Morgan Rich brings heart, soul, humor, and passion to anything that he undertakes. This book and its ideas exemplify his commitment to play huge in life and to be the change he wants to see in the world; because of that, this book and its concepts will make a HUGE difference in the lives of the people who read it. Morgan's conversational style, heartfelt earnestness, and concrete examples from real life are compelling, yet he also incorporates comic-book elements that inject lightness and inspiration simultaneously. Anyone who chooses to not only read this book but also to work with Morgan as their Play Huge coach will launch their life into a trajectory of unparalleled success, fulfillment, and fun. Ready? 1—2—3...LET'S GO!"

AMORÁH ROSS, MCC
Partner & Director of Training, inviteCHANGE

"It is a rare book that bares its soul for all to see. *Launch Your Life* is a deeply personal exploration of what it means to live a life of Meaning and Fulfillment—a life well-lived. In a world awash in complacency, consumerism, and shallowness, we need new models and compelling visions to imagine how things might be otherwise. In *Launch Your Life*, Morgan Rich has provided a powerful vision forward that should be required reading for every young person who has ever wondered, questioned, and hoped for something more out of life."

JAY ROBERTS
Assistant Professor of Education and Environmental Studies
Earlham College

"*Launch Your Life* by Morgan Rich is the kind of book that we could all wish to have read at the age of twenty-something, but soon realize that its '5 secrets' are strong points of reference for living a life of purpose and meaning at any stage of life. The secrets hold true for launching a life, a school, a business, or any dreams of ordinary and extraordinary proportions."

JUDY GRAVES
Founder, Opal School of the Portland Children's Museum